ANCIENT EVENINGS

NINE PYRRHONIAN DIALOGUES

Adrian Kuzminski

imprint-academic.com

Published in the UK by
Imprint Academic, PO Box 200, Exeter EX5 5YX, UK

Distributed in the USA by
Lightning Source,
La Vergne, TN 37086, USA

ISBN 9781788361194 Paperback

A CIP catalogue record for this book is available from the
British Library and US Library of Congress

Based on surviving material from Sextus Empiricus, Diogenes Laertius, Timon of Phlius, Aristotle, Cicero, Plutarch, Epicurus, Philodemus, Lucretius, and Epictetus, among others

Contents

Part III: Dialogues on Life and Death

Prologue

Ancient Evenings is a literary philosophical work of historical fiction in dialogue form. It unfolds as a series of discussions among a circle of family and friends, set in the Antonine era of ancient Rome in the second century CE. There are three parts with three dialogues each, for a total of nine dialogues. The first series, on Good and Evil, is set at mid-summer in a villa in Campania; it is followed by a second series, on Truth, in the following mid-winter in Rome; and it concludes with a third series, on Life and Death, in the following mid-summer, once again in the villa in Campania.

We moderns still have much to learn from the ancients. The educated classes of Greek and Roman antiquity lived in a secular, multicultural world, in many ways a precedent to our own. They wrestled, as we do, with the prospects for human life and death in the absence of divine intervention. The Pre-Socratics had already recognized the physical world to be a self-contained and self-determined sphere of activity to be understood in its own naturalistic terms. Socrates subsequently folded all human social activity, or ethics, into the same natural sphere. Thus was born the secular world inherited by the Hellenistic philosophers, a world based on a thoroughly naturalistic understanding of human experience.

Earlier presumptions of an independently existing divine power controlling nature and human affairs from the outside — manifest in the cults of the traditional gods — were quietly put aside by all of the major Hellenistic schools, including Stoics, Epicureans, and Sceptics. Aristotle had already reintegrated Plato's pure, divine forms back into the natural world; his pure abstraction of a prime mover took its place as an object of secular worship, of naturalized philosophical contemplation. The Stoics recognized this naturalized divinity as the providence whose hand they saw directing the rational flow, or *logos*, of human affairs. The Epicureans, following Democritus, went even further. They reduced all of nature to material atoms in motion, while the Sceptics, who took over Plato's old Academy, undermined any belief in any divinity at all, or in any extra-human powers, external or internal.

The spirit of this first age of secularism is perhaps best captured in the philosophical dialogues of Cicero. In his sceptical, fluid mind, the major schools jostle together and prod one another, much as they surely did in discussions among leisured and educated people in his day. The philosophers of that era continue to speak to perennial questions of good and evil, truth and falsehood, and life and death in compelling ways which arguably match, and perhaps exceed, what contemporary discussion on these subjects has to offer. Plato and Aristotle and earlier Greek philosophers had focused on what we can know about the natural physical and social worlds. Hellenistic philosophers took a different tack. Although a secular understanding of the world remained fundamental to their work, for them the leading question of the day became how the individual should react to the natural world in which he or she must live.

The format of philosophical dialogue employed here has a distinguished history, yet it is surprisingly little used in our time. At its best, it has been an unparalleled genre for original and powerful philosophy of the first order. Plato's dialogues are by far the best known, but we also have classic dialogues by Xenophon, Plutarch, and Cicero, and, in modern times, by Berkeley, Diderot, and Hume, among others. Serious philosophical dialogues, now lost, are also attributed to Democritus and Aristotle, among other ancients. Lucian, the Cynic satirist, and other authors wrote more popular dialogues as well. The classic texts of the Buddha's discourses are cast as dialogues. The work offered here can only aspire to the standard set by such examples. Nonetheless, *Ancient Evenings* attempts a serious dramatization of a sustained exchange among a half dozen characters, including an Epicurean, a Stoic, a Peripatetic, a Sceptic, a Platonist, and a Pyrrhonist, in an intimate setting at the calm height of the Roman Empire.

Most philosophical schools, then as now, perpetuate their philosophies internally, following a lineage of teachers and disciples. Their works are normally presented didactically as monologues, usually as speeches, essays, treatises, and monographs, under the command of a more or less omniscient voice. The dialogue format, by contrast, has the virtue of integrating into a single narrative direct exchanges among competing voices normally kept apart. Only in a dialogue format do otherwise independent ideas unavoidably confront and interact directly with one another. No voice, in a real dialogue, enjoys a final command over the others. The alternating exchanges set up a pattern of reciprocity, a dialectic, in which, at best, the contrasting views mutually modify and deepen one another, whether or not they reach a point of resolution.

The dialogues presented here, though voiced by fictional characters, aim to create a plausible account of what an actual exchange among the major philosophical schools of the Hellenistic and Roman Imperial periods might actually have been like. *Ancient Evenings* is an historical re-enactment in the sense advanced by the British philosopher of history, R.G. Collingwood. He argues that the past can best be retrieved and understood by reconstructing the thinking, or reasoning, of past actors. This means entering their minds through an act of imagination, and following out the implications of their thinking in arguments and conclusions plausible in light of their assumptions.

Just as a detective works with factual clues to construct a narrative adequate as a convincing explanation for a crime, so the author of an imaginative re-enactment of a philosophical discussion must work with available evidence to construct a narrative adequate to illuminate exchanges among philosophers. Such a re-enactment is not a mere fiction; nor is it an interpretation. It is properly a reconstruction, hewing as closely as possible to what a group of ancient Hellenistic thinkers might actually have sounded like talking to one another.

The major Hellenistic writers whose extended dialogues have survived were Cicero and Plutarch. Both were inspired by Plato's dialogues, but both also faced a world unanticipated by Plato and dominated by the new schools of Stoicism, Epicureanism, and

Scepticism. They adapted the dialogue format to this new setting to compare and contrast the principal features of the competing Hellenistic schools. The most important surviving philosophical dialogues are those of Cicero, especially his *On Ends, Academica, Tuscan Disputations*, and *On the Nature of the Gods*. Plutarch's dialogues —important if less comprehensive than Cicero's, including *Oracles in Decline, Socrates' Daimonion*, and *Eroticus*, among others—are gathered together in his *Moralia*.

Ancient Evenings takes the same dialogical approach as these ancient writers. Additionally, it aims to contribute to the historical record by adding a Hellenistic voice which Cicero and Plutarch regrettably ignore, that of Pyrrhonism. As other important ancient sources make plain—especially Sextus Empiricus in his *Outlines of Pyrrhonism* and other works, and Diogenes Laertius in his life of Pyrrho in his *Lives of Eminent Philosophers*—Pyrrhonism was a major school in its own right which offered a significant and unique challenge to all the other major schools. The intent of these dialogues is to use that challenge to illuminate both Pyrrhonism and its Hellenistic competitors, and to present a fuller picture of the scope of philosophical debate in high antiquity.

The Pyrrhonians brought a new perspective to Greek thinking. Pyrrho had accompanied Alexander the Great in his Asian conquests as far as India, where contacts with Indian holy men, possibly including early Buddhists, apparently inspired in him a new form of scepticism, one which suspended beliefs and relied solely upon direct experience to guide human conduct. This suspension, said to result in a state of tranquillity and imperturbability he called *ataraxia*, was remarkably akin to the enlightenment or *bodhi* of the Buddhists. The Pyrrhonian sceptical school Pyrrho inspired avoided the positive dogmatic claims of Epicureans and Stoics rooted in their speculative beliefs about the natural world; it also avoided the negative dogmatic claims of the most radical Academic sceptics, who believed that no knowledge at all of the natural world was to be had.

It is important not to confuse Pyrrhonian and Academic sceptics. The radical Academic sceptics, led by Arcesilaus, head of the Academy in the early third century BCE, and later by Carneades, were arguably nihilists. They appear to have concluded from the uncertainty and controversy surrounding speculation about the nature of things, or beliefs about the world, that nothing at all could be known. The Pyrrhonian sceptics, by contrast, argued that controversy over our speculative beliefs itself is insufficient reason to either affirm or deny them. They proposed instead that we suspend all judgments about our beliefs, and that we live a life without belief, relying on the sufferance of our immediate experience, by which we respond to the demands of the physical and social world we cannot evade.

The Pyrrhonists sought a middle ground between the positive and negative dogmatisms of their day—between speculative assertions about the meaning of the natural secularized world, such as those advanced by Epicureans and Stoics, and the equally speculative denials, by the Academics, that all such assertions are false. These alternatives continue to bedevil not only modern philosophy as they did ancient philosophy, but they also continue to set widespread patterns of thought in modern science, religion, politics, and culture. Pyrrhonism not only offers a middle path between these extremes for the human understanding of experience, as does Buddhism, but it does so in a philosophical idiom native to Western thought—the language of classical Greek and Latin philosophy.

The price of dogmatism, whether positive or negative, ancient or modern, is the exaggeration of emotion manifested in the instability, conflict, and anxiety which accompany many beliefs. Epicureans, Stoics, and Academics, like the Pyrrhonists, seek liberation from inherited beliefs, but their strategy is to replace them with new and better beliefs. The Pyrrhonists, by contrast, seek, like Buddhists, to live without any beliefs at all. The promise of Pyrrhonism, like Buddhism, is the peace of mind which follows the suspension of judgment about the truth or falsehood of beliefs, accompanied by a clarity of understanding which such suspension makes evident. *Ancient Evenings* reminds us that a philosophy of personal liberation from all forms of belief was already a sophisticated practice in the classical ancient Western world.

The Hellenistic schools were famously open and cut across social classes and roles. Women in the Hellenistic era gained more freedom to divorce, to retain property rights, and to live independently of men. In contrast to earlier schools, both Stoics and especially Epicureans welcomed women into their ranks. They set equal and open standards of participation not only for men and women, but for any seeker who might come forth, even a slave. The educated women of the day would likely have expressed their views not only in the schools, but among family and friends. The major roles played by Harmonia, Philia, and Aurelia in *Ancient Evenings* reflect the times in which they lived. No doubt, a setting of family and friends remains, at its best, one in which greater honesty in mutual exchange can be tolerated, suffered, and even expected, more than elsewhere. The family is one place where prejudices accepted in the larger society—in the schools, at work, in assemblies, in courts, and in civic societies—can be suspended in a free exchange of ideas. The reader is invited to a re-enactment of such a free exchange.

Part I

Dialogues on Good and Evil

Characters:

Rufus, a Roman Senator

Harmonia, a Stoic, daughter of Rufus

Lucian, student of Pyrrhonism, son of Rufus

Philia, an Epicurean, a friend of Harmonia's

Petronius, a Peripatetic, a friend of Rufus's

Saturninus, an Academic, neighbour of Rufus's

Time:

The Reign of Antoninus Pius, second century CE

Place:

The Villa of Rufus in Campania,
Overlooking the Sea

The First Evening

Do Good and Evil Exist?

RUFUS: Hear, hear, everyone! Listen up, please, and come along with me. The stars are out. Let's go out to the garden and enjoy the cool of the evening. We'll have new wine with honey-cakes and continue the conversation we started over dinner. Perhaps because I took the trouble to have both my children—Harmonia and Lucian—study philosophy, the gods now favour me with the advice I get from them, and from their young friends.

We are especially glad to have Philia this evening, Harmonia's good friend, who arrived just today for a visit. We hear she's been living for some time with the Epicureans, who are famous for telling us that pursuing pleasures and avoiding pains is the only way to live, and to be happy. Perhaps I'm too old to believe it. It seems to me to miss the tragedy in things. The pains of life will have their way with all of us, more or less, and when they do, the ideas of Epicurus, I fear, will be but cold comfort.

But what does an old man like me know? With time and age there seems less and less to be sure about. Scepticism, and the humility it brings, seems to be the wisdom of old age. We are all more or less philosophers here, after all, so let us take advantage of our gathering together and have a proper philosophical discussion. We have three evenings to share, and I can't imagine a better way to spend them. We all know how it's done: assertion and response, or better, question and answer, with the host posing the topic. Let me propose, then, for our subject tonight, to ask what good and evil are, whether they are the pleasures and pains of the Epicureans, for instance, or whether they are something else, as other philosophers claim. Good and evil, after all, stand for values in general, for virtues and vices, and for all the discriminations we make in life, however else they may be understood, because we think something is good, or bad.

Perhaps we can learn something. Are we agreed?

[All nod in approval …]

Well, then, who will start?

PHILIA: Senator Rufus, if I may. Thank you very much, kind sir. It's most generous of you to have me a guest. It's an honour to be welcomed into your family. But I must say I fear you misunderstand us Epicureans, if you'll excuse my boldness in saying so.

RUFUS: There is no philosophy without boldness. So perhaps you could enlighten me. What do you think I'm missing? It wouldn't be my first misunderstanding.

PHILIA: All right, I'll try to explain, if I can. It isn't just a matter for us of pursuing pleasures and avoiding pains, but rather of calculating how best to maximize pleasures and minimize pains. We accept some pains if they lead to greater pleasures, or benefits, and avoid some pleasures if they result in greater pains, or harms. Pleasure isn't just fun, I should say, or only physical pleasure. Epicurus himself distinguished what he called the kinetic pleasures of impulse from the static pleasures of satisfaction. The mind, the most subtle part of our body, allows us to calculate and so navigate among our pleasures and pains. Mental pleasure is the peace of mind which comes when we are liberated from the anxiety which inevitably accompanies the false beliefs we hold about our physical pleasures and pains. Our mental calculations aim to smooth out our pleasures and pains, to bring them under control, and to enjoy them for what they are, not for what we fear they might be, such as some silly wrath of the gods. The deepest pleasure is the calm steady-state which emerges when we are able to harmonize our pleasures and pains, for only then can we overcome the disruptions they can inflict upon us.

Our master Epicurus teaches us that the world, including our bodies and minds, is composed of a steady stream of atoms flowing through empty space. We can easily picture this, even though the atoms are invisible. Imagine, for instance, an army marching over a field in lockstep order. From a distance the individual soldiers, like our real atoms, are invisible; what we actually see are only the grosser resulting formations, or the ranks and files into which our 'soldier' atoms are combined as they move over the field. Now imagine further that a few soldiers here and there are randomly hit by the enemy's arrows and missiles as they march along. They fall out of the line of march and disrupt and entangle the flow of the whole. The smoothness of the flow is interrupted and what we see from afar — the moving formation — is altered and broken, even if we can't see the individual soldiers. In just the same way, everything we see in nature is composed of invisible atoms whose swerves or disruptions of order account for the changes apparent in our experience. How we see an army marching in the distance is exactly how we see, hear, and think, as well as taste, touch, or smell, anything at all.

Now to the point: in this world of simple elements, there is no evidence of evil forces — gods or demons — interfering in our lives. Our experiences arise entirely out of the interactions of neutral, random, invisible atoms. Once we realize that, our anxieties begin to dissolve, and we are able to relax, and eventually to find *ataraxia*, or tranquillity and serenity, a state beyond physical pleasures and pains. Death, for instance, is nothing to fear, for 'while we exist', as the saying of Epicurus goes, 'death is not present, and when death is present we do not exist'. For our existence is no more than a temporary aggregation of atoms, and our death no more than its dissolution.

Not only that …

HARMONIA: Hold on a moment, my dear friend! My goodness, so many questions come up, and you speak so eloquently, and so quickly, and in such a flood of words, that I, for one, need to start asking my questions before I become totally distracted and end up forgetting what it was that puzzled me in the first place. The Epicureans may be to your taste, but my loyalty, as we all know, lies elsewhere, with the Stoics, who I think got it right about pleasures and pains, or what you call compulsions and repulsions.

So then let me ask you this: who can be confident that your calculations to balance out pleasures and pains, presumably to neutralize them, will give you the results you seek? How can you be sure, in the end, that your pains will not outweigh your pleasures? We Stoics take no such gamble. Nor do we measure by calculation. Nor are we so sure the gods, or the force behind them, can be dismissed outright. We seek the deeper virtue, if I may say so, which includes rather than evades our pleasures and pains, as you seem to be advocating. Our world is organic and purposeful, motivated by a divine and purposeful Providence, while yours is mechanical and random, a dead end. We see meaning in its purpose: the realization of virtue through the unfolding of reason. The Stoic idea is something like this: if we can but understand the order of things, the *logos* or law or rule of nature, if you like, we will see that pleasures and pains are both essential to the scheme of things. It is not a question of figuring out what to pursue and what to avoid, but of accepting both in their rightful places, of facing the world as it is, not as we might like it to be. The world is no machine as you imagine—it's not like one of those complex celestial clocks, like the one Saturninus has in his villa, but an unfolding drama written by the rational hand of Providence.

And if I can slip this in, Philia, there's a sly side to you Epicureans. You think you can smooth out pleasures and pains into a calm flow of experience you call the highest pleasure, as if we could take out an insurance policy in pleasure to offset the claims of our pains. This seems a kind of vanity of self-control. We Stoics are no doubt more plodding, and more sober. Our duty is to be vigilant, to accept and not deny what life gives us. We have a lot in common. Like you, we too are naturalists, though more organic than mechanical; we agree with you that what unfolds in the physical world is the common ground we share. But for us the lesson is to recognize what we cannot control, to find our destiny, so as to better accept it. To this end, we need to come to a rational understanding of the world, of what we can control in it and what we cannot. Our role is to bring ourselves out of ignorance and into knowledge. When we do that, we come to see how our reason is a reflection of divine reason. We become more rational agents guided by well-reasoned choices. The choice for Stoics is not to try to escape normal pleasures and pains, but to accept their proper roles in determining our fate. Acceptance is virtue, acceptance is all. Conforming to a rational world turns out, perhaps ironically, to be a form of liberation. You want to beat the system, as it were, whereas we counsel embracing it.

PETRONIUS: That's quite a speech.

HARMONIA: And I'm not done yet. Let me put it another way, before I give the floor back to Philia: the Stoic Sage, our ideal, is neither elated by pleasures nor distressed by pains; he or she takes them equally in stride. Evil is a necessary complement to the good, just as a shadow is to the light. You can't have one without the other. Nor should you confuse them. The point is to understand the unfolding rationality of experience—wherein all things have their place—against the resistance of irrationality, and thereby to gain some tranquillity beyond the noisy, endless contest of pleasures and pains. This allows us to accept pain as indispensable to pleasure, and vice-versa, as the way things are, not as something to be evaded. Our good and evil are not pleasure and pain, but knowledge and ignorance.

But—and this is important—even if our pains turn out to outweigh our pleasures, we can take comfort that such pleasures as we may enjoy we would not have had at all without the world as it is. Our pains in this way become ennobled. To understand all is to forgive all—whether we like it or not. There is a peace in this understanding beyond pleasure and pain, beyond feeling, which the Greeks call *apathea*. Unless we accept pleasure and pain as part of the larger order that is nature, we cannot hope to live peacefully and act properly, that is, virtuously.

PETRONIUS: Young ladies! Can an old man have a word?

PHILIA: Another interruption! Even among us Epicureans I suppose some precedence is due the older and presumably wiser. All right, only I insist on a chance to finish what I started earlier.

PETRONIUS: By all means. I'll yield back to you in a moment. Just let me add this observation: any view, it seems these days, expressed by any philosopher or anyone trying to understand the rational way of things, their *logos*, invites attack by another. Just as the Stoics think they can improve upon the Epicureans, so my fellow Aristotelians, or Peripatetics, believe they can go one better than either Stoics or Epicureans. Virtue for us is not merely a resigned understanding of the world, as you Stoics seem to claim; nor is it a calculation of pleasures and pains, as you Epicureans believe. It's rather something like an active process of development and self-realization. We are happy as individuals only when we are active and productive. You Epicureans are active enough, but you're slaves to your sensations and to the randomness of pleasures and pains. You Stoics recognize that things have a destiny or end towards which they move, but you give away too much in your embrace of Providence. You have more agency than you think, not just whether to go along with things or not. We Peripatetics combine what both of you separate; we are active in the pursuit of our ends.

Consider this: our productivity, our creative activity, is what allows us to become the individuals we turn out to be. That's where we find our identities. I must not only understand my potential, I must actualize it, as much as possible, if it's to have any real value, and if I'm to discover through it who I really am. It is what I can achieve in life that counts, and therein lies my happiness. My understanding of knowledge and science is but a means to realizing my true end. It is only natural for us to apply ourselves productively in the world, for we can realize ourselves only insofar as we are able to bring order out of chaos. And for that investment we expect some kind of reward. Honours and wealth are the natural marks of anyone's success in the world, in being productive. That's what it means, at least to us Peripatetics, to live properly. In the end, it is this discovery of the self through productive activity, we believe, which is the highest good. Call it self-realization, if you like. All right, I'll stop there. I apologize for the interruption. The floor is yours, Philia.

PHILIA: I trust, Petronius, you're not patronizing us as 'young ladies'. While it may sound good to invoke some kind of supposedly 'deeper' understanding which contains both pleasures and pains, as the Stoics say, or to talk about productive activity in the world as the key to finding happiness and one's true self, as you followers of Aristotle claim, there is no need to do so, we Epicureans maintain, and there is considerable harm in the prospect. We live by experience, by the physical world, not by some mysterious deeper abstract or conceptual understanding—an understanding, I should add, which remains elusive to most people. It may seem plausible to say that happiness comes from a deeper grasp of the world, as Harmonia says, or from acting productively on that understanding, following your Aristotle, Petronius, but both of these amount to pursuing a chimaera—living in a dream world—while remaining exposed to the buffeting of real fate and experience.

HARMONIA: A chimaera! That's pretty bad!

PHILIA: It gets worse. Even if you could achieve some kind of deeper understanding of the world, or produce some satisfying creation, you would not thereby be in a position to live fully and happily; nor would you be able to separate good from evil. Stoicism requires eternal vigilance to figure out what depends on your actions and what does not, and on what the virtuous thing to do is, and what it is not. How do you know if you're being rational enough, or rational about the right things? Aristotle's idea of a productive life, like Stoic vigilance, requires unending effort. Both of you—Stoics and Peripatetics alike—presuppose a constant struggle to recycle our sensations through our understanding, which we use to filter and distil our sensations, and so on, round and round, a treadmill which never stops. There is no peace in either of your philosophies, whatever you say, only constant fear of failure to live up to your own theory. How exhausting all that must be! We Epicureans take quite another path: we confront our fears directly—for it is fear which obscures the pleasures of existence—and in that way we make the best of life as it comes to us everyday. We do this by stilling the mind, by turning it into a smoothly functioning machine, like an abacus, whereby we can sort out our sensations and figure out which pleasures to pursue and which pains to avoid. The pretentiousness of the mind, its airy creations, are put aside, leaving only material function.

PETRONIUS: Calculating pleasures and pains ends up on that same treadmill, it seems to me. You Epicureans seem to be interpreting experience just as much as any of us. But, be that as it may, you can't deny that achievement brings satisfaction, that it's a kind of pleasure, which makes it an end for you?

PHILIA: Well, yes and no. Aristarchus was a great scientist, who went so far as to suggest that the earth revolves around the sun, but he was not necessarily a happy man because of his brilliance. Sculptors like Phidias and Praxiteles produced great works, but that too does not mean that they found happiness. The pleasures they got for a time were sooner or later matched by the pains they ended up enduring. We are all acquainted with talented people who have a deep understanding of nature, or who can produce moving poems and powerful histories, but who are nonetheless melancholy and restless—think of Catullus, or that charlatan Peregrinus, restlessly moving from one set of beliefs to the next. Such people are far from what we could consider happy or content. Not infrequently, they are miserable wretches, for all their talent. As for the wealth and honours you extol, Petronius, they often bring only more anxiety and insecurity, not to mention the resentment and envy of others.

PETRONIUS: But …

PHILIA: Now hold on and let me finish! There's one more thing: happiness—which is surely part of the good, if not all of it—requires something less than what you two both propose. The maximizing of pleasures and the minimizing of pains is all we need to get us there, something you Stoics and Peripatetics rush past all too quickly. That means learning to focus on the immediate experience of our sensations, which are subject to change and uncertainty, to be sure, but which also exhibit enough stability and reliability to allow us to observe and calculate, and what we calculate are the advantages of pleasures and the disadvantages of pains. There's nothing mysterious about our experience; we know it when we're having it. Every

moment something is happening to us, generating feelings which stir
our souls, which comes from grosser particles affecting more subtle
ones. Feelings are waves which pass through the soul. Those feelings, I
dare say, are what life's all about. The challenge is to put ourselves in
a better position to experience good feelings, or pleasures, and avoid
bad feelings, or pains. The only good which exists is pleasure, and the
only evil is pain. It follows that no pain at all is the highest pleasure, or
good, since it means that our consciousness is filled entirely with
pleasures and entirely void of pains. Beyond pleasures and pains there
is nothing else, save illusory opinion on the one hand and peace of
mind on the other. There! I've said my piece.

[Pause …]

SATURNINUS: Well, since you are all staking out lines of defence, like
soldiers before a battle, let a man who appreciates the old Academy
have a word, before you dig in your positions too deeply. There is
indeed harm, or at least danger, in seeking for any understanding
beyond experience, either of good and evil or of anything else. So far I
agree with Philia. Let's not forget, however, that any experience can at
any time turn out falsely, not to be as expected, not to be what we
thought it would be. Now Aristarchus, Archimedes, Erastosthenes,
Hippocrates, Galen, Theophrastus, or any other great scientist you can
name will tell you that science is rooted in the observation of
phenomena, of nature, of physical reality, and, just as important, in
tracing the correlations evident among phenomena, and *not* in
speculating about what we might or might not actually experience.

What we actually experience are the phenomena of which we are
directly aware, by which I mean those sensations—sights, sounds,
touches, smells, tastes—along with thoughts, which are immediately
present to us in consciousness at any moment. The trouble is that we
can also be fooled at any moment. Anything can turn out to be something else. One man sees water ahead in the desert, while another sees
only a shimmering blur. Another may hear voices where the rest of us
hear nothing. The wine is tart to this woman, but sweet to that man. A
letter brings news upsetting my expectations. Apelles, they say, made
paintings so real in appearance that birds would fly at them, trying to

pick at the grapes he put in his pictures. The moon appears much larger near the horizon than when high in the sky. In a misty fog we may easily mistake a statue for a person. One twin is easily confused with another, as are different eggs from different hens. There are endless examples of us being fooled by the phenomena we experience.

The point is that appearances can't be trusted. Never. You presume, Philia, with the scientists, that we can agree about what is pleasure and what is pain, or what is beautiful or ugly, or what counts as evidence and what doesn't, but that is hardly so. The same experience — say exercising in the gymnasium — is judged a pleasure by some and a pain by others. There are people who appear to enjoy pain, and actually take pleasure in it. Indeed, there is no experience which cannot be taken as a pleasure in some circumstances and a pain in others, and perhaps sometimes even both at once. It's impossible to calculate pleasures and pains, as you Epicureans propose to do, because they are not phenomena but judgments about phenomena, and there is no end to judgments. So, at the end of the day, even your phenomena are not what they seem to be.

PHILIA: But Saturninus, aren't some things beyond doubt intrinsically pleasurable or painful? Being branded by a red-hot poker, when a surgeon cauterizes a wound, is surely a pain to anyone, even if it may be beneficial in some way. Any pleasure we take in the utility of such an act surely cannot cancel out its pain.

SATURNINUS: I'm not so sure. Ascetics and holy men, like the gymnosophists from India, are able, it seems, to somehow disconnect themselves from such experiences. No doubt you've seen them in the forums at Rome, as I have, or outside the games, where they stand frozen for hours in one bizarre posture or another. It's quite remarkable. They also suffer the hot iron, to be sure, like anyone else, but the pain which would be so overwhelming to most of us is somehow reduced by them to such insignificance as to virtually disappear. Or so it appears. Some of the holy men from India have even immolated themselves publicly, as we know, unflinchingly burning to death with no apparent discomfort. Didn't Strabo write somewhere about a holy man who accompanied a delegation from India in Augustus's time, who did exactly that in Athens, with the Emperor and many others present? And of course there's that gymnosophist, that naked philosopher or Indian holy man, as they're called, called Kalanos, who accompanied Alexander back from India to Persia, who also famously peacefully immolated himself before the entire court.

In any event, this kind of self-control should not really surprise us. A lion who springs into our path threatening to devour us fills us with terror, but a lion observed behind the bars of a cage is no more than an object of curiosity, albeit a striking one. In fact, if we are bored or distracted enough, or as used to the lion as his trainer might be, even a lion in a cage could become an indifferent sight, so that after a while we might not even notice him. It should be clear, if these examples make any sense, that we need not—and indeed cannot—identify any phenomenon as intrinsically anything at all. It doesn't necessarily mean any one thing instead of any other.

Phenomena are not explained by saying that they are made up of unobservable, eternal, elementary, independently existing entities in which we are asked to believe, such as your Epicurean atoms. You call your atoms 'nameless' and without qualities, and yet qualities are what we actually experience, not atoms. By trying to create qualities like colour out of colourless atoms, you are trying to create something out of nothing, which Epicurus denies can be done—an unfortunate contradiction.

Of course, we all presume that for things to be stable and reliable, they must be unchanging and permanent, that they must have some kind of unchanging intrinsic essence, some kind of independent existence or enduring identity. The problem is that our fluctuating sensations fail to provide this support, so unchanging entities can only exist elsewhere—in some non-sensory or non-physical realm, as Plato taught. However, that's no more than a belief. In fact, we cannot find such independently existing entities at all.

It's better, then, to be free of this useless quest to find the essence of things, and to accept the flux of experience as the illusion that it is. Epicureanism appeals to the passions of youth, for whom the pleasures are strong; but it turns out that trying to capture experience through pleasure and pain dissolves into fleeting nothingness when we try to get a hold of it, just as if, were we to try to grasp with our bare hands the water over there at the fountain, it would run through our fingers. The same thing applies to the various beliefs which distinguish Stoics, Peripetics, Platonists, and all the dogmatic philosophers. Our mental fingers, so to speak, cannot hold them. None of them, in the end, can be relied upon.

HARMONIA: Well, you are very hard on us, Saturninus, and I'd suggest rather dogmatic in your own way. You say that pleasures and pains, and all goods and evils generally, do not really exist—even though we certainly seem to feel them, don't we?—and that any peace of mind we might hope for in fact requires no less than their elimination. But isn't that just a clever way of redefining, not eliminating, good and evil? It is beliefs which are evil and their elimination which is good, you're telling us, and in this way you reintroduce at least one belief through the back door. You accuse the Epicureans, and us Stoics, and the Peripatetics, and I suppose the Platonists and others as well—and I imagine anyone with any positive doctrine at all—of falling victim to one or another insubstantial belief. You advance no positive belief of your own, it is true, but you embrace, it seems to me, an enormous negative belief, namely that liberation of a sort follows from the elimination of all positive beliefs, which are necessarily mistaken, and therefore evil. You not only believe in nothing, you hold there are only beliefs, all of which are illusory. Sounds like nihilism to me.

SATURNINUS: I don't mind pleading guilty. In fact, I'm happy to do so. My method, my *via negativa*, is in my opinion precisely the path to liberation, to the good, which lies, as Plato long ago suggested, beyond both phenomena and our opinions of phenomena. And, of course, it was later, in Plato's Academy, that the *via negativa* was developed, by Arcesilaus first of all, and then by Carneades and Clitomachus and the others. They all harkened back to Socrates' sceptical dialectic of question and answer. It turned out that the assertions of any dogmatist were liable to neutralizing counter-assertions. You say this is a kind of negative belief, or even nihilism, and that may be so, but there's all the difference in the world between positive and negative beliefs. The latter have no content and therefore do not bind us to anything; and therein, I suggest, lies our true liberation. Insofar as dogmatism persists, as it seems to, it is surely better to capture and domesticate it, rather than trying fruitlessly to kill it. Confining it to negation is one way to do that while getting rid of all the positive versions.

The *via negativa* was a hard morsel to swallow, I'll admit, and it became especially hard for the Academy. They became afraid, perhaps, of such a drastic step. Some of the later Academics, like Philo and Antiochus, and even Cicero, tried to fend off the charge of nihilism, which the Stoics threw back at them. It embarrassed them not least because they continued to presuppose the belief of Stoics and other dogmatists that anyone in principle should be able somehow to grasp the truth of things, even though they had convinced themselves that such a truth could not be found. They continued to hold a standard of truth which, it turned out, they could not realize. The moderate Academicians suggested, in defence of this predicament, that even if we don't know exactly what we are really seeing, feeling, etc., we can at least make some good guesses about it.

For example, I see a shape in the distance I can't quite make out: I might first guess it's a man; if the shape comes closer, I might see that it's in fact a man, and even closer, that it's Socrates. But on still closer inspection, however, I might see further that it's not Socrates at all, but Glaucon. I see I was wrong, but I also see that I'm able to correct myself. I accept or assent to my latest and most tested belief, that this is Glaucon, unless something else turns up to make me change my mind again. This kind of refinement is what allows us to function practically, as animals do, thus preserving a power of discrimination which allows us to come to plausible if not absolute conclusions.

Sounds reasonable, you might think. But why should anyone take plausibility as a substitute for truth, since even the most plausible thing can turn out to be totally wrong? It is plausible, for instance, to assume that most people, most of the time, are healthy and act accordingly; it is what we expect every day when we go to market or the baths, or to court, assembly or temple, or anywhere. But if the plague comes to the city, for instance, and most people are suddenly wretched or dead, health becomes the exception and illness the norm, and the plausibility of encountering healthy people is replaced by the plausibility of encountering sick people. Our reality has been reversed. It's a reminder that anything plausible may at any time be entirely confounded. Far from avoiding nihilism, then, I must embrace it, following the deepest thinkers of my school, as the conclusion which frees me from holding any beliefs at all. I find that liberating. For me, the good is nothing at all, and evil is everything, that is, every illusion which pretends to be something, and not nothing.

[Pause …]

RUFUS: Lucian, you've been listening quietly to all this, but now I see you shaking your head. You've been attending lectures by the Pyrrhonists, and especially by that unusual doctor in Rome, what's his name …?

LUCIAN: Sextus Empiricus.

RUFUS: Ah, yes, Sextus Empiricus. Well, then, tell us something about these Pyrrhonists, if you can, and how they understand this problem of good and evil. I suspect they have yet another view.

LUCIAN: Well, yes, they do. They have a peculiar approach which I'm still trying to figure out. The Pyrrhonists seek to question our beliefs, like Saturninus here and the radical Academics. But, unlike Saturninus and his nihilistic sceptics, Pyrrhonists do not conclude that all beliefs in question are necessarily mistaken, nor that positive beliefs are pernicious and negative ones liberating, nor that our sensations are illusionary, nor most of the other things we've just been hearing. They conclude only that we lack sufficient evidence either to substantiate or refute any belief, positive or negative. They neither reject nor accept beliefs, but instead suspend judgment not only about some of them, but about all of them. Further, unlike the Academics, they do not conclude that our appearances are meaningless without some belief or other to anchor them.

Appearances, the Pyrrhonists maintain, are not merely a function of what we might or might not believe about them, or how we choose to interpret them; rather they have their own peculiar integrity. They somehow contain their own meaning. They impress themselves involuntarily upon all of us in the same way under normal circumstances, that is, provided our eyes, ears, and bodies in general function as they usually do. The Pyrrhonists would have us follow our appearances as our only guide, and put aside all our beliefs about them, where beliefs are understood as non-evident judgments variously expressed as opinions, theories, creeds, oaths, dogmas, prejudices, and so on; beliefs usually take the basic form of an assertion that some X is actually something else, namely some Y.

HARMONIA: That sounds too neat. How can we know when something is actually an appearance as opposed to a belief or an opinion about an appearance? How do we know that we aren't mixing them up? And how can we be expected to rely on appearances after what Saturninus has just said?

LUCIAN: Let me put it another way. Phenomena, the Pyrrhonists say, are undeniable and common to us all, they are the evident appearances which affect us, which is how we know them. If I have eyes to see, and I'm normal and healthy, and I am asked to go out and look at the blue sky on a sunny day, I cannot help but see the blue sky on a sunny day, and so on for all the other phenomena we experience in sensation and thought. Many of Saturninus's examples of illusion depend on some abnormal or pathological condition, but healthy bodies under normal conditions do not fall into those errors, the Pyrrhonists maintain. Nor is it merely plausible that we see the blue sky as we see it; it is in fact real just as it is, and is not to be judged by some other standard.

Similarly, we cannot calculate pleasures and pains, Sextus maintains, because they are not simple phenomena but ever shifting judgments about ever changing phenomena. Indeed, Saturninus, you go so far as to claim that there are no phenomena at all, if I understand you, only judgments about what we mistake to be phenomena, such judgments themselves being only illusions. But what occurs in consciousness, what appears, remains prior to any judgment about it. If there are uninterpreted phenomena that actually occur, the question is what exactly these phenomena might be? What does it mean to be a phenomenon?

Let's take a clue from Saturninus. It's true that the same phenomenon can be seen as a pain at one moment and a pleasure in another, and that both of these are judgments about that phenomenon, about the different roles that same phenomenon can play in different contexts. We are in the habit of evaluating the appearances we experience in relation to one another, in one or another context. We can't avoid doing so, yet that's where we are liable to go wrong; that's where we can be taken in by the illusion, like the birds who were fooled by Apelles' painting. The birds mistake one context for another — a real fresco on a wall for a real vineyard — precisely because they are having the same visual experience of grapes, grape leaves, stems, vines, etc. in the painting as they would if they saw a regular vineyard outdoors. Both in the vineyard and in the painting they see, as far as they're concerned, the same visual objects.

HARMONIA: But these visual objects cannot be the same. We have daubs of paint on a wall in one case, and real grapes in a real vineyard in real nature in the other.

LUCIAN: They appear to differ only if we confuse the different contexts. For the birds — or even for us, who also can be fooled by a good painting, or a mirror image — certain shapes and colours appear as immediately indistinguishable in one case as in the other, as indeed they are. Once they bang into the wall, however, the birds realize that they have made a mistake, and fly off the wiser. And, once we see that a painting is only shapes and colours on a wall, or that an image is only a reflection in a glass, we too can see our mistake in judgment. But we also continue to see the phenomenal identity between the images and the things they represent. After all, there is no doubt on a literal level when a representation succeeds for us, when it somehow captures or re-presents something that exists apart from it. Look at the Emperor's face on his coins; it is surely him we see there. We can be confident of that, the Pyrrhonists say, precisely because we see the same visual arrangement of elements — the line of his profile, the familiar curve of his nose, and so on — in each case. We find the same forms displayed on both the coin and the living man. The former we can retrieve from a purse or money chest and examine it, and the latter we can sometimes see in person at the Senate or in court, or in the theatre, or at the games, or with the army.

HARMONIA: Let me think about that. In the meantime, remind me what this hair-splitting about appearances has to do with our subject, good and evil.

LUCIAN: As a first approximation, let me suggest that what we call good and evil have to do with different contexts in which the same appearances can be found, not with those appearances as such.

HARMONIA: But aren't there appearances we would want to judge as good or bad apart from their context? Saturninus used the example of a hot poker to make the point that any experience, even feeling a red-hot poker, can be virtually eliminated. You seem to be agreeing with him.

LUCIAN: We can separate ourselves from our judgments about our experiences, if Saturninus is right, to the point of radically minimizing them. But minimizing an experience is not to eliminate it entirely. An involuntary residue remains, no matter what. We can't count on a lion we see in a cage, for instance, simply disappearing because we are distracted or bored, though we can detach ourselves to some degree from him, even if we remain in his presence. Similarly, I cannot help but suffer the hot poker whenever it is applied to my flesh, even if I am able to detach it from all judgments and interpretations, and so reduce its effect. I will still feel something, perhaps pressure rather than pain. The only consolation, Sextus says, is that if what I feel rises to the level of pain, it will be brief if sharp, while more chronic pains will be more moderate and intermittent, and thereby more bearable.

HARMONIA: So pain remains part of the involuntary residue, part of what there is to be experienced.

LUCIAN: Yes, though it can be reduced insofar as we can reduce the judgments and interpretations which magnify the pain—which is something that we (or at least some people) seem able to do. It should hurt less if I am able to identify less with the pain, but it will still hurt —or at least it will be felt—to some degree. No doubt the techniques of meditation and concentration developed by the gymnosophists of India and other wise persons seem to reduce pain dramatically without eliminating it. They can mortify their flesh, even consume themselves in fire, after all, without losing their composure. No doubt much can be learnt from them—but that's a topic, perhaps, for another day.

HARMONIA: Sorry, but I still don't understand. Let me put my question this way: to go back to pleasure, isn't it a property of the good as much as pain is a property of evil, as Philia suggested? And the same for other examples of what is good and what is evil, even those which the Epicureans dismiss: for instance, virtue, reason, self-realization, justice, the ideal world, and so on for what is good, and the opposite of these for what is evil. We might add still others: that the good is desirable, useful, and satisfying, and the opposite is the case for evil. Of course, some of these qualities may be in conflict, and we may disagree about them or even about what counts as good or evil, but then our challenge is not to throw up our hands and suspend judgment, as you seem to be suggesting, but to persevere in our inquiry and determine which of these are the true attributes of the good (and of evil, as the case may be). Isn't that so?

LUCIAN: The Pyrrhonists claim never to abandon inquiry; on the contrary, they embrace it. That's why they call themselves sceptics, in the sense of seekers, not doubters. Saturninus and other nihilists sometimes call themselves sceptics, but one might be sceptical of their scepticism, if I can put it that way. They do not seek the truth any longer, and are content merely to deny it exists. But here's the rub: if we knew what the good was, we would be able to determine which properties belong to it and which do not. But—and the Pyrrhonists insist on this—we can't hope to know even that much, at least not on any basis we can establish. There is not only no agreement about the good, or evil, there are conflicting views about them both, as I think we have already seen in our discussion so far tonight.

Perhaps I can bring this out more clearly if I ask you a series of questions, if you don't mind me pretending to be a prosecutor in court trying to elicit testimony from a witness.

HARMONIA: Go ahead.

LUCIAN: So tell me, Harmonia, conflicting properties or qualities cannot be instances of the same thing, can they? If something is a pleasure in one situation and a pain in another, then it seems that that thing cannot be either a pleasure or a pain?

HARMONIA: I suppose not.

LUCIAN: So as far as that's the case, we do not share collectively a notion of a single good, or a single evil?

HARMONIA: It would seem not.

LUCIAN: So, also if that were the case, we wouldn't be able to tell whether some phenomenon, something which immediately affects us, is a property of the good or of evil? A taste of wine, for instance, we might judge to be a good thing if we are lying down at dinner, but at the same time a bad thing if we are worried about our health, or have trouble sleeping. And to go back to the hot poker, to the extent to which we can free ourselves of contents which amplify its terror, which are mostly interpretations we imagine about our pain, the less significance it will have, the more tolerable it will be.

HARMONIA: But just what are these properties, or qualities? You call them phenomena. Can't I know what a property is—like a taste of wine—without necessarily knowing what it's a property of? I may be entirely ignorant of what a horse is, for instance, but if I hear just the neighing of a horse, I surely know that I'm hearing the neighing, even if I don't know what that sound may mean. I do know the sound. It's a distinctive sound, one I would recognize again.

LUCIAN: Exactly. That sound, the neighing, is not nothing; it has some kind of compelling presence of its own. It is not entirely determined by something else. It is not in itself an illusion. That's why the

Pyrrhonists stick to calling properties or qualities, like a sound or a taste, simply appearances, or things directly and immediately present to consciousness just as they are. A property or quality implies being a part of something definitive. Appearances just appear, and in various combinations, but not exclusively as part of one definitive thing. They are evident to us as the involuntary thoughts and sensations we necessarily suffer—sights, sounds, touches, tastes, smells, and thoughts. We don't know any more about them than that. We are— with regard to nature as a whole, or the totality of appearances— exactly like someone who hears the neighing of a horse for the first time. Such a person knows nothing of horses, does not know it is the neighing of a horse he or she is hearing. It is like listening to the speech of barbarians. We hear the sounds they make, but we do not know what, if anything, they mean by them.

That is how we live in the world of appearances, as the Pyrrhonists understand it. Nature—the flow of appearances through time—is like a language we hear, but which we don't understand, just like music, for instance. Not understanding what if anything music represents doesn't prevent us from admiring its beauty, or appreciating the structure and patterns it exhibits, or being overpowered by the various feelings it induces. We feel something like understanding or recognition when we hear music, but we cannot articulate *what* it is we are understanding or recognizing. The sublime beauty of nature is the same, as are our dreams, for that matter. Like music, or art in general, we can't explain what our natural appearances mean, that is, what if anything they represent, even when they affect us strongly, as they often do.

Now positive dogmatists—the three of you, Philia, Harmonia, and Petronius—try to define our appearances by coming up with some explanation of what they really mean, while negative dogmatists, like Saturninus here, maintain that no such explanation is to be had. The Pyrrhonists, by contrast to all of you, suspend judgment on whether appearances can be explained or not by something other than what they are. Instead of affirming or denying that appearances are other than what they appear, they accept them as they must for what they seem to be.

Dogmatists of all kinds persist in trying to advance some final definition of good and evil—even a definition which rejects all definitions, like the nihilists'—in hopes of settling the matter once and for all. You are not necessarily wrong to seek such a definition, and the Pyrrhonists are more than willing to entertain this as an open question, but their point is that no definitions so far proposed have been convincing, or evident, which leaves those definitions unsupported and open to objection. They are no more than beliefs.

HARMONIA: This still seems confusing to me. People say they might not be able to define something—say pornography, if I can be a little off-colour—but they also say that they know it when they see it. Can't we know good and evil when we see them in just the same way? Without having to define them?

LUCIAN: That's exactly what the Pyrrhonists maintain, but it's you dogmatists who are holding out for some definition. Since anything we can think of as a property of good can turn out to be a property of evil as well, and vice-versa, we are left with no clue as to what good and evil might be in themselves. Nonetheless, without knowing why, as with the beauty of music or nature, we continue to similarly respond to some things as good in one situation and as evil in another. Just because we don't seem to know what good and evil are doesn't mean that good and evil don't exist, or that we can't experience them. We obviously do.

HARMONIA: I'm not sure I'm ready for that conclusion. It seems to leave us with no basis of morality. You're saying that we have no understanding of good and evil apart from specific contexts in which they immediately affect us. But then good and evil seem to disappear beyond contradictory appearances, and we're left with no control over our own behaviour. You can't be serious!

RUFUS: Let me interrupt to see if I follow all this. So good and evil, as the Pyrrhonists tell the story, are not banished or overcome, but rendered manifest through phenomena, or the ordinary things that come to us in life, even though any specific phenomenon might be part of something good on one occasion, or something bad on another.

This reminds me of something we've all experienced. In the theatre, as we know, any actor can play any role—a man can play a woman, a woman a man, a coward a hero, a hero a coward, a wise man a fool, a fool a wise man, and so on—and similarly, if I follow you, Lucian, any experience can be experienced now as good, now as evil, now as indifferent, perhaps, and now good again, and so on. We naturally pursue those shifting appearances which we think can play the role of the good for us, and try to avoid those which can play the role of evil, even if it means embracing one appearance in one situation and avoiding it in another. Is that a fair summary of what you're saying, my son?

LUCIAN: I think so, yes.

RUFUS: So if the same appearance is good when it is a part of one context, that is, one complex of appearances, but bad when it is a part of another—as marital sex is good, we might say, and adulterous sex is bad—then sex as such is neither good nor bad. And since, it seems, we can find no appearances which are consistently and exclusively the parts of anything we can determine as good or evil, it remains, as a practical matter, that we can determine nothing at all to be good or evil, or even indifferent, not even our pleasures and pains, yet we continue somehow to experience good and evil. This seems an odd view of things, leaving one a passive observer of life at best, since we never can know what is actually good or evil. This hardly seems an improvement over Saturninus's nihilism.

[Pause …]

HARMONIA: So, Lucian, do you dispute Saturninus's point that our immediate experiences are unreliable, that they are no more than fleeting particulars, subject to change, and not stable, recurring universals?

LUCIAN: Yes, I do. Notice that if our sensations and thoughts are unreliable particulars, then the only way we can make sense of them is by interpreting them, or trying to, in terms of something else, something more enduring and therefore more reliable. Most commonly, that means positing some kind of continuing entity of which they are but imperfect expressions, an entity which exists independently of appearances, but which nonetheless is presumed to determine their nature. That's what positive dogmatists like you, Harmonia, try to do, and Philia and Petronius too. Saturninus simply despairs that any such independently existing, reliable entities can be found, but notice that he still presupposes that they are the solution needed to solve the problem of fleeting phenomena. You were quite right, Harmonia, to notice his negative dogmatism.

HARMONIA: How do we know when we're not misinterpreting our direct experiences?

LUCIAN: We don't have to interpret our direct experiences. We need only to let them speak to us directly.

HARMONIA: But, again, how do we know the difference? Don't our beliefs also speak to us directly?

LUCIAN: It is our imagination which allows us to interpret the things we experience. Normally, this is not a problem, and indeed a useful thing. If I see smoke in the distance, I interpret it as a sign of fire; if I see a scar on a soldier's arm, I interpret it as a sign of a wound. These interpretations are reliable because we can verify (or falsify) them with corresponding phenomena. We can go and see whether or not there's a fire where the smoke is coming from; and we can ask the soldier where he got the scar, and his testimony that it occurred in battle, say, is usually good enough to satisfy us.

HARMONIA: So to interpret something is to take it as a sign of something else.

LUCIAN: Yes. But here's the problem: we often interpret things without being able to produce what it is that we take them to signify. When we see thunder and lightning, for instance, we can interpret them, as many people do, as signs of Zeus stomping around in the heavens. But so far no one has ever actually seen Zeus up in the sky doing anything like that, or anywhere else for that matter. You dogmatists are in a similar predicament, though it's more subtle. The ideal Sage of the Stoics, Harmonia, is an imagined perfect person: someone who always does the right thing. But that's someone who doesn't seem to exist in reality. And the Stoics imagine the cosmos to be a reflection of a natural rational order which they say it somehow exemplifies, an order also not necessarily evident. Petronius follows Aristotle in a similar vein, imagining productive activity to be the vehicle of self-realization, when it might be just tedious or laborious. The Peripatetics, like the Platonists, imagine that the particular things which make up our experience are imperfect and changing realizations of independently existing ideal forms. And, not to leave Philia out of it, the Epicureans imagine invisible, impermeable, unchanging atoms which somehow make up the world around us. But there is no evidence at all for the real existence of these abstract atoms, nor of any of these other things. They are all imagined. They are no more than pictures we paint for ourselves in our minds.

HARMONIA: So we're supposed to suspend judgment about all these imagined things, according to the Pyrrhonists?

LUCIAN: That's right. But that doesn't mean falling back into the nihilism of Saturninus. We still have the ordinary world of regular experience, along with some ability to anticipate what it may bring.

HARMONIA: But the ordinary world is too unpredictable and dangerous for us to just throw ourselves on its mercy.

LUCIAN: Perhaps, but we can hardly avoid it. It remains our world, the only one we have. The flow of experience — the *logos* in the broadest sense — is certainly no continuous idyll, though it can contain idyllic moments.

HARMONIA: I don't see how that helps solve anything. It's the suffering and terror of life which disturbs us; it certainly haunts me.

LUCIAN: Which is precisely why dogmatism — positive and negative — is so tempting, or so say the Pyrrhonists. It seems to offer a way out, but its practice so far has been neither secure nor reliable. The

Pyrrhonists say of dogmatic belief that it's not only unnecessary, but harmful, or at least an unsatisfying burden. We might say that the good for them is the suspension of belief, and evil the embrace of belief.

RUFUS: You say we're better off without beliefs, or dogmas, but I am not yet persuaded. Since anything, any appearance, according to what you report the Pyrrhonists to say, can be good or evil in some circumstances but not in others, nothing is inherently or essentially or naturally good or evil in itself. So our judgments of good and evil evaporate from our experience, if I follow you, leaving us with no morality at all.

LUCIAN: Only with no morality we can articulate, any more than we can articulate the meaning of music or art or nature, as we said earlier, but which we nonetheless feel. But our inability to articulate meaning doesn't show that there is no meaning, only that we don't seem able to express or represent it. We are ignorant of it, at least in our current state, it seems. The Pyrrhonists follow as best they can the guidance of nature, as I've been trying to say, and recognize what seems to be good or evil in what they experience, just as they experience it, without being able to define it. Having beliefs about nature only distorts our reactions to what we experience. It's their view that we experience good and evil, but that we can't explain them or understand them, at least not so far.

RUFUS: But how can we judge what cannot be explained? How can we judge this experience here and now to be good and that same experience then and there to be evil?

LUCIAN: We don't have to judge. The uninterpreted experience judges for us, so to speak, and that's all we need—not the fictional context of belief but the real context of appearances. Appearances judge themselves, as it were, at least if we let them, and don't insist on confusing them with beliefs. The only way we can learn that the sound of neighing comes from a horse is if we are able to see the visual horse as it's neighing in addition to hearing its neighing. And the only way the birds will know that the grapes of Apelles are not real grapes is if they recognize the difference between his picture and a vineyard.

RUFUS: But then we are thrown on the mercy of a world at once beautiful and terrifying, a world where everything is subject to change. No wonder we hunger for peace of mind, for tranquillity.

LUCIAN: And we can have it, at least in part, by suspending beliefs. The Pyrrhonists call it *ataraxia*, a term the Epicureans borrowed but don't understand, I'm afraid. But nonetheless nature is something we continue to suffer whether we suspend beliefs or not.

[Pause ...]

RUFUS: I can see by their wrinkled foreheads and nervous eyebrows that our dogmatists here—Philia, Harmonia, and Petronius—are not yet persuaded, and, no doubt, have a further line of defence in mind for the utility of belief. And Saturninus too looks restless and ready to object. But the hour is late and nature calls an old man like me to bed. So let me invoke the prerogative of the host and adjourn us for this evening. Tomorrow after dinner we will gather again here in the garden and continue our discussion.

Do Things Exist Independently?

RUFUS: Well, relax everyone, and take a seat. Here we are again in the garden at twilight. It's another beautiful evening; the stars are beginning to peek out. The octopus and shrimp were a little extravagant, I suppose, but delightful, and perhaps we've already had a bit more to drink than usual. If 'in vino veritas' has any truth, then indeed we might make some progress tonight!

[Gentle laughter …]

It seems to me that Lucian here gave everyone a good run for their money last night, but you dogmatists — as he calls all of you, including Saturninus — you've had a quiet day to think, and perhaps you've found a way to rescue good and evil from the limbo, or at least uncertainty, to which Lucian seems to have cast them. So let's hear from the dogmatists! What say you Petronius? Age before beauty!

PETRONIUS: Well, there's no doubt that young Lucian here has become quite skilled in dialectic. Those Pyrrhonian disputations in Rome must be very sharp! But, as I mused about all this walking along the sea this morning, my thought was that Lucian and the Pyrrhonists come at the question of good and evil in the wrong way. Lucian is quite right that good and evil continue to elude us in the sense that any definition advanced so far is vulnerable to challenge by another which contradicts it. And while Lucian tries to avoid nihilism by suspending judgments about beliefs, without concluding, as Saturninus does, that they are all false, this general approach is too despairing, it seems to me, to be useful; it leaves us with nothing, it seems, and we can only wonder if we can ever make any progress at all.

The Pyrrhonists are always searching for the truth about things, or so they tell us, but I'm not sure I believe them. Any worthwhile search needs some clues, or at least a sense of direction, or some other sign of progress. But they don't provide any of that that I can see. If the search for truth is to be kept up, it needs to show some promise of reaching a conclusion. Still, Lucian's Pyrrhonism, to be fair, leaves open the question of whether one or another dogmatic view might not yet turn out to be true and finally clarify what we mean by good and evil, or some other understanding we're searching for. Even our current views shouldn't be dismissed just because they are challenged. Further debate might well elicit a deeper insight or implication on the part of one school or another that finally silences its critics and brings on a consensus. Isn't that what each school hopes for?

I'd say we've hardly begun to explore in depth the arguments of the various schools. That takes skill, something which requires not only knowing how to think, but perseverance. Only a person expert enough to distinguish between good and evil, or any of the other pressing issues of the day, would be in a position to be truly happy, it seems to me. It's a matter of learning how to make such distinctions, something the philosophical schools are all trying to do—except for Academics like Saturninus, who appear to have given up on the possibility. It would be rash, I think, to go so far as to conclude that our efforts are in vain.

PHILIA: Excellent, Petronius. You and I and Harmonia would agree, I take it, against Lucian and Saturninus, that at least some beliefs we hold about good and evil are true, or could be true, and provide us with the guidance we need to know how to live, how to find happiness, and that it is our job to seek them out. We differ over what those beliefs might be, to be sure, but not over whether there is a right belief out there somewhere, one which is necessary to determine in order to resolve the question of good and evil, and how to live.

RUFUS: Still, these beliefs, if they exist, would seem to have to do so independently of our phenomenal world. Saturninus says they can't be found at all, and has stopped looking. The rest of us may have found them, it seems, but can't be sure. Lucian can't find them either, but argues that we should suspend judgment about whether or not they exist. So I suggest we take as our subject tonight whether or not independently existing beliefs can actually be determined. Can we really expect to find them? Do we agree with the topic?

[All look at Lucian.]

LUCIAN: That's fine with me. Let us proceed, by all means, to see if such independently existing things can be established. I'll be curious to see how far we get.

PHILIA: Okay, then. What we so-called dogmatists seem to share is that there can be a science of how to live well, or properly, or virtuously, and that it starts with certain hypotheses, or ideas, which we can imagine and which we believe to exist independently of us, that is, of our imagining them, and which we then apply to our experience, to see if it explains what is going on. We ask, for instance, whether nature fits our idea of nature. Are we agreed so far?

HARMONIA: Yes, very much so.

[Petronius and Harmonia nod in assent, but Saturninus raises his hand.]

SATURNINUS: Before you start, let me object once more, before my views are rejected out of hand. The only hypothesis an Academic sceptic can accept is that there is no such hypothesis. What results from trying to isolate true beliefs, as we imagine them, is not any kind of guide to experience and happiness, as most of you seem to think, but the frustration of finding any such guide at all. Not that that has to be a bad thing. The idea that we have no guide at all to follow is the only liberation anyone needs. It's better to throw ourselves in the hands of fate and the gods, and to give up this futile struggle to find the right belief. Call it nihilism, if you like.

HARMONIA: But your idea of rejecting any hypothesis is itself a guide, a belief like any other, as I pointed out last night. You proceed by trying to reject every theory you encounter, and generally succeed. But that's a method just the same as any other! I'd say you share the dogmatic idea of a true belief, but despair of ever finding it. Yet that doesn't seem to bother you. Why not?

SATURNINUS: Because my method, as you put it, only tells me what not to do, and unlike yours, never what to do. Call it Socratic nihilism, after our true founder. Socrates claimed that he didn't know. That's a very different thing from thinking that you do or can know something, and yet it is sufficient for my purposes, or, I dare say, yours. You, Harmonia, along with Philia and Petronius, all think you can find a final guide to good and evil, or a happy life. I can only wish you luck.

HARMONIA: But how is your way a sufficient guide? It removes any possibility of meaning, or rather, it turns meaning into nothingness. What kind of liberation is that?

SATURNINUS: Let's be honest. The hard lesson, I would say, is that the world in fact has no meaning; that it's a chaos of experiences, a hall of mirrors where nothing is what it seems to be. We think we know so much, but we know nothing. As I suggested earlier, the best course is to leave it all up to the gods.

HARMONIA: Hard to see how that's liberating.

SATURNINUS: Because there's nothing left to lose.

HARMONIA: That's just not good enough for me. The nothingness you so smoothly promote seems terrifying, and the justice of the gods you invoke may not be any more to my liking than to yours.

PHILIA: Yes! It's outrageous, really. Not to use the intelligence the gods have given us to find our way in the world seems shocking and sacrilegious.

SATURNINUS: Academic nihilists use their minds to find their way like anyone else, only it's a negative path not a positive one.

PETRONIUS: Well, Saturninus, if philosophical issues can be decided by voting, I'd say you're voted the odd one out here.

SATURNINUS: Perhaps I am. But truth is not determined by majority vote. Just ask Lucian.

[Pause …]

LUCIAN: I have to agree with that. But, before we go further, let me add something more. Like Philia and Harmonia, I too see no advantage, and only detriment, in your nihilism, Saturninus. It's true that Academics and Pyrrhonists—you and I—both doubt beliefs. But the Pyrrhonists make the point that Harmonia just made: the Academics —certainly at their most notorious—turn doubt itself into dogma by leaping to the conclusion, as you do Saturninus, that nothing can be known.

This overlooks what our appearances have to teach us by dismissing them as illusions opaque to deeper realities. For the nihilistic philosophers, appearances have only a negative value as self-cancelling signs of nothingness. But Pyrrhonists see no reason to judge our appearances by any other standard than by what the appearances we suffer supply in themselves, as modifications of the soul we cannot escape. If appearances are not necessarily something to be explained by something else, by some particular belief, or set of beliefs, as the positive dogmatists hold, neither are they necessarily false, as the nihilistic negative dogmatists hold.

PHILIA: Lucian is lumping us all together as dogmatists, whether positive or negative. And I have to say, Saturninus, that I find it hard to see how your practical behaviour differs from that of us Epicureans, or any other dogmatist. After all, even if you reject all belief, you still have to blindly navigate the world of appearances, of pleasures and pains, just like the rest of us. And surely, you make the same kinds of calculations we all do. You eat when you're hungry, sleep when you're tired, and so on. Perhaps you are an Epicurean — or perhaps even a Peripatetic or Stoic — in spite of yourself?

SATURINIUS: Of course I make all those calculations, as we all must, but I'm not looking for some kind of resolution, or final solution, as you are. I have no clue where my calculations will lead, and I no longer worry about it. I only do what seems best at any given moment. You think, Philia, you can manage pleasures and pains to your advantage, if you're clever enough. And you put a value on pleasure over pain, as Harmonia puts a value on virtue over vice, or Petronius on self-realization over ignorance. I just try to cope as best I can, without any of those expectations. You're bound to be disappointed if your pleasures don't outweigh your pains, and so on for the rest. I simply roll with the punches, or try to. Nihilists can be quite humble, really.

   In the meantime, Rufus, how about another glass of that very good wine?

RUFUS: Of course, my friend! I don't think the servers have all crept off to bed yet. Steward! Call up the kitchen slaves! More drinks and refreshments all round!

[Pause …]

PETRONIUS: Rolling with the punches sounds well and good, by the way, especially for a man like you, Saturninus, neither young nor old, in the prime of life, if I may say so. You're a wealthy man with a fine estate, and proud of it, as you might well be, so, since we are among friends, let me be frank: perhaps you can afford this kind of Academic nihilism more than some others. If the gods didn't favour you so prodigiously, Saturninius, I venture you might sing a different tune.

SATURNINUS: Don't think I feel guilty about my good fortune. I don't. After all, there's no reason to feel guilty about anything since a countervailing reason not to feel guilty about it can always be found. You can bet on it. How things will turn out in the end, time alone will tell. In the meantime, maybe I'll feel remorse someday about my wealth, and maybe not. Who knows? But there's no getting past the illusory meaninglessness of all things, as I keep reminding you all, and any lingering hope, such as the Pyrrhonists seem to harbour, that our inquiries might turn out differently seems like a fantasy to me, like trying not to have your cake, but eating it too. I've made my views clear, I think, and I see no reason from anything said so far here tonight not to stick with them. You all can argue all you like, and I'll be content to sit back and watch the spectacle, unless I'm provoked, for I'm pretty sure you will reach no resolution.

LUCIAN: I can't share your certainty, Saturninus, that we are necessarily driven to a negative belief in nihilism, but neither do I, insofar as I follow the Pyrrhonists, see any merit in the idea of embracing some positive hypothesis—as Harmonia and Philia and Petronius here all do—on no more than the hope that it will lead to virtue or happiness or whatever is desired, or, if that fails, then trying on some other hypothesis, and so on, until we presumably strike upon the right one.

PHILIA: Well, that's exactly how we 'dogmatic' philosophers proceed, isn't it? We take up some positive hypothesis and apply it to life. Happiness is something we seek and value, and the good is whatever produces happiness, even if we have to invent it. So among our several philosophical schools we share a general standard or criterion of the good in spite of our differences—it's whatever truly promotes happiness—and we test our various definitions of the good against that standard. The Happy Man turns out to be the Good Man, also known as the Epicurean Sage who, like the Stoic Sage, does the right thing by consistently distinguishing between good and evil, or the beautiful and the ugly, or whatever demands discrimination.

HARMONIA: So far I have to agree with Philia, but how are we to test or apply these various views? Let us take seriously the rebuke Lucian keeps giving us, and return to my father's challenge and see if we can do better. Our starting points may be different, but we all aim in the same direction. We can expect that Philia here will propose the pursuit of pleasure and the avoidance of pain, and you, dear Petronius, will propose the fulfilment of the self through productive activity, and I dare say I will propose holding steadfastly to virtue, to the rational order of the universe, whether or not it brings us pleasure or pain, or self-fulfilment. But how can we adjudicate among these approaches? Although I can't agree with everything they say, Lucian and Saturninus have a point that the very differences of opinion about good and evil threaten to undermine the claims of each one of us, unless we can do better than we have.

PETRONIUS: Why can't we say that it's a matter of personal prefer- ence or individual disposition as to what works for each of us? Not everyone can or should be a Stoic, or a Peripatetic, or an Epicurean. If anyone is dissatisfied with one view, then by all means try another. Aren't there many paths? When students went to Athens to listen to the philosophers, they'd first sample one, and then another, and make the rounds until they found one they liked, or else they gave up on the whole enterprise. I agree with Harmonia that a presumption of some kind of independently existing good and evil—some belief or mental picture about these which makes sense—is what is needed to become a Happy Person, or to achieve a Happy Life. But it has to match the intuitions one already has. It has to fit your needs and your per- sonality. Without that, we are left in the lurch, like our friend Saturninus here, I would say, with no values at all, except nothingness itself. He says he's happy, but he seems the very example of the Unhappy Man, restless, and I would guess rather bored. How else can you describe someone who denies he can find the beliefs he believes are required to understand Good and Evil? As for Lucian and his Pyrrhonists, this suspension of judgment seems a clever evasion.

RUFUS: This merry-go-round of different views reminds me of the old story that used to be told in the Academy. Suppose, as the tale went, that each of the things said to be good presented itself in the theatre, with a prize to be voted by the audience for which of them was the genuine good. First on stage came Wealth, with a fine if somewhat self-satisfied speech, describing all the advantages which money can buy, which are considerable, as we all know. Meeting with roars of approval, Wealth was about to be acclaimed the ultimate good straight off, when Pleasure suddenly took the stage, pushing Wealth aside.

Wealth, as Pleasure pointed out, while singing a gay tune, is easily lost and never secure, and is of little benefit in gaining the things that really matter most, such as love and beauty and the like, which cannot be bought, but are intrinsically good. The crowd at once abandoned Wealth and cheered instead for Pleasure, and would have awarded her the prize, except that Health then took the stage, stepped in front of Pleasure and reminded all, in a sober speech, that, without her, Wealth and Pleasure are meaningless. If you don't have your health, after all, you don't have anything. The fickle crowd, suddenly quiet and thoughtful, again changed its mind, and solemnly resolved that Health should take the palm. But then Courage quietly came forth and brushed the others aside, and calmly in epic verses declaimed that none of his competitors could hope to thrive unless Courage himself guaranteed everyone's security, making it clear that valour trumps all the rest. And so it went, with every conceivable good taking its bow, with the last one invariably carrying the day. It is only the novelty of the good which is on current display, combined with the strength of its presence, it seems, which makes it temporarily persuasive, not any comparative measure of its attributes.

LUCIAN: A charming and disturbing story. Doesn't it show that beliefs are based on imagining something to be the case, not on any common evidence which shows that they are in fact the case? The audience is asked after all to imagine being wealthy, or physically fit, and so on. Since we can imagine different and often incompatible and even contradictory things, as if they existed independently, and since we tend to identify with, or at least approve, much of what we can imagine, our beliefs often end up at once self-fulfilling and self-defeating. Self-fulfilling because we seem free to identify with and control whatever it is we imagine the good to be, and self-defeating because we can imagine the good as now one thing, and now as some-thing quite different, even inconsistent with the first thing, as we've already seen in our own discussions. In this situation, even the Pyrrhonists would say, we have not yet distinguished successfully between good and evil, so it is necessary to keep on searching.

PETRONIUS: Of course. But the Happy Man or Woman has succeeded where these others have failed, haven't they? Such people do exist. They called Democritus the 'happy man', didn't they? 'Happy' people are recognized and admired precisely because of their ability to distinguish those things which are good, and to avoid those which are evil. They exemplify steps in the direction of the Sage, or the perfect person.

LUCIAN: We may doubt whether the Happy Man or Woman really exists, let alone the Sage, but if so, then he or she succeeds by somehow discerning or learning what is good and what is evil. Isn't that what you've been maintaining?

PETRONIUS: Absolutely.

LUCIAN: And we learn what is good and evil by gaining some sort of understanding through moral training, let's call it, which allows us to identify what is good and what is evil.

PETRONIUS: Yes, that's the idea.

LUCIAN: And some people identify one thing as good (or evil) and some another; some, as we've just heard, might conclude that Wealth is good, and Poverty is evil, and others that it's Health on the one side, and Sickness on the other; and so on. But we don't know who's right or wrong. Sextus in his lectures offers the example of several archers shooting at a target in the dark. Whether they hit or miss the target, no one can know, as long as they remain in the dark. Similarly, whether or not our beliefs hit the target of truth remains unknown. We're still waiting for the light to illuminate the truth, aren't we?

PETRONIUS: Well, the difficulty of knowing who hits the mark and who misses is precisely why understanding and training are necessary. Perhaps someone, like the Sage, will suddenly come along with a bright torch so we can see where all the arrows we shot in the dark ended up. It's no easy thing to identify good and evil, obviously, but that doesn't mean it can't be done, as even you Pyrrhonists admit. We dogmatists, as you call us, maintain that good and evil exist by nature—who could doubt it?—but admit they are not easily discovered. It's not just that we take them on faith, and are content merely with what we can imagine; we aim to establish them firmly, one way or another. When we say they exist by nature we mean they exist, like any other truth of nature, independently of us, consistently and reliably. Surely Pythagoras's triangles exist independently of us, as do the stars in the heavens, and all the things we find in nature. And to discover them is clearly a sure way to be happy, or at least to gain what happiness we can. We are born ignorant of most things, after all, and therefore must learn about them. Good and evil are no different from any of the other less than obvious things we must learn about in life.

LUCIAN: A nice speech, but one might well doubt that good and evil, or for that matter any of the other things you say exist independently by nature, in fact do so exist. Where is the evidence they do? More to the point, why presume that anything exists independently in the first place? Indeed, doubting is possible only where there is such a presumption, or preconception.

So let me ask you something, Petronius, and this applies to Philia and Harmonia as well. You hold, do you not, that the good is desirable for its own sake? Isn't that right?

[Petronius, Philia, and Harmonia all nod yes.]

And anything good desirable for its own sake would have to be recognized by all, isn't that so? If we could show that, we would move beyond faith towards knowledge, as you claim, wouldn't we? Who will answer?

HARMONIA: I will. Yes, what is truly good must in the end be good for all; it must be something we can all hold in common, once we find it, of course. For Stoics, of course, the good is virtue, discovered by attention to nature, to the changing course of events, through which we recognize the destiny of our lives, which we believe can be achieved by anyone to their satisfaction. Indeed, it is from this virtue, as from a fountain, that all good and useful things—proper conduct, friendship, justice, and all the rest—spring.

LUCIAN: It all sounds noble enough, but how do you get past the apparent divergence of views of the good before rushing on to their common essence? Do you still believe everyone really must come to the same conclusions over belief? Hardly. Beauty, some say, is a common good, or should be, but when men, at least, inquire into the comely features of women—I trust the women here will pardon me!—we find that the Ethiopian prefers the blackest, and the Persian the whitest, and others have still other preferences, a slim body vs. a plump one, and of course vice-versa, and so on. The preference for any one option implies the exclusion of the others. Just how then do we determine, for instance, the essence of feminine beauty? The ideal woman, it seems, can be neither black nor white, snub-nosed nor aquiline, nor any other quality, and, if we pursue this line of investigation, we discover that there is nothing at all she can be! And similarly, one person's virtue may be another's vice. Some say greed is bad, but others embrace it as good. Where's virtue to be found? Isn't there honour among thieves? It looks like Saturninus has a point.

HARMONIA: All I hear you saying, Lucian, is that neither the good nor the bad can be explained, as many of us believe. For, you say, there seems to be no end of diversity and contradiction in the senses, at least so far, and no end to it at all, as Saturninus maintains. Fortunately, however, there is a way out. It is through reasoning about sense experience that we are able to refine our ideas into concepts, and arrive at the truth of the good and other non-evident ideas. The use of reason is how true philosophers differ from untutored folk—who are easily diverted by games and bread, or myths and rituals, or fame and fortune—as well as from nihilists and Pyrrhonists. Here's the point: we are not left with nothing at all when we exercise our reasoning, as Saturninus would have it. On the contrary, our reason is not a dead end, but the road to truth. It allows us to sort out the vagaries of sensory experience in order to isolate what they have in common and make progress in understanding. So we reason about, say, ambition or courage or justice, and try to determine when and where they can be found and applied, if at all. Reason is our guide in life because it alone illuminates independently existing truths.

LUCIAN: But how is it that even the philosophers who rely on reasoning come to different conclusions? We've seen this with all of you in this discussion, and we can't seem to get around it. Zeno, the founder of your school, Harmonia, came up with his rational intuition, as we might put it, of virtue, which you just invoked. And Epicurus, Philia's mentor, ends up with pleasure as something we can focus on and calculate, and, of course, your Aristotle, Petronius, settles on productive activity and the honours it brings, while Saturninus, taking things a step further, uses reason against itself to show that it's self-defeating, and that we should be satisfied with nothingness.

[Pause …]

RUFUS: I hope we're not going round in circles. I appreciate that this appeal to independent, non-evident assumptions to somehow explain experience seems an elusive business indeed. It puzzled me when I made the rounds of a few philosophers in my youth. It seemed then as now a technique or practice, well-honed by most philosophers, especially the scientists, to illuminate truth, as they claimed. But sceptical philosophers, such as nihilists and Pyrrhonians, opposed the non-evident assumptions of their opponents against one another to perplex them, and undermine their beliefs, and reduce them to silence. It turned out that no one's beliefs were safe from their criticism.

LUCIAN: Well, reasoning serves only to elucidate something already presumed, something felt or intuited, perhaps, but not known. Reasoning is no better than its premises. It brings out the implications of what someone already believes. The beliefs of the dogmatists are really matters of faith; they believe that a leap can be made from what they regard as the shifting, chaotic, and contradictory experiences of life to some safe landing in a presumed unity of being, in an independently existing truth.

It is not that the dogmatic philosophers reach a conclusion which must be binding on us all—even if that's what they think—but rather that they present one or another imaginative vision, a myth, if you like, something we are free to accept, or not. They offer us an appealing vision of some kind of harmony and unity underlying the surface confusion and sadness and tragedy of life. Once you assent to it, you're hooked. What you call reason, Harmonia, is really the logical unfolding of some imaginative projection we entertain, and which can enthral us, even if it can't be established to everyone's satisfaction.

HARMONIA: Not so fast. I'd rather not get technical, but we Stoics aren't just making leaps of faith. A rigorous method of truth has been worked out by the Stoics—from Zeno, who may have got the idea of living by nature from Diogenes, through Cleanthes and Chrysippus and Antipater and Posidonius and all the rest, down to Seneca and Epictetus—and you're just ignoring it. The heart of the matter, as I'm sure you're aware, but perhaps do not fully appreciate, is what the Stoics call an apprehensive presentation—as assent to an appearance as a representation of something independently existing. We think it makes more explicit what Aristotle and the Epicureans already suggest about how we gain knowledge.

LUCIAN: Well, let's hear what you don't think I understand, which I very well may not. Remind us of how Stoics think we can apprehend knowledge of things.

HARMONIA: The question is how we know which of our thoughts and sensations accurately represent what they seem to represent, and which do not. Saturninus is right that we can be fooled by our impressions when we take them to be a sign of something which they are not. The Stoics push back by saying that that does not prevent some appearances from being true impressions of an external object, say this goblet I'm raising up right now. This goblet, just as we see it, is grasped by our souls, just as a hand grasps a stone, or a net grasps a fish. The result is something captured by consciousness, some particular reality constituted by a complex of phenomena. That reality is retained and somehow stored in consciousness and subsequently compared with other realities similarly captured and stored by consciousness, thus building up a rational picture of the world in our minds of how all these things are linked together. Through such careful examination—we call it science—we learn how the world works, and how best to navigate through it. This knowledge is virtue, since it displays a kind of beauty in its inevitability, and gives us solace for the place evil and pain have in the scheme of things.

LUCIAN: The question of how we can tell the difference between these two kinds of appearances—the true and the false—remains. You say the goblet you raise is the real thing, that you somehow grasp its substance, its independent existence or reality, somehow in your mind. But there is nothing there other than some passing phenomena of shape and colour and texture, momentarily combined. What you imagine is some kind of essence or enduring form behind that momentary conjunction, but there is no warrant to conclude the independent existence of something simply because you can imagine it. To do so is to speculatively interpret your experience of vision and touch. Now we can disagree, it seems, about any interpretation of any experience, including the most basic; we can disagree about the proposed reality of the goblet. On the other hand, no one disagrees about their own appearances, about whether they themselves feel hot or cold, pleasure or pain, light and darkness, love or hate, and all the rest.

SATURNINUS: Lucian, I have to ask you something before you go any further. Last night I was about to object to your confidence in appearances, but the conversation went off in a different direction, and I let it go. But since appearances have come up again, I have to press you on this again. Our appearances, it seems to me, are far from reliable, as I have already argued, and if they are involuntary as you say they are, then it's all the worse for us. We are easily confused by them, a point on which Aristotelians, Epicureans, and Stoics all agree with the Academics. You're the odd man out on that. I can be fooled by a counterfeit coin, or a slave I buy in the marketplace may look healthy and strong, but might turn out to be sick and weak. I may be impressed by the beauty of a woman, but that same beauty can turn into a curse if she spurns me for another. Or the grapes in my vineyards may look promising when the vines first bud out in the spring, but might still turn out to make poor wine. I could go on and on.

Let me put it this way: I agree with you, Lucian, about the failure of reasoning to get at the truth, as the Stoics and others claim it does.

There is no apprehensive grasping of the reality of things, or any similar mechanism. On that point, we agree. But I can't follow you in putting your trust in appearances, in spite of that, to somehow save the day. I have to stand with the dogmatists, that our appearances play us false. And if one rejects—as I do—both appearances and reason as criteria of truth, then nothing is left as a foundation for saying anything is true or false, good or evil. That leaves no alternative to nihilism.

LUCIAN: Well, the Pyrrhonist response to this objection is to begin by distinguishing between our appearances and our interpretations of them, as I tried to point out last night and again just now.

SATURNINUS: Yes, I get it. You want to say that we go astray not with sensations as such, but with how we interpret them. That's a nice distinction you've introduced, but I continue to argue that there is no end of interpretation, no way to separate a sensation, even Harmonia's goblet, from some interpretation of it. You say we can't help but see the blue sky under normal conditions, or the goblet, which sounds convincing, but invoking normal conditions begs the question, doesn't it? How do we know what is normal? Does a baby know it's seeing the sky? Maybe we suffer a mass delusion, inflicted by some god, which leads us to interpret the sky as blue? Maybe our 'normal' vision is only the way human beings happen to see things. A dog or an eagle or a bumblebee might not see a blue sky at all. There is no 'blue sky', for all we know, just a subjective sensation we, or some of us, think we happen to have. It is an illusion because it seems to represent something external, yet it cannot actually be shown to do so.

LUCIAN: Nicely put, but when you say there is no blue sky you are still positing an independently existing reality lying behind our visual phenomena as the standard of what would reveal the truth about the colour of the sky, except for the inconvenience that we can't seem to find it. You conclude that there is no way to be sure that the appearances we actually have in fact represent any independently existing reality. And I have to agree with you.

SATURNINUS: I'm glad to hear it.

LUCIAN: But here's where we differ. The appearances we actually have—such as the blue sky which at least you and I and other human beings can agree that we see—are not necessarily in question. We don't know about the dog or eagle or bumblebee, or even the baby, it's true; we can't ask them what they see and get an answer. But there is nothing in their behaviour that contradicts the notion that they see more or less, or at least some, of what we see. My dog may or may not see colours as I do, but when I show him a bone he responds, at least in part, to something to which I am also responding, namely, the bone. That we respond together to something is crucial. Very tellingly, in contrast to animals, we humans are able to ask one another about our appearances, and, by pointing and comparing and so on, we can make it as evident as we need that we are looking at the same sky, and that we see the same colour, and so on. We can compare what we see in the sky with colour samples, for instance, and agree that what we're seeing together is something to which we can give a name, say, blue. The key point is that there is no reason to think otherwise.

SATURNINUS: Really? Just how do we know that what we agree to call 'blue' is the same for each of us? I might be seeing something totally different in colour than what you see in the sky, even if we agree to use the same colour word to describe it, or point to the same samples.

LUCIAN: Well, I can look up through the portico here in the garden, and I can point to the sky beyond, dark as it is at this hour, and you can do the same, and there's no reason for us not to say that we are each looking at the same dark sky, meaning that we share an appearance. That's how we test, at least in part, whether we share the same phenomenal experience or not. Now maybe you are a semi-blind person, or jaundiced, or somehow otherwise you do not in fact see the same blue sky I do. But what's interesting is that we are also able to determine that we don't see something in common in just the same way as we are able to determine that we do see something in common. We can similarly determine if, say, you are jaundiced or otherwise visually compromised through physical gesture, comparison, symbol, language, and so on. In fact, that's how we know that someone who's ill or injured can have different appearances from ours. We can be clear, apparently, even about our differences.

SATURNINUS: Ah, but that isn't necessarily so. I might still see different colours than you do in every case, without any kind of test showing any difference. What is blue for you whenever you see it might be red for me whenever I see it, but as long as this difference is experienced consistently, and privately, no one can tell it is there.

LUCIAN: But the point you make remains a moot one as long as there is no actual appearance of a difference, for then there is also no basis for postulating a difference, as you do. That you can imagine that we see different things without them appearing different doesn't establish that in fact we do see different things, as you seem to think. You are driven, in order to maintain your view, to imagine how things might appear differently to each of us without showing that they in fact do so. You require an unsubstantiated belief about what might be the case to make your point, but without anything at all to show that it is actually the case.

SATURNINUS: Yes, and that's all I need.

LUCIAN: Unfortunately, the price you pay for embracing your belief is to discount what the *only* evidence we have actually says — namely, that under ordinary circumstances we seem to see things in common, and that we can confirm and agree about that to our satisfaction. The Pyrrhonists are content to stay within appearances. Even if we did see different colours without being able to tell the difference, it remains that whatever colours each of us sees plays exactly the same role in our vision. Insofar as they are perfectly interchangeable, and do not appear otherwise, there remains no reason to say they are not the same. It is, in fact, only reasonable to say that they *are* the same for our purposes, at least insofar as we can tell. Your view seems self-defeating, even perverse. You are forced to use an unfounded belief, a speculation, to support your view of what you think is real, but it doesn't really help you. The Pyrrhonists, by contrast, prefer to follow what our appearances actually tell us, and not to interpret them.

HARMONIA: But then nothing we see can gives us absolute knowl-edge of the sky as it really is. It only provides us, if you're right, with the right to conclude whether or not we are sharing common appear-ances, without knowing what they are. That doesn't seem very satisfying, or take us very far. It may look like we share appearances, but we still don't know for sure whether we are or not.

LUCIAN: Well, we should remember that we have to rely on our appearances. They are all we have. Saturninus doesn't think we can distinguish between our appearances and our interpretations of them, and dismisses them all as illusions, but in fact even he relies on common appearances every day. It's one thing to say that your goblet is an illusion, but that doesn't prevent you or me or Saturninus from drinking from an illusion. We can even share it in a common illusory libation! The proof is in the pudding, as they say, in the phenomena we actually share, not in speculation, of which there is no end.

HARMONIA: I think you're giving up too much Lucian. If we can't penetrate to the essence of things, it's hard to see how we can hope to understand the world, or, for that matter, what is good and what is evil. You dismiss the Stoic analysis of the apprehension of real things, like other dogmatic claims, as just more speculation, yet it remains, to me at least, a comprehensive account of how we can begin to know our otherwise problematic universe. It shows that opposites like good and evil make sense in relation to how rational we understand the world to be. How can we suddenly be expected to rely on appearances?

But, if we must do so, and suspend judgment on the real nature of things, I ask again, what is left? If there is no independently existing world somehow represented by our appearances, then I can hardly conceive of where that leaves us. And if it can't be proven that we share the same appearances without a doubt, then we seem to be plunged into our own private worlds which at best seem to be super-ficially or indirectly connected, if at all. That seems to make our appearances look just like the illusions Saturninus thinks they are.

LUCIAN: Lots of questions! Let me try to back up a bit to address them. If the Pyrrhonists are right about appearances, then indeed we are not subjects living in an external, independently existing world governed by reason or pleasure or some other principle. Or at least we can't conclude that. On the contrary, what is interpreted to be an independently existing world can just as well be something which exists within us, at least as a first approximation, as you suggest. That is, our appearances — sensations as well as thoughts — can be presumed to be located in our souls, as it were, that is to say, somehow inside of our bodies, in our minds, or imaginations; similarly, they can just as well be presumed to be located outside of our bodies, that is, in externally existing things. What we take to be the external world does not, as far as we can tell, really exist. Yes, of course it might, but so far we have no evidence that it does, and certainly we have not earned that conclusion. By the same token, however, if we cannot establish the existence of an external world, neither can we establish the existence of an internal world. Based on the only evidence we have — of our own existence as souls which suffer sensations and thoughts — then space and time, or inner and outer, do not exist except as secondary constructions out of something more basic, something neither external nor internal.

HARMONIA: That seems pretty bizarre. You're suggesting we live in an indeterminate dream world out of which arises what appears to be an external world of objects in which we find ourselves, along with a separate but parallel internal world of thoughts. But if we cannot establish that we actually share these appearances, but only seem to do so, then we seem sunk in isolated subjectivism. How do the Pyrrhonists get out of that?

LUCIAN: To answer that we need a sense of what primitive, or unconstructed, or uninterpreted appearances actually are. We're used to thinking of them as bundled together into the common objects of everyday life — a woman, a dog, a horse, a road, a tree, the sea, a house, a city, and so on. Like the Epicureans, the Pyrrhonists presume that ordinary things are made up of parts, or elements, or atoms, if you like. But while the atoms of the Epicureans are unobservable fictional entities, those of the Pyrrhonists are actual phenomena, the smallest parts of our sensations and thoughts which we directly experience. The grosser objects we experience are but combinations of elemental sights, sounds, touches, smells, tastes, and thoughts.

Remember the distinction we made last night between the neighing of the horse and the horse itself? The neighing horse is the horse we hear; but the horse we see—the visual horse—is quite something else; so is the horse we touch, and the horse we smell, and the horse we taste (if we dare to eat horse meat!). These are all entirely distinct 'horses', corresponding to the different senses—sound, sight, touch, smell, and taste—and quite unpredictable and completely unrelated to one another. There is nothing about any of these 'horses' which remotely suggests any of the others. There is nothing about the 'horse' we hear that suggests the 'horse' we see, or the 'horse' we touch, and so on for the rest of them. You cannot get from one to the other. Someone born blind, for instance, has no way of imagining what a visual horse would be like. The senses are entirely heterogeneous, as far as we can tell.

When I say they are unpredictable, I mean there is no apparent way to infer, say, the visual horse from the audible horse, and so on. No rational inferences seem applicable. We should perhaps add as well the 'horse' we can only imagine, or think, which the Pyrrhonists consider a sixth sense. Of course, there is no doubt about any of these 'horses' in themselves. It is the idea that they are the qualities of some independent essence or substance that is in question. That is the truth, according to the Pyrrhonists, which we cannot say exists, even if it does; nor can we say it does not exist, even if it does not.

So here's the Pyrrhonist observation about independently existing things: there is no underlying 'horse', no such thing as an apprehensive conception which brings them together. As far as I can see there is only a congeries of radically different sensory things contingently but consistently associated together, which we find convenient and useful to call a horse. There is no external, independently existing horse, no common essence or substance of horse, at least not that we can find. Nor is there an internal, independently existing horse we can find either. These different 'horses' are no more, but also no less, than mere items of consciousness. They are simply things which appear. There is no need to assume any kind of independently existing horse at all; we can do quite nicely without that notion.

HARMONIA: But don't the associations between the audible, the visual, the tactile, and the rest point directly to the independently existing horse? Isn't that a compelling conclusion? Doesn't the consistency of their correlations demand it? And the question still remains of how we can establish that the phenomenal atoms are shared in common rather than subjectively and perhaps differently experienced.

LUCIAN: Well, think of the alphabet. We have the visual letters—A, B, C, and the rest—and we have the audible or spoken letters—'eh', 'bee', 'see', and the rest, just as we pronounce them. We do not conclude that there are independently existing letters underlying the distinct visual and audible letters, that is, that there is some kind of common essence informing A, B, C, etc., as well as 'eh', 'bee', 'see', and the rest. It's the same with the phenomenal alphabet of sensations and thoughts, if we can call it that, where the smallest visual elements, audible elements, thought elements, and so on are combined together to create the gross objects of our experience, like the visual horse, the audible horse, and so on. As for sharing these phenomenal elements, keep in mind that if they exist prior to any distinction between inner and outer, between object and subject, then there is no reason to think they must be subjective and so cannot be shared. It is when we use our beliefs to interpret the phenomena we share in common that distortions arise.

What the Pyrrhonists say is that by suspending judgments on independently existing things, on the essence or nature of things, we are liberated from the anxieties which come with making those judgments. You dogmatists argue over whether such things exist or not, over being and nothingness, as it were. Such mind-splitting puzzles! The Pyrrhonists avoid these extremes, and pursue a middle path between them; they acknowledge only the appearances they cannot deny, and set aside speculations about their true nature, or lack thereof.

HARMONIA: But the perceptions you say we must suffer are of every which sort, good as well as evil, pleasures as well as pains. So we cannot hope to avoid the ups and downs of life.

LUCIAN: That's right, there's no telling whether a specific perception will always be good or evil, as we've seen. The difference is that the Pyrrhonists avoid, or say they avoid, the anxieties connected with our beliefs about things, that is, our opinions or interpretations of them. It's one thing to experience physical pain; it's quite another to fear the harm that will come because of some belief you hold about the pain. If you believe, for instance, in health as a value, anything which seems to threaten your health, such as pain, will give rise to anxiety.

HARMONIA: But isn't health a value?

LUCIAN: The Pyrrhonist, like anyone else, tries to avoid pains and enjoy pleasure, and cultivate health as a value, yes, but he or she will not make a fetish of it. The idea is to keep fit in a moderate way, but not spend all day long at the gymnasium, or obsess over what foods and herbs and drugs are best, or who the best trainers are. There are also situations in which health can play an evil role for us. A healthy adversary, say in battle, is more likely to be harmful to us than one who is wounded or sick. By a belief in health the Pyrrhonists mean what we might call a health nut; and similarly for any other such obsession, such as love of money, or fame, and so on. Even the love of wisdom can be a fetish. Anyone with beliefs has more to lose, and so will suffer more than is needed.

HARMONIA: So the person without beliefs is the one who is the happiest?

LUCIAN: It appears so. Or the least unhappy. Of course, it's a relative happiness. No one can escape the ills and pains of life entirely.

HARMONIA: I don't know. 'Relative happiness' doesn't sound that exciting. We dogmatic philosophers, and I'll include Saturninus here with the rest of us to please you, aren't so easily disabused of what I assume you suppose to be our fetish: a love of wisdom. Are you giving up on wisdom?

LUCIAN: Well, perhaps it's possible to worry about it too much …

RUFUS: Ah, Lucian, pardon my interruption. It's been another interesting but long evening. Before you continue, and perhaps provoke some further objections among the dogmatists, let me invoke the prerogative of the host, and of a father, and call our session to an end, at least for tonight. An excellent discussion. But once more the hour is late and our beds beckon, whether they exist 'out there' or in our minds, or perhaps nowhere at all! We have one more day together. Perhaps tomorrow's discussion will come to some resolution. So, for now, let us say good night and look forward to the morrow!

The Third Evening

Is There a Middle Path?

RUFUS: Now that we are gathered together for our last evening, let me share something odd. I don't know about any of you, but I had a restless sleep last night. In a disturbing dream, I found myself puzzled about whether I somehow existed in the external world, or whether the external world was in some way hidden within me! I first dreamt finding myself going, with a flickering torch, down one dark tunnel after another, searching for the good, hoping to avoid evil, and coming up empty-handed. Then, as the dream wore on, I found the world, so to speak, suddenly spinning faster and faster inside of me as I turned into a charioteer going faster and faster round the track in the Circus. In each circuit of the race, I could see flashing by me, a bit blurred, the bright and crowded galleries, with their many flags and streamers waving, over and over again in round after round, with accompanying shouts, groans, and cheers, all in rapid sequence. It seemed to me, upon suddenly waking with a start, and thinking quietly a bit, that the flurry of the race captured the fleeting nature of our senses in the everyday world, but also that their involuntary, repeated recurrence promised a kind of stability even in the midst of change. On the other hand, my empty-handed nocturnal excursions into the tunnels left me cold and depressed, like the seemingly endless search to find the nature of things.

If dreams are any kind of an omen, this one at least seems to portend that the world is within me, or at least is somehow dependent upon me, as I think Lucian was suggesting last night, rather than existing independently of me. Or maybe I just couldn't find the right tunnel to explore, the one which leads to the light of a world beyond, or maybe the tunnels and spinning vision of the Circus are both illusions, as Saturninus would say. What does a dream signify anyway? Perhaps just the vapours of last night's wine.

I suggest we spend our final evening of our visit together by looking more closely at the notion of whether or not there can be an art or science of life, something we have circled around but haven't directly addressed. In our time, that means, from what we've been saying, learning how to live in a world of conflicting beliefs, where good and evil, right and wrong, or almost any values are up for grabs. You dogmatists, except for Saturninus, seem intent that there can be some kind of a science, or practice, of life. Saturninus seems equally intent that no such thing is possible, while Lucian seems to seek an alternative path, a sort of middle way between the extreme of positive dogmatic beliefs, and the negative dogmatic extreme of the Academics, if I understand him at all. Who shall begin? Saturninus?

SATURNINUS: All right. I agree that a science, or even an art, of living presupposes knowledge. And by knowledge we mean some kind of underlying or unifying understanding of things, a description of their unique essence, if you will. The question which set us off the first night was whether or not we can have knowledge of good and evil, and we might as well ask whether we can have knowledge of anything at all. How do we know that we know anything? Or do we only think we know? We might, to pick an example from last night, ask what is a horse? Of course, there are many different kinds of horses—big ones, little ones, strong ones, weak ones, white ones, brown ones, not to mention mares, colts, and stallions, and so on. Since all these particular horses divide up what it is to be a horse into many kinds of horses, there must be something else, some general concept or notion or idea of a horse apart from any particular horse, which unifies them together, and finding that concept or notion is the business of inquiry or science. My point, however, is that we can never get there, that there is no concept or notion that can do the job. So there is no real science, and certainly no science of how to live.

PHILIA: But surely there is something you're overlooking about all these particular horses, something which distinguishes them from animals which are not horses. Why is it that we're not confused by this in ordinary life? We know a horse, as they say, when we see one, or hear one, or touch one. There are perhaps borderline cases—such as mules—but surely we somehow seem to know what a horse is, especially a real one, don't we? Just as we somehow seem to know what good or evil are, I would add, so it is with horses. Of course, some cases are harder than others, and difficulties arise. Our discussion has shown, if nothing else, how hard it can be to clarify what we think we know, but that doesn't mean we should give up, or that our intuitions should be abandoned. Maybe there is something about horses we haven't yet discovered, but when we do, we'll be able to distinguish them more precisely from other animals, and therefore know more clearly how they and other animals might or might not be related. Maybe there is something, for instance, about the mixture of particular atoms which make up horses. Perhaps a certain combination of atoms gives us a horse, and another combination, a chicken, and so on? Perhaps there are families or varieties of combinations of atoms which give us the various kinds of anything? Who knows? But if we knew that was so, then we might be able to breed horses more scientifically, or understand how they should be better nourished, or treated better when they are ill, and so on.

By saying that there can be no knowledge at all, Saturninus, you're saying that there can be no science at all. But we do have science! Look at geometry, for instance, the science of how things are laid out in space. How can you doubt that points and lines and planes and shapes and solids and so on are the essence or underlying structure of objects?

SATURNINUS: Well, the notions of geometry are so many lovely fictions, are they not? Are you so sure that Euclid's postulates and definitions are final? If we changed even one of them we would get a very different geometry describing a very different world, which very well may exist out there somewhere. In the meantime, our perceptions, or appearances, come and go, and need not correspond with any geometry we can invent. Indeed, we can interpret our appearances to fit with many geometries.

We see here once more the futile effort of the mind trying to extract the *logos* out of the flow of experience and distil it into a concept. Lucian, how can you keep open the prospect that some interpretation may yet be the right one? What would that even look like? What would the Pyrrhonists say?

LUCIAN: The Pyrrhonists would say these exchanges among you dogmatists show the need for a middle path, a way between these extremes of knowing something and knowing nothing. Saturninus, you who denies the realities posed by you Stoics, Epicureans, Aristotelians, and any others, even the Platonists, think that we know nothing. On the other hand, Harmonia and Philia, and you too Petronius, you trio of philosophers, you all think that you know something, only you can't agree on what it is. In any event, what's left over are appearances. But our appearances, you all tell me, are confused, unreliable, illusory, fleeting, and above all impermanent. They can give us no comfort, for there seems to be no way to spring from the constantly morphing and changing phenomenal flow of immediate reality to reach an understanding of a separate, unchanging world, which Parmenides called the One.

HARMONIA: Well, then, what then is this middle way you propose?

LUCIAN: Let me try to start this way: Saturninus has a theory or interpretation about appearances, a theory the rest of you seem to share, namely, that they are confused, unreliable, illusory, fleeting, and so on. Is that fair? Perhaps Saturninus can answer for all of you.

SATURNINUS: Fair enough, I think we would agree.

LUCIAN: Your view too, it seems—that there is no underlying, unchanging reality—remains an interpretation about appearances, does it not, just as the claims by the rest of you for one or another underlying reality are also just so many interpretations of appearances.

SATURNINUS: I am happy to say that everything is an interpretation. And if everything is an interpretation, if there is only interpretation, then nothing is reliable and all is in flux, as Xenophanes and Heraclitus taught us, and later Arcesilaus and Carneades as well. The interpretation that 'everything is an interpretation' is itself an interpretation of everything, of course, but far from refuting the truth of infinite interpretations, or nihilism, as you call it, it rather demonstrates it.

LUCIAN: I would have thought it demonstrates the absurdity of nihilism. It's rather like a mirror or an echo chamber; it refers only to itself. It's a closed-off dead end. You talk about our perceptions as illusions, but let me say why I think you're jumping to an interpretation of perceptions, not assessing them accurately for what they are. We're all familiar with the illusion of a mirage in the distance, for instance, especially when it's hot and dry. It often happens in the desert, but also, on hot days, on roads or on large paved spaces like Trajan's forum, or outside the Circus. We occasionally see a shimmering something that looks like water in the distance, but when we approach it more closely, what looks like water disappears and we're left with more of the same surface we see all around.

SATURNINUS: Well, what's your point?

LUCIAN: That there is no mistake about what in fact we see. We see a patch of shimmering colour in the distance. It looks like water to us, but when it disappears, when we discover it isn't water but a mirage, that doesn't mean we didn't see what we just saw. It's just that we interpreted it, we jumped to the conclusion that it was water, no doubt because it looked like water. But there is no mistaking that we saw something, call it a patch of shimmering colour.

SATURNINUS: But doesn't that plainly show that things are not what they seem to be? What about the oar of a boat which appears straight when raised in the air but crooked when lowered into the water? The blur of the mirage is the same whether we interpret it or not, but the bent oar is different from the straight oar. The illusion is in the appearance, not the interpretation.

LUCIAN: Not really. If we feel the oar with our hand when it is submerged we find it to be straight, just as it appears out of the water. That's a test, just like walking up to see the mirage to inspect it. The difference between seeing the straight and bent oars is like the difference between seeing the mirage at a distance and seeing its disappearance as we approach it.

SATURNINUS: So we discover our appearances don't make sense.

LUCIAN: Quite the opposite. Our appearances always make sense. They are simply and undeniably what they are. What doesn't make sense is our interpretation of what appears, not what actually appears.

To be sure, our ordinary interpretations of our appearances are, for the most part, for better or worse, quite reliable and predictable. We might be surprised at any time, but mostly we know what to expect. When we encounter an illusion, however, it's a sign that we are misinterpreting what we actually see, not that what we actually see is unreliable. A good magician, like one we might see at a court entertainment or in the theatre, or even in a street fair, will cleverly induce us to misinterpret what we're seeing. We've all seen it done.

SATURNINUS: But how do we know that everything isn't an illusion? Aren't we constantly interpreting everything? Isn't that what you are complaining about? How can any phenomenon exist on its own? It wouldn't make any sense; it would be no more than a passing item in an incoherent, chaotic stream of consciousness.

LUCIAN: But appearances are not always, or even usually, chaotic. They may be chaotic at first to a newborn, say, a baby who is seeing sights, hearing sounds, etc. for the first time. He or she has no idea of how they are correlated to one another from one moment to the next, or with his or her body. Yet it turns out that there are very reliable correlations which emerge, and this is why our appearances make sense. It may take a while, but soon enough the newborn settles down, gets comfortable, and learns what to expect. We grow up on the basis of such reliable connections; indeed, they form our world, and what we call science is really no more than the systematic, in-depth study of such correlations. Ordinary life depends wholly on the reliability of our appearances. We assume that the sun will rise, that crops will grow, that children will grow up, that our lives will run their course, and so on endlessly. Sometimes, of course, there are exceptions—an unpredicted eclipse, a famine, an earthquake, a child's death—but these do not overturn the overall reliability of things upon which we depend. And yet we know, at the same time, that it's all impermanent, and could end, for us, at any moment.

SATURNINUS: Nonetheless, we have no idea what all these appearances mean—even if they are consistent and reliable, as you claim. For all we know the gods are playing with us, as they will, putting phenomena into our minds the way they put dreams into our sleep.

LUCIAN: Yes, for all we know they might be doing just that. But that is just another belief, isn't it, regarding which the Pyrrhonist must suspend judgment. Suspension of judgment is the respect philosophy pays to opinion. It is the middle path to tolerance, to the mutual respect paid to all beliefs as possible truths, which is piety. There is no warrant to cancel the customs and rituals of a tribe or city. Rather they should be obeyed and observed, though not embraced. Who knows if the beliefs they reflect might or might not be realized in due course. It might well be that the world is a kind of theatre set up by the gods, as you seem to suggest, with us trapped inside. Plato had a similar idea with his famous cave. The only way we can figure out if we're in such a situation is if we stumble across an exit, or find our way around behind the stage machinery and see for ourselves the actual gods, like so many puppet masters, manipulating what we see in the theatre.

SATURNINUS: You concede, then, that the world has no meaning, that is, no reference outside itself, at least not one available to us.

LUCIAN: That such a meaning is not available to us, at least not up to this point, I am happy enough to concede. But that it doesn't exist, no, we have no evidence to conclude that.

SATURNINUS: So we live in a world that doesn't have meaning for us, at least, which is what I've been trying to say all along.

LUCIAN: It's a fine point, perhaps, but the fact that we do not seem able to find the meaning of the world as a whole is not to say it doesn't have meaning. The Pyrrhonists neither affirm nor deny a deeper meaning or truth to things, but allow it a possibility. They leave the question open, rather than insisting on a resolution.

SATURNINUS: Yet it has no meaning for us, at least not now.

LUCIAN: It might or might not. The point is that we don't know. I'd rather say that the question of meaning remains up in the air. I may not know the meaning of a barbarian language, for instance, but it would be rash to conclude that it has no meaning, or that the meaning it has, which we don't know, might not affect us. If you live with barbarians for a time, and get to know them, you will quickly see how their words are correlated with certain things, that in fact their words have a meaning, just as ours do, that they speak in their way just as well as we do in ours. Perhaps the same is true of birds and other animals, or even the sounds and sights of nature. Don't the augurs try to draw conclusions from the flight of birds? The trouble with our phenomenal world is that we don't seem able to get outside of it to see if it's correlated with anything else. Perhaps we might wake up one day to discover that our appearances were indeed a dream, and now left behind, but so far we still seem to be asleep.

HARMONIA: Okay, let's assume, then, at least for the sake of argument, that the conclusion that life has no meaning is better suspended than taken at face value. But we've gotten off the subject of whether there's a science of living. I for one want to know more about this middle way of the Pyrrhonists, which sounds like a notion of a science or practice or art of life of some kind, which father raised as our question for the evening. Let's return to our subject, or we will be disappointed.

LUCIAN: All right, let me back up a bit. I'll get to why the Pyrrhonian middle path is not exactly a guide to life. And I'll try to explain why I keep coming back to appearances to make my point. The Pyrrhonist whose lectures I've been sitting in on in Rome, Sextus Empiricus, is a physician. He talks about how important it is to pay close attention to appearances, by which he means both sensible and mental phenomena —the things which are immediately and directly experienced, such as a patient's symptoms, in addition to what he or she thinks and says. To understand disease and health, the physician looks carefully at the state of the body, what a person eats, his or her habits, and so on. If an illusion crops up in any of this, it's a sign that the physician is entertaining some interpretation which distorts what he or she sees, just as with the examples of the mirage and oar. The point is to recognize the regularities and correlations which occur so as to be able to make a diagnosis, or prediction of the likely course of events, and offer a treatment, if possible. In this sense, the Pyrrhonists proceed scientifically and gain knowledge, even if it is confined to the world of appearances.

HARMONIA: But what about how to live? What about good and evil? Or the other values? Where do they come in?

LUCIAN: Don't forget, there is no avoiding the appearances that come to us, involuntarily, as we have seen. The Pyrrhonists, like everyone else, avoid pains and seek pleasures and so try to navigate the world of appearances as best they can. They seek health, and aim to avoid illness. It is in this sense they recognize what is good and what is evil.

PHILIA: So why aren't you an Epicurean, if it's only a matter of recognizing good and evil through pleasures and pains?

LUCIAN: Because, as I think the Pyrrhonists are right to point out, and as we discussed our first evening, that it's not only that pains can be good and pleasures bad, but that that undermines any attempt to define good and evil, as you Epicureans and others try to do. If any appearance can be good or bad, we can never get to some sense of good and evil apart from appearances, as you Epicureans—and Stoics and Aristotelians and all dogmatic philosophers—believe we should. That would take some new kind of evidence beyond appearances, which we don't seem to have, or some new and surprising appearances, but—so far—we most conspicuously lack any such evidence.

The only knowledge we can have, it seems, is knowledge of appearances themselves, which is knowledge by acquaintance, and such knowledge by definition never goes beyond appearances.

Knowledge is no more than the experience we actually have, which is delivered to each of us, as it were. You Epicureans, by contrast, believe that everything is made of something you call matter, the invisible atoms of which you claim make up phenomena. But that is just another interpretation of appearances — something, however pleasing, which might be right or wrong, a speculation, but one whose truth we cannot seem to determine.

PHILIA: So we can learn how phenomena are more fully correlated and interrelated, but nothing more? Sounds disappointing.

LUCIAN: Disappointing or not, that seems to be how things are, at least as far as phenomena go. But suspending judgments or interpretations of phenomena changes our attitude towards them, once the impulse to embrace or reject them is set aside. Recognizing that is the first step towards the liberation of which Pyrrhonists speak. I suppose the gods could infuse our souls with some kind of extra-phenomenal knowledge, or create in us some kind of special state of consciousness, or perhaps we could wake up from the dream we are living and find that all is somehow explained, but none of these circumstances, at least not yet, have materialized. Some mystics might claim to take us beyond appearances, but mystical states are not easily shared, if at all, so it's hard to evaluate what they say about them. Some drugs induce new appearances, but they too do not take us beyond appearances; they only give us more and often different appearances.

PHILIA: So, if we cannot learn what good and evil really are in themselves, and while we're waiting around until someone figures it out, then it seems that there can be no science of life. We can have no guide to life apart from, or in advance of, life itself.

LUCIAN: That's exactly right. Currently, we are unable to produce a common definition of good and evil as a standard by which to live, as Saturninus keeps reminding us. Those who nonetheless believe they have something to teach us about what good and evil really are are prone to strut about and pontificate. They have lost confidence, it seems, in reality as it is, and long for a purer version of it, and seek to replace it with something else, something to be imagined. They are magicians who hypnotize us, or try to. On the other hand, those who have little if any education, or pretention—a humble peasant, even the roughest slave—can be as honest in repaying debts, or as dutiful in caring for parents, or as scrupulous in fulfilling any other virtue as any so-called 'wise person' or 'sage'. There is nothing about the 'wise man' or 'wise woman', no virtue, which cannot be found among those who are far more modest. So the notion of a 'wise person' or 'sage' may be little more than a convenient conceit.

PHILIA: You don't sound very tolerant of sages.

LUCIAN: I can tolerate the believers as persons, even as friends, as long as respect is mutual, but not their beliefs. Should anyone be above criticism, even the Sage?

PHILIA: But surely the wise man, or wise woman, or the Sage, the person who is said to know the nature of things, is like the artist or the physician; they have a recognizable skill, with special knowledge, which sets them off. Just as the artist can produce beautiful objects beyond anything a person untrained in the arts can produce, and a physician, like your Sextus, can treat patients in ways that can help them get better, unlike an ordinary person untrained in medicine, so surely, the wise sage, like Epicurus, or Socrates, or your Pyrrho, as well as the Stoic ideal sage—all of them possess a special skill—let's call it virtue or wisdom or knowledge—which allows them to distinguish good from evil. Isn't that obvious?

LUCIAN: But, alas, unlike the artist or physician or some other crafts-person or expert, whose skills are widely recognized precisely because they can achieve results, it is not at all clear that there is some skill demonstrated by the so-called wise person which differs from what can be found among ordinary people. An ordinary person, as I've just suggested, even the humblest, is as likely as any 'wise man' to act virtuously, that is, to exhibit courage, modesty, honesty, piety, duty, justice, or any of the other things which might be recognized as virtuous. This is no speculation, but a fact of life I think should be obvious to all.

PHILIA: But surely the wise person, whoever he or she may be, is marked by self-control and discipline, while the foolish and ignorant person is marked by inconstancy and confusion. If even an ordinary person may be wise, as you suggest, it is surely because they display steadiness of character and consistency of behaviour, signs of the sage. Perhaps anyone might turn out to be a sage? Who knows for sure?

LUCIAN: Well, whether an orderly and consistent life of self-discipline is virtuous or not depends on the situation. Often it may be wise to proceed in an orderly fashion, but at other times, the best thing is to be flexible, to be able to abruptly change course as circumstances demand. Self-discipline, after all, can turn into rigidity, a desperate attempt to control inner turmoil and insecurity. The circumstances of life change, and no one skill or attitude seems adequate to all the changes, just as no one tool in a toolbox is adequate to all the jobs we confront when building a house or repairing things which are broken. And any tool can be used for a destructive purpose, say as a weapon in a crime, and so can be turned into an evil thing.

PHILIA: Oh, Lucian. You are being perverse. If there can be no science of a good life, how can we expect to raise children to do the right thing, to have happy families, let alone to secure a happy and virtuous city, or a peaceful and prosperous empire? If you are right, we are thrown into a confusion and despair as bad as the nihilism of which you accuse Saturninus. Your clever suspension of judgment about interpretations, or beliefs, such as virtue, is just as effective at leaving them beyond our reach as Saturninus's nihilism. Hardly an improvement, it seems.

LUCIAN: Well, it's true the Pyrrhonists hold there is nothing to teach or learn, as they are themselves fond of saying, and not just for its shock value. For them, it's a literal fact. You realize, with regard to suspension of judgment, that you're no more than a witness, both to your sensations and your thoughts, and to your body and the world as well as your mind. Yet, somewhat paradoxically, this suspension becomes a liberation from anxiety and fear. Saturninus, like any dogmatist, thinks he has something to teach us. In his case, it is the lesson that everything is interpretation, that nothing is what it appears to be. But the Pyrrhonist has nothing to teach, no lesson to offer. Not even that. There are no Pyrrhonian teachings.

PHILIA: That sounds crazy. Mothers teach their children, scholars their students, craftsmen their apprentices, generals their soldiers, philosophers their disciples, and on and on. What can you possibly mean? Why do you attend Sextus's talks? Does he teach anything? What does he do?

LUCIAN: Appearances, as the Pyrrhonists point out and I keep repeating, are experienced involuntarily. None of us actually *learns* to experience anything. We don't need to. We can't help it. We simply experience phenomena as we involuntarily encounter them, as they appear. The actual experience of any phenomenon remains direct, immediate, involuntary, and in the present. It is always in the now. You aren't trained to see the blue sky, or to smell a rose, or hear a song. These things all just happen in the present moment. This is why there are no teachers, and no students, as the Pyrrhonists provocatively maintain. We are reminded of this when we have a shock, when we suddenly fall ill, or have an accident. We can hardly believe it. Everything changes in an instant, involuntarily.

PHILIA: But doesn't the apprentice learn to play the flute or the lyre from a teacher? Don't the students of the sophists learn rhetoric? Isn't there some kind of instruction involved?

LUCIAN: Well, we can imitate what other people do. The master isn't explaining to the apprentice what's going on; he or she is instead showing what can be done. That's instruction, to be sure, but it's not interpretation. The apprentice will either choose to copy the master, or not. You can bring a horse to water, as they say, but not make it drink. There is no understanding needed here of cause or effect. There is only the replication of the task, with greater or lesser success, or indifference. Some students are able to replicate the desired effect, because they imitate closely, and others are not.

PHILIA: This still sounds like a version of Saturninus's nihilism.

LUCIAN: Well, the Pyrrhonists offer no interpretations. But Saturninus does. He would have us believe, as we've seen, that all is nothing, that appearances are illusions, not at all what they seem to be. To discount appearances is to blunt our interest in them; we end up less curious and less likely to learn the useful things experience can teach us. We would rather rush on to our beliefs, where we seek comfort. The Pyrrhonists hold rather that our phenomena, our appearances, are neither the projections of some unchanging, independent essences, nor are they nothing at all. They simply try to describe them, not interpret them.

PHILIA: So what are they?

LUCIAN: They are dependently, not independently, existing things, a dependent reality, if you like. They are dependent not only on one another, but on us, that is, on our consciousness of them, without which they would not exist, at least not for us.

PHILIA: Well, that's odd.

LUCIAN: Not really, if you think about it. As far as we can tell, we are souls, that is, conscious or sentient beings, who are constrained to encounter various phenomena. Doesn't that describe your experience? And haven't all the phenomena you've experienced been accompanied, as it were, by your presence as the witness of those phenomena? There are no phenomena for us without us being conscious of them, it seems, and no consciousness without it being conscious of some phenomenon.

PHILIA: Well, I suppose it could be like that. But what about this consciousness or soul stuff you are suddenly invoking? Sounds like a belief. We Epicureans are materialists. We recognize no special soul, but only atoms and the void. In other words, any 'soul' we might acknowledge is but a subtle material substance which interacts with other less subtle material substances. Aren't you suddenly going beyond phenomena to posit a mysterious entity, this witness, just the sort of thing you've been objecting to?

LUCIAN: The Pyrrhonists point out that we have an intuition of a self which arises out of the realization that we are distinct from any of our appearances, even from those of our bodies. But this intuition of ourselves is an intuition of an absence, of *not* being this or that. I am somehow attached to my body, profoundly so. I never seem able to find myself without it, even in my dreams. But my body is no more than a series of phenomenal states, and I cannot find my conscious self in any of those states, hard as I look. There is no evidence that I am my body, only that I am very closely and consistently attached to it, and that I am aware of the world, or the flow of sensation through my body, which is itself part of that flow. I am as involuntarily conscious of being conscious of phenomena as I am involuntarily conscious of those phenomena themselves.

PHILIA: So then what can we say about this mysterious consciousness you're now invoking, which sounds like a kind of soul? How can we know what it is if it does not appear to us?

LUCIAN: We can't. But we can call our intuition of consciousness a soul, if we like, with the understanding that this is a negative intuition, an intuition of an absence, as I am trying to suggest. If phenomena are the objects of consciousness, then the soul, this absence, is the subject of consciousness. The soul, we might say, is evidently non-evident. It is somehow missing in action. It is an absence or lack—an indeterminate space, if you will—that somehow nonetheless accompanies our evident phenomena. It is the strange empty space we recognize as consciousness.

In the Pyrrhonist discussions we've had in Rome, someone mentioned a school of thought in India in which the soul is recognized, though only as an indeterminate reality, neither something specific, nor nothing at all. They are called the Pudgalavadins, I believe, after their word for soul, *pudgala*. An obscure group, no doubt, but perhaps they are on to something. The soul, we might say, is a negative appearance; it is the very lack of a positive appearance, such as a thought or sensation. But that very lack as something of which we are aware, though only in a negative sense, is an absence, or, to put it paradoxically, the presence of an absence. There can be no presence without absence, and no absence without presence.

PHILIA: How can we have a negative appearance, or the presence of an absence? Mysteries seem to abound here.

LUCIAN: It's quite simple. A teacher notices when a student does not come to class; in other words, he or she notices the absence of the student. More generally, we notice, if we think about it, that a kind of absence accompanies all our appearances. The very fact that our appearances are present in the moment, we learn, does not mean they will always be present; their presence now implies their possible absence later, as we see in the coming and going of appearances. Yet *we* are always there, so to speak; *we*, meaning each of us individually, are always witnesses to the phenomena we suffer, even as we are somehow distinct from them as well. It is in that persistent absence alongside the persistent presence of appearances that we find the soul. In this negative way, we can talk about the presence of an absence. By the same token, the soul is no phenomenon; it is nothing discrete. It is what is left over, which is wholly indeterminate, indefinable, ineffable, and resistant to any and all description. But it is not nothing.

PHILIA: You say the soul is not a phenomenon. Yet you also say that it is not nothing, that it's something indeterminate. How can that be? Why isn't not being something just being nothing?

LUCIAN: Your question gets us to the middle path between being something and being nothing, the path which the Pyrrhonists try to discover. For the dogmatists, to be something means to be an independently existing thing, say a person, with a permanent and unchanging essence which underlies its impermanent and changing appearances. For the Pyrrhonists, however, being something means being a dependently existing appearance, or phenomenon, apparent to consciousness, but without any evident permanent or changing essence. Appearances are dependent by virtue of being present to consciousness; essences, by contrast, in their supposed independence, are notoriously not present to consciousness.

Among appearances, the Pyrrhonists distinguish thoughts from thoughts, sensations from sensations, thoughts from sensations, and sensations from thoughts. They eschew or suspend judgment, or interpretation, about any of these appearances. Appearances are impermanent, but not illusory, for there is nothing available to us for them to be illusions of. Although subject to change, they also recur with regularity. Like everyone else, Pyrrhonists notice the correlations among appearances evident in the recurring patterns of phenomenal experience by which life and the world are organized. Apart from ordinary life, as in medicine and the sciences, for instance, they explore these correlations in depth and deepen our understanding of appearances to the point where anomalies like diseases and eclipses can be predicted and normalized in the course of our experience.

Pyrrhonists also distinguish the absence of thoughts and sensations as a kind of emptiness in which neither of them is to be found. Since absence too can be distinguished, though only by contrast, we must give it a kind of reality or being, I would think, which is what keeps us from saying that absence, or consciousness, is simply nothing.

Maybe it's only potentiality—a kind of invisible sea or medium out of which appearances arise. Perhaps we can say that absence is invisibility rather than nothingness. The fish in the sea see each other, after all, but not the water in which they are born and live and die. To call the absence of thoughts and sensations simply nothing is to deny the potentiality of absence—an extreme conclusion, really, which goes beyond the facts into speculation. Potentiality, on the other hand, goes hand in hand with suspension of judgment.

PHILIA: That's a lot to think about. All this 'potentiality' seems rather mysterious. I'm not sure what it all means, nor how you get to the soul, or consciousness, from the absence of thoughts and sensations. How about another way to liberate the truth?

LUCIAN: I can only say that my soul is a seemingly empty self, a kind of space which is filled up with my thoughts and sensations, but which is not itself either a thought or a sensation, yet which somehow remains implied by their presence. Not sure I can say any more than that at this point, or that anyone can.

PHILIA: So, putting all that aside, but accepting what you say if only for the sake of argument, where are we left? The answer to father's question—can there be a science of life?—seems to be no.

LUCIAN: Yes, the answer is no, at least provisionally, at least as far as the Pyrrhonists are concerned. The middle path is not a science of life but a simple balance to be struck, or not.

PHILIA: But you are also suggesting that there is something like a science of appearances. And how can we have science and knowledge without the discovery of essences, of what is not evident?

LUCIAN: Let's say Pyrrhonian science means something different than is commonly understood. It is not about finding the essence of things—that's pseudo-science, a kind of mythology of reason. Pyrrhonian science means attending to our fluctuating appearances, separating them from our confusing beliefs, resolving illusions, and letting phenomena speak for themselves. We can study our appearances, or phenomena—they're the same thing—and their relations, and that's what science is. It's the middle path because it abandons the extremes of imagining what lies beyond the veil of appearances on the one hand, and on the other hand proclaiming that nothing at all lies beyond those appearances.

PHILIA: But if that's so, we still need some clearer sense of how to think about how to live our lives. And we're still left with the uncertainty of appearances which brings pain as well as pleasure, death as well as life.

LUCIAN: The Pyrrhonist point is to suspend all beliefs, all interpretations, all views, all theories, all speculations. To do that one must recognize the distinction between beliefs about appearances and what actually appears, between interpretations and what is being interpreted. Anyone who can do that will be able to recognize appearances for what they are, and respond accordingly. And they will be able to recognize as well the mysterious and indeterminate emptiness of the soul. The Pyrrhonists do not offer a solution to the mystery of life. They only offer relief from the burden of belief. The problems by which we are burdened by our beliefs trouble us all. It is our beliefs which unnecessarily magnify and distort our pains and pleasures, after all—something you Epicureans insist upon as well. So the Pyrrhonian suspension of belief offers just what you want—the elimination of self-induced disturbance which allows for the peace of mind you seek. The problem with you Epicureans is the dogmatic beliefs you continue to hold, especially your materialistic version of atomism and the soul. But that's perhaps a topic for another time.

PHILIA: I'm afraid it must be. It's getting late, and suddenly we're all looking tired, it seems. At least I am. In the meantime, accepting what you're saying, again if only for the sake of argument, I continue to be puzzled about this middle path you advocate. You say it's not really a path but some kind of balance between extremes we can achieve. What exactly are we supposed to do to realize it? Is there some practice we can follow?

LUCIAN: Well, there are people in Rome who practise a technique which I think comes from India where one sits quietly and simply observes the passing of appearances without making any judgments about them. I tried it myself, with modest results at best, but there are those who swear by it. The idea is to contemplate the contents of consciousness, and for that quiet and solitude are helpful. Another technique, perhaps more amenable to our schools here at home, is to attend to our language, to our words, and particularly to avoid speaking in ways which are not directly correlated with appearances, to recognize beliefs as confusions about appearances, and to question them when others use them, as I've been trying to do in our discussion, I'm not sure how well. This questioning method, or dialectic, is familiar to us all, it is our common philosophical heritage, dating at least from Socrates.

PHILIA: Well, I'm still not sure what more to say. Attending to appearances, to the phenomena of which we are actually conscious, is I think too general a description to be useful. Dialectic we are all familiar with, but it seems there is no end to it as you and Saturninus practise it, nor to the endless interpretations it seems to encourage. Beliefs seem too well entrenched to be so easily disposed of.

LUCIAN: Well, then, I'm not sure I can satisfy you. The Pyrrhonists take experience seriously and are open to what it offers. They are curious; they are seekers, even though there may be no end to inquiry.

PHILIA: But experience, even with beliefs dampened, troubles us as well as elates us. How do we keep this balance you propose? I'm reminded of Senator Rufus's dream of spinning around the Circus in Rome.

LUCIAN: We keep our balance, or try to, by being wary of any interpretation or belief about experience, as best we can. That's the trick, though, as you suggest, it is no doubt easier said than done. It's precisely when we try to explain our experience, to grasp it in some final way, whether by some positive idea — like virtue, or pleasure, or achievement, or the other things we've discussed — or by a negative idea like Saturninus's nothingness, that we lose our balance. We get in trouble when we try to stop our experience, to control it. Even Saturninus's nothingness is a form of control.

PHILIA: So we just give up trying to control things?

LUCIAN: Precisely. Like it or not, we find ourselves part of a moving panorama of perceptions. As long as we are alive, it seems, we are like the chariot driver father dreamt he was. We are in constant motion. Round and round we go, day after day, as our appearances swirl about, yet whatever happens we are always somehow in the midst of it all. It is the same charioteer, after all, who is always there, who experiences every round of the race. He experiences his own activity, his own driving. He is the witness of each succeeding experience, and if he's lucky he enters what athletes call the 'zone', where everything seems to be happening automatically, even his own responses, where everything is somehow balanced. Outside the 'zone', the charioteer is liable to be distracted and to second guess himself, thinking he's in charge. If he does that, he's more likely to overturn and crash.

And the same goes for good and evil. I tried to say this in the first evening: good and evil depend on the appearances we suffer, for better and worse, so that what is good in one context turns out to be bad in another, and vice-versa. It's not that we don't experience good and evil, it's just that we don't know what they are apart from our conflicting and even contradictory experiences of their realization for us at any given moment.

PHILIA: So how do we know how to behave? Or how to recognize something as good or evil when we experience it?

LUCIAN: If we put aside our interpretations of things, the appearances which remain will speak to us directly and honestly. Just as we naturally recoil from a snake, or are drawn to a beautiful sunset, we spontaneously do the right thing, unless we're distorted by belief.

PHILIA: What about more complex cases? If I'm threatened with torture unless I betray others, what should I do?

LUCIAN: The Pyrrhonists say that one will react in such a situation just the same way—spontaneously. As long as one resists one interpretation or another of the phenomenal facts at hand, one will do the right thing. Here the Pyrrhonists are close to the inevitability of the Stoics. But the thing is, you won't know ahead of time what you will do. A soldier might be a coward at one moment, and a hero at the next. And the more you think you know, the less likely you are to do the right thing.

PHILIA: That sounds like the Pyrrhonist version of the sage.

LUCIAN: Perhaps …

[Pause …]

RUFUS: Once again, Lucian, you've left us with much to ponder. This old man, at least, would be relieved to see, if you're right, that he doesn't have to really worry about good and evil, or trying to learn what they really are. There's enough else to worry about! I can see how the dogmatists make life harder for themselves (and their students!), but even so I doubt they will be satisfied by your advice. You would have us surrender to life, not resist it, and, as you admit, that is perhaps easier said than done. Maybe only someone long in years, like me, may be ready for that conclusion. Most people, it seems to me, are not. So, as it is late, let's end this discussion, at least for now; perhaps someday we will have another occasion to visit together and ponder these matters. Maybe next winter when most of us will be in Rome? We'll see what we can arrange. So to bed, then. Tomorrow's another day, and they say the weather will be fine for everyone to travel on their way.

Part II
Dialogues on Truth

Characters:

Rufus, a Roman Senator

Aurelia, wife of Rufus

Harmonia, a Stoic, their daughter

Lucian, a student of Pyrrhonism, their son

Philia, an Epicurean, a friend of Harmonia's

Gaius, a Platonist, brother of Aurelia

Saturninus, an Academic, neighbour of Rufus's

Time:

The reign of Antoninus Pius, second century CE

Place:

The House of Rufus and Aurelia in Rome

Does Truth Exist?

AURELIA: I am pleased to have so many of my family here in Rome this evening and for the rest of the holiday, especially my children, and dear Philia, and my brother Gaius, and Saturninus, old friend and neighbour in Campania. Thank you all for coming. This year's *Parentalia* went very well, I'm pleased to say, and after visiting the family tomb today, and leaving our offerings, I think we've done our duty, and deserve to relax this evening.

Our Rufus, as most of you know, was called away to the Senate and I don't expect him back until late tonight. Some urgent discussion there about this new sect we've been hearing more and more about, the so-called Galileans, or Christians, who follow, it seems, that strange God of the Jews, and who seem to have some new ideas about him. Their prophet, Jesus, claimed to know the truth, which he offered to his followers, saying it would make them free and immortal, and it looks like they believe him. As you probably heard, there have been disturbances in the city. The Galileans refuse any compromise. I'm concerned, like many of us, that they are unwilling even to utter the *sacramentum*, the oath of loyalty to our beloved Emperor in the name of the gods. Only their God, it seems, is worthy of such honour, not ours. I wonder where all this will end.

GAIUS: It will not end well. The Christians, and the Jews before them, are hardly the first to claim to know the truth. To be honest, our poets and philosophers have all made similar claims. Our philosophers in particular have insisted that what they call the truth about things—about the gods, or the stars, or nature, or the soul, or politics, or justice, or you name it—can be determined. Still, to their credit, more often than not they were content to argue their points, and to take the trouble to listen to their opponents, even as they tried to refute them. Plato, above all, recognized criticism and objection, even as he hoped to get as close as possible to what he thought was the most likely truth about things. Even our poets, Homer above all, and our own Virgil, were mostly content to let their stories speak for themselves, and mostly to find correspondences rather than contradictions in what they and others were describing. But now attitudes seem to be hardening.

SATURNINUS: What a lot of foolishness, if you ask me. I know you are a tough crowd to convince of this, but all these attempts to insist upon one truth or another are doomed to fail, as I keep maintaining. There is no truth about things, I tell you, no deeper understanding of them. If the old philosophers were more polite, as you suggest, and didn't actually beat up on each other, it's because their speculations were usually a step or more removed from everyday experience. When they did get involved in real life—like Plato's attempt to turn Dionysus, the great tyrant of Syracuse, into a philosopher king, or Seneca's Stoic tutelage of Nero—things didn't go so well. Only one of them was lucky enough to barely escape with his life. Mostly philosophers sat around the agora, or the stoa, or some pleasant villa or garden—just like us here this evening—and freely debated with each other. It was and remains a pleasant but serious, even compelling, passtime, which we honor here. But it's when claims to truth collide with one another in real life that real trouble arises, and this is why the Galileans are a problem. They would substitute their god for the authority of the Emperor, and if we let them do that all hell would break loose. Believe me.

HARMONIA: Saturninus, your consistent nihilism continues to baffle me. Let's not be so dismissive about the prospects for truth, in spite of the challenges you and Lucian advanced in our discussions last summer, in Campania. Finding the truth about things is no easy matter, to be sure, but that doesn't mean we should throw up our hands and walk away. Especially when we know there will only be more trouble if the collision of conflicting truths can't be resolved. The response should be to get things right, to methodically sort through the issues and the varying views, and to try to determine which of them is closest to the truth. Who would disagree?

PHILIA: Hear! Hear!

AURELIA: I agree with Harmonia. If we're serious we must honour the effort to try to clarify what we mean when we try to talk about how to determine the truth about things still unclear to us. Let me suggest, if I may, as my husband would, for our edification and entertainment this evening, that we pool our talents in a further discussion to see if we can't make some progress towards truth, or at least how we understand truth. I hear Harmonia has met Flavius Arrianus, once a student of Epictetus, who has introduced her into discussions with some Stoics here in Rome, and Philia has become well known among us for her passion as an Epicurean, and of course Saturninus here is notorious as a our relentless Academic. For my part, I try to keep up, but mostly as a curious amateur, I'm afraid. As for young Lucian, my beloved son, we all know he has become interested in philosophy lately, and I think we'd like to hear more about what he may have discovered.

LUCIAN: I hope a son can live up to a mother's praises. I'm curious really about all the schools. But most recently I've been listening, as most of you know, to Pyrrhonian lectures, especially by Sextus Empiricus. Last summer, down at the Villa in Campania, some of us here now had a long discussion then about good and evil. I'm sure you heard something about that. Father was there, as well as Saturninus, and Petronius, and Harmonia and Philia too. I'm not sure what we resolved as a group, though it helped me to rethink the approach of the Pyrrhonians. I think I made some progress, anyway. I'm not sure about anyone else.

SATURNINUS: I'm not entirely the curmudgeon some of you may think I am. I'm happy enough to follow along, as long as you let me chime in when I feel compelled. At least it promises some amusement. I warn you, though, I'm pretty sure you're not going to get very far. In the meantime, the least we can do is have some more of that fine

Sicilian wine, Aurelia, and maybe some of those oysters you've promised us.

AURELIA: Yes, let's have the slaves to bring them in. [Clap! Clap!] Steward! Wine! Oysters!

Shall we begin to talk about truth? Gaius?

GAIUS: Okay, then, let me suggest, if I may, how we might start. If we already have the truth, there's no problem. But if we don't already have it, then we need to find it. Can we agree with that?

LUCIAN: Perhaps. But shouldn't we first ask what it means to already have the truth?

GAIUS: Well, to have knowledge of it.

LUCIAN: And what's knowledge?

GAIUS: I must say, Lucian, you quickly cut to the chase. Well, then, let me try this: knowledge is certainty. To know something is to have no doubt about it.

LUCIAN: How about some examples?

GAIUS: Well, two plus two equals four. Or the fact that the server has just put a cup of wine in front of you. We do not disagree about these and many other things. We know them with certainty, don't we, as much as we know anything?

LUCIAN: No doubt we might think so, but there are also things people think they are certain about with which others disagree. We were talking about the Galileans a moment ago. They are certain that their god exists, and that he's the only god; others are equally certain he does not exist. Still others are certain that other gods exist, like Jupiter or Isis or Serapis, and that there are many other gods, like Isis and Serapis, for instance, and also there are those who doubt that there are any gods at all. And so on. How can we sort all that out?

GAIUS: You're saying that certainty might not be certain?

LUCIAN: Exactly. People can be certain about something, but they can turn out to be wrong about it too. We see it all the time. I might insist, if I couldn't find it, that I left my hat in the carriage on my way over this evening; but maybe I didn't. Maybe I forgot that I brought it in and left it in the courtyard or entryway. So it seems that certainty can't be knowledge.

GAIUS: Let's slow down a bit. Do any of us doubt that two plus two equals four? Or that you're now drinking the wine that was set before you?

LUCIAN: Of course, we don't normally doubt such things. But there's a big difference between being certain and not doubting. We don't have a reason to doubt these examples, and lots of reasons to accept them, but it's not impossible that even in these cases we might be wrong. The waiters might have made a mistake, for instance, mixed something up, and brought me beer instead of wine, and no one (except me) might have noticed.

GAIUS: What about two plus two equals four?

LUCIAN: Again, we don't have a reason to doubt it, but remember that the number system we are talking about is a convention—it consists in certain signs which we, that is, our ancestors, made up in the first place, and agreed to use in certain ways, following certain rules. An Egyptian or Persian might not know how to use them as we do; our written numbers might make no sense to them, apart from being visual images which they can experience like any others.

GAIUS: But we can be certain, can't we, that we are using the numbers correctly according to our conventions for doing so?

LUCIAN: I would prefer to say that we have no reason to doubt that. At least not yet. Peace of mind is not having a reason to doubt any-thing. Even the slightest doubt about anything can upset us. We don't need to invoke certainty here, which seems to me an emotional judg-ment, especially when we know that emotions and judgments can be wrong. I would rather say that there is a consistency or reliability in how we add numbers when we follow the rules we've been taught for doing so, just as there are reliable consistencies in nature, say between the sound of drops of water I hear when I'm walking in the city in the rain, and the drops I see falling at the same time on the paving stones in front of me, not to mention the feeling of rain in my face, and so on. As long as my experiences are consistent with one another, no doubt arises, and therefore no uncertainty.

GAIUS: Nonetheless, there is some possibility, however remote, that even two plus two doesn't equal four? That's hard to believe.

LUCIAN: Yes, it's hard to believe, and I'm no mathematician, but consider this. Counting by number depends on a regular succession of appearances, as we see in the fingers of my hand as I hold them up. I accept the convention (that I count one finger at a time) because it's what I was taught as a child, along with everyone else. But there might be some other world in which the phenomena we experience (including our fingers) have some different order. If we had four fingers on a hand instead of five, perhaps we might have a different number system. We might count in multiples of eight integers, instead of ten, or almost any other multiple. Or maybe even the rain we might see falling in another world is suddenly not accompanied there by any sound, as it normally is for us in this world. That's certainly how it is for a deaf person.

HARMONIA: This is getting pretty far-fetched.

LUCIAN: Perhaps, but the point isn't to produce far-fetched examples, of which philosophers tend to be overly fond, but the fact that such examples can be imagined at all. That should be enough to give us pause about attributing some kind of certainty to anything we can imagine, no matter how obvious it seems to be.

SATURNINUS: So you're saying we should doubt everything?

LUCIAN: Not at all. It might be clearer to say that our understanding of anything we experience is not necessarily exempt from doubt—for instance, how two and two are used as symbols, or what the server actually poured into my goblet. But, until that actually happens, until our understanding of some otherwise obvious experience—like the waiter pouring something in my cup, or the calculation two plus two equals four—is shown by some counter-example to perhaps be somehow wrong, or in error, and so called into question, until then we should accept our understanding as a fact, take it for granted, and proceed accordingly. Indeed, absent any reason to the contrary, we can't help doing so.

SATURNINUS: But can't we find reasons to doubt anything and everything? Once more, isn't everything an interpretation? You keep saying it's not so, as you argued last summer in Campania, but you need to do more convincing to establish, for instance, the distinction you introduced in our earlier discussions between uninterpreted and interpreted phenomena, or what you call beliefs, before you can hope to have it be accepted, or even made plausible.

LUCIAN: All right, let me try this: if the server brought me beer instead of wine, as I suggested earlier, and if you had been told, as you were, that he was bringing all of us wine, then you would have fallen into error insofar as you accepted an interpretation of what was actually brought, or expected to be brought, not because of any problem with the facts. And why wouldn't you have? And similarly, normally there is no question that we are using the notations of 'two' and 'two' and 'four'. But a young student just learning numbers might interpret what he or she is being taught in some odd way. They might indeed believe that 'two' and 'two' add up to something other than 'four'.

HARMONIA: But, still, how do we know what's an interpretation and what's the thing being interpreted, the latter apparently being the truth. This problem keeps coming up in my mind. We need some criterion by which to distinguish them, don't we?

LUCIAN: Okay, then let me turn the discussion back to you. What do you think such a criterion might be?

HARMONIA: Are you asking how, or by what standard, we avoid error and know the truth of our appearances?

LUCIAN: Well, let's start with that.

HARMONIA: The best answer given by our philosophers, as far as I can tell, is that we have an ability to grasp the truth of what appears to us, to understand that it actually represents something existing out there. We grasp the truth with our rational mind, our *hegemonikon*, as our founder Zeno put it, just as we grasp a stone with our hand. He famously called this comprehension, or the mental act of *katalepsis*. I think we talked about this last summer.

LUCIAN: What does it mean to grasp something with the mind?

HARMONIA: Well, first we have to attend to our appearances where we see not only the appearances themselves, but also that they can be a mark of something else. Let's revisit the Stoic notion of grasping the truth of things, their essence, which we briefly discussed in Campania. When I see an apple, I don't just see what appears to me, that is, some colour and shape; when I hold it in my hand, I don't just get a certain tactile feeling. Rather, through what repeatedly appears over time I am able to recognize, or grasp in the mind, that I'm seeing an apple, something coming to me from outside, something beyond the phenomena which appear directly and immediately, which are actually present in the moment, something which, in making its mark on me, shapes and modifies my soul or psyche, something which I recognize I've experienced before. When I grasp that, I grasp knowledge. This recognition follows from employing the subtle *pneuma*, the force or power of rational mind unique to us humans, by which we can arrange and compare the phenomena we experience and bring out the order they exhibit. *Pneuma* literally means 'breath', the basis of active human life, which Stoics take as a metaphor for the power of mind.

LUCIAN: But how do you know that an appearance is the mark of something external, outside of you, which so affects you? In the Eleusinian Mysteries and other rites, and even in our dreams, and with wine and herbs, people have visions of things that do not exist, but which they believe exist.

HARMONIA: An apple is always an apple, even in a dream. I might even eat an apple in a dream.

LUCIAN: So any presentation we grasp of an apple means that the apple really exists?

HARMONIA: Yes, when we really grasp it.

LUCIAN: But we just had the example of what appears to be a cup of wine turning out not to be a cup of wine. Why aren't we similarly in error if we take something to be an apple when it only looks like an apple? We've all seen those decorative, faux apples made of wax sold by the vendors in the porticos at the baths. They look totally real, certainly to sight, but they're not.

HARMONIA: To grasp our phenomena correctly we need to understand the full range of circumstances in which they reliably appear over time. An ordinary person has accumulated enough understanding to correctly grasp what's behind most presentations. Only a truly wise person—such as the Sage of the Stoics—would have sufficient experience to correctly grasp the meaning of any presentation. You have to broaden your experience to more accurately grasp things. That's the job of the *hegemonikon*, of your guiding faculty. If you just look at the wax apple, you might be fooled. But if you take a step further, if you pick up the wax apple, you will know immediately it's not the real thing.

LUCIAN: But even the Sage can be fooled by the wax apples if he doesn't pick one up.

HARMONIA: The Sage is an ideal person, someone omniscient, virtually a god, not a regular man or woman. Imagine someone who simultaneously lives and relives all possible lifetimes, past and present, constantly, and so comes to know fully what's happening at any given moment, and indeed what's ever happened. To say that such a god-like Sage knows all is only to say that he or she has been there before and has already picked up that apple; it is to recognize that all knowledge is really recollection, which the Sage alone is able to fully access. And all this comes out of the endless succession of experiences, ultimately of one universe after another, as they are born, grow, decline, and flame out. Don't you ever get the feeling that something you're experiencing is a recollection?

LUCIAN: Sometimes, yes.

HARMONIA: To me that's knowledge, or the mechanism of knowledge. Let's see if I can understand what you're saying. You're telling us that it's not just the immediate grasping that's necessary and sufficient to reach certain knowledge, but that something else is needed as well: what you're calling a broader, comprehensive understanding of things, something only the Sage, or a god, can be confident about. What more can you say about this broader understanding?

Stoics believe that the world is a rational place, governed by *logos*, the inherent order of things, and that everything happens for a reason. The world is complicated, and we are limited creatures, to be sure, so normally we do not have all of the reasons or evidence we need to understand a particular situation. I might not know, for instance, that the thing I grasp with my eye as an apple is in fact a wax object made by an artisan, or that the waiter gave you beer instead of wine, or even that some other way of using numerals would turn out to make two plus two not equal four. But if I had fuller knowledge of what was going on in each case—which the rational mind can give me—I would not be fooled. Ultimately, perhaps only great Jupiter, who directs the course of the universe, has such knowledge, but the Sage can come close.

LUCIAN: Is this reason, or the *logos*, which you say governs things separate from the things it governs?

HARMONIA: Yes. It is the active principle, or *pneuma*, which animates what would otherwise be passive matter. Nature is defined as those things which can act (or force) or be acted upon (or matter).

LUCIAN: So you're distinguishing between something which animates and something which is animated, but I'm not clear about what these are, let alone about how they can be distinguished. Let me put it this way: everything we experience, if I follow you, seems to be a blend of activity and passivity. But, if that's the case, then everything is subject to change. Nothing I can think of can be totally passive. Nor can I imagine pure activity. Indeed pure activity and pure passivity seem to be as indistinguishable as they are incomprehensible! It seems they cannot have an independent existence.

HARMONIA: Nonetheless, I'm saying that everything is at once both active and passive; that's a basic Stoic point.

LUCIAN: But if we can't separate out activity from passivity—or *logos* from matter, or reason from our appearances, or whatever we want to call this supposedly basic dichotomy—then how can we possibly recognize them when they are said to be inevitably mixed together?

GAIUS: Let me interrupt here. My head is starting to spin. Don't the philosophers, the Stoics certainly, but most others as well, including Plato, who is closest to my heart, and the scientists, don't they all teach us that the world makes some kind of sense, indeed that it's rational, by which they mean that it follows predictable rules? And that we can extract those rules, which have a fixed and enduring being, from the ordinary stream of changing phenomena? Aren't these the forms Plato taught us to seek out? Don't some philosophers also tell us that nature is in motion, or that it is in the process of becoming, that there's a kind of plan or fate or destiny to things, a chain of events? I've heard that's what the Indian holy men call *karma*, a kind of unchanging logic to the changes we experience among phenomena. And aren't *logos* and *karma* perhaps the same thing? Isn't all that reflected in the common sense shared by ordinary people? Isn't respect for the gods, or piety, just a way of acknowledging this basic dynamic? Isn't that what you're saying, Harmonia?

HARMONIA: Absolutely.

LUCIAN: Really! I didn't think Stoicism would turn out to be a mystery religion! You're asking us, Harmonia, to embrace a providential force we can't understand as the vital principle of a nature that you say would otherwise be incomprehensible! Even the Stoic wise man, the Sage, would have trouble making sense out of that!

HARMONIA: Be a little more patient, Lucian. Think of it this way: experience, the unfolding of events, is our greatest teacher. If I see one person, then a second, then a third, and yet another, and so on, then at some point—when I've seen enough people—I am able to grasp the essence of persons, to form a cognitive presentation, a concept, which synthesizes many examples. I am able then, and only then, to understand and recognize what it is to be a person; and so on for what it is to be a dog, or a tree, or almost anything. Once I've developed the concept in question, it becomes the standard by which I know whether or not some future appearance of sights, sounds, etc. is in fact a person, or a dog, or whatever. At that point I have real knowledge of what really exists independently of myself.

LUCIAN: Well, you've argued this before, and I'd object once again that one person is short and fat, another tall and thin; one is black, another white; one is young, another old, one a man, another a woman, and so on. There is no single image of any cognitive presentation of a person that can represent all these distinct persons; it can only represent one particular person, or perhaps some of them, but not others, and clearly not all.

HARMONIA: But look more closely. All these people have certain common features, do they not? They all have heads, eyes, noses, ears, arms and legs, fingers, toes, and so on! I come to recognize the common features and disregard the differences. It is this collection of common features that we use the word 'person' to signify.

LUCIAN: But blind people don't have eyes that can see, nor deaf people ears that can hear, and so on, and yet we still say they are persons. It's not so clear that there really are any common features that can be grasped, or cognitively presented, as you say, or that any one of them are essential to what a person is.

HARMONIA: You're being a little perverse. I concede that not every instance of every person has all the essential qualities. This person, or that one, may be missing one or another feature which most other people have. We would say he or she is a defective or incomplete person, perhaps, but a person nonetheless. We draw the cognitive presentation of person from the general run of people, from the cumulative sum of the qualities common to most people under most circumstances. That's the point. It's the overlap of the faces we have seen which creates the concept behind them, just as the lines a painter repeatedly sketches in on the wall finally overlap to gradually bring a singular figure into focus. No one line in the sketch is determinative, but collectively they are entirely so. That is what gives us the standard for recognizing a person. How else could it happen?

LUCIAN: You know, Daedalus was such a clever craftsman, they say, that he made statues that not only resembled people in some pose or posture, but moved and acted like them as well. He was so good at this that people couldn't tell the difference between real men and women and his artificial men and women.

HARMONIA: Yes, we've all heard the story, but it's only a myth, a beguiling fantasy.

LUCIAN: I'm not so sure. It's a story that might one day come true. Even ordinarily, under certain conditions, we can mistake a shape we see for an actual person. A scarecrow in a garden, for instance, is a crude approximation of a Daedalean figure, but, seen from a distance, by a stranger, perhaps, or in poor light, it can be mistaken for a real person. Indeed, it's meant to fool the birds! A very artful Daedalean figure might fool us permanently. Imagine a figure that walked and talked and behaved exactly like a real person. Indeed, as the story goes, didn't Athena and Hera create a phantom of Helen which Menelaus mistook for the real Helen?

HARMONIA: Yes, and what of it?

LUCIAN: Well, then we would have a case where the conditions for what you call a cognitive presentation would be fulfilled, but the presentation would be false, wouldn't it, as when we mistake one identical twin for another?

HARMONIA: But we can discover the difference between a true and a false presentation. We can find the other twin and put them side by side to settle the issue. As for Daedalus, perhaps there are wires and pulleys inside the artificial body we take to be real, instead of flesh and blood, and perhaps we can visit his workshop and see that these are machines he's making, not real people. There will be a point of discovery that will reveal the truth.

LUCIAN: But let's say the skill of Daedalus knows no bounds, or that at least matches or exceeds any bounds we can imagine, and that his machines are fashioned from flesh and blood as well, which he has somehow learned to produce. And maybe his machines give birth to other machines in his workshop as well, just as human beings do. Maybe his workshop closed long ago, and his creations have reproduced on their own and mixed with us so that we can no longer detect any difference between us and them.

HARMONIA: If there's no difference that we can see between us and his machines, then I suppose we have to say that they are the same as us, as far as we're concerned. But, in recognizing that, don't we continue to grasp the defining essence involved, just as Zeno pointed out long ago?

LUCIAN: I have to agree; if there's no detectable difference, we'd have to admit an identity, and admit that Daedalus figured out how to make real people.

GAIUS: Score one for Harmonia.

LUCIAN: Yes, indeed. She's clarified something very interesting. She's established that an identity consists of two or more things which are completely indistinguishable, and entirely interchangeable, like two of Caesar's coins which have the same metal and weight and stamp. No one can tell the difference between them.

HARMONIA: I sense I may regret this 'clarification' you're giving me credit for.

LUCIAN: Well, let's see. Remember that persons, our subject here, are not identical, except perhaps for those identical twins, not to mention identical triplets, and so on. Zeno's idea of a cognitive presentation isn't about grasping a series of identical things, like a stack of Caesar's denarii. There's no problem with Caesar's coins, precisely because they are identical with one another. What Zeno was trying to do was something different—to grasp an identity not obvious but hidden in a series of similar, but not identical, things. And that's what you are trying to do as well.

HARMONIA: Precisely. And why not? We need the cognitive or rational part of the soul to grasp the more subtle essence of a thing. It's what allows us to extract or recognize the underlying identities which unite and define the things we experience. Without such an ability we're left with nothing more than the flow of diverse phenomena as they appear to us successively, in time.

LUCIAN: Tell me again how the *hegemonikon* does the job?

HARMONIA: It sees a pattern. It sees that similar if not identical recognizable forms recur in various discrete things over and over again. They may not all be there in every instance, as they seem to be with Caesar's denarii, but it's enough that a certain number of them— say, certain shapes and features, etc.—recur consistently enough to give us a kind of reliable recognition. Again, we see this dog, and that dog, and many other dogs, all different but similar to one another, and at some point we form a concept which enables us to grasp what a dog is. The same goes for persons, or anything else, which may differ from case to case (say, men and women, or actual individuals) but who also overlap, who share enough to justify a common identity. The mind can grasp similarity as well as identity.

LUCIAN: Clearly many of the phenomena which appear to us, including those of various dogs, or horses, or persons, or whatever, are similar rather than identical to one another. That's obvious. But

then you go on to say that we need a special mechanism or faculty—
somehow exercised by the mind—to separately grasp what you presume to be an underlying identity in any such series of similar things.
Why is this even necessary? Why do we need to resolve the similarities that are displayed spontaneously in perception? Why search for
an identity there at all? Why invent this mental machinery at all?

HARMONIA: If we have to rely on what we find among appearances
to have any hope of knowledge at all, as I hope we all agree we do,
then we need some mechanism to bring together all the similarities
they display in order to fuse them into the identities we call dogs,
horses, persons, and most other things, as you yourself were
suggesting just now. Similarity can be striking or obscure; it can be
concentrated or diffused. Many human features are shared by animals
—monkeys most notably—and more distantly by dogs and horses,
and so on. Even fish and insects have some common features with us:
they have heads, eyes, mouths, bodies, legs, etc.; they move and eat
and reproduce—all things we do as well. Insofar as we grasp what a
person is, or a dog, or a fish for that matter, we define what that thing
is, what its major features are, distinguish from those of the others, as
well as its limitations. We are able to turn similarities into identities in
this way, and thereby to recognize and understand them. Isn't that
pretty basic?

LUCIAN: Yes it is. It's a very basic belief nowadays, thanks largely to
your Stoics and the other dogmatic philosophers who preceded them;
one thinks, for instance, of Aristotle and his classifications of genera
and species, and as Gaius suggests, it goes back to Plato and his forms.
It's not clear, though, that this imagined picture of how the mind
works describes what actually happens, or that it's necessary at all.
Animals, for instance, don't seem to do any of the sort of reasoning
you describe, yet they get by pretty well. In fact, isn't this notion of
mentally grasping the essence or *logos* of things what Stoics and most
philosophers claim distinguishes people from animals? *Logos*, it seems,
can reveal a concept, like 'dog', or any kind of pattern displayed in
experience, like cause and effect or other correlations. Humans are
rational, it's said, meaning that they can extract the *logos* present in our

experience in a variety of ways, as you describe, inscribe it in memory, and present it as something independently existing, but animals can't do anything like that.

HARMONIA: Absolutely.

LUCIAN: But it's a curious thing, this *logos*, isn't it? The other attributes of persons we've been talking about—especially the shapes and features we might recognize as parts of the human figure—turn out to be more or less shared by many animals, as you've pointed out. They at least are things we can actually observe in experience—such as eyes, ears, arms and legs, an upright posture, and so on. But the *logos* as such is conspicuously not something we can observe in experience, can we? Nowhere is the *logos* actually displayed among our appearances, is it? No one sees the *logos* at work, do they, only its effects, as it were?

HARMONIA: Yes and no. It is the mind which allows us to distinguish the *logos* embedded in our sensations. Our thoughts are not sensations; we cannot see or hear or publicly share them as we actually experience them, to be sure. They are the private images we all have in our minds; they are the things we remember and imagine. But, although our thoughts are private, we can, once we have them, use them to recognize the order of things; we can then translate them into public sensations. We do this whenever we speak or write, and that's how we share our thoughts. Speech, the mark of the rational mind, is the best evidence of how we can isolate *logos*; indeed, some philosophers would say speech is *logos*. And, yes, animals have practically no speech, which is how we mainly distinguish persons from animals.

LUCIAN: Well, of course, we have thoughts as well as sensations, and indeed our thoughts are somehow private and our sensations somehow public. And yes, we can represent our sensations in private thoughts, and private thoughts in public speech by the sounds we make with our voices, most obviously, but also by the words we write on scrolls, or the diagrams we make in the sand, and so on. Paintings and sculptures are physical replicas of things we imagine. And, to agree even further, this does seem to be the main difference between ourselves and the animals.

HARMONIA: So much agreement from you!

LUCIAN: But my agreement goes no further than that. For while it's true that our thoughts are things we actually experience—things we recall or imagine—we do not find among them any thought which we actually experience of any underlying similarity of objects.

HARMONIA: What do you mean? It's created through our power of abstraction. By virtue of seeing many similar people, I can infer or grasp the concept of a person.

LUCIAN: Is abstraction something you can imagine? Could you draw a picture of it? What would an abstract person look like?

HARMONIA: Well, think of an abstraction as a kind of diagram. Let me give you an example. At the old frontier between Italy and Gaul, at the Rubicon, there's still an Imperial post station, with an inn, a checkpoint, and an army garrison. Some of us have passed through it in our travels north to the mountains and lakes. The soldiers, at least when I was there last, were pretty lax. They asked us to say only who we were and where we were going, before waving us through. At the milestone before you get to the checkpoint, there's a sign on the side of the road—it shows a head and shoulders outline, no more than a silhouette, of a man with a centurion's helmet on his head, with his right hand raised in warning. It's a symbol that the checkpoint is coming up. That's an abstract person, or a diagram of one, or close to it, and we all recognize it as such. That's what an abstraction looks like.

LUCIAN: To be clear, that's only a diagram, or pictogram, of some-thing you can barely imagine after you've eliminated most of the details.

HARMONIA: Exactly so. It's constructed—through the process of abstraction, I would say—to show us the minimal defining features not only of a person, but of a soldier, and specifically a centurion. It's what you asked for, isn't it? Abstraction is the process not of describing something as fully as possible, but of the opposite, of outlining it as simply as possible. With imagination we are always going forward, adding more details. With abstraction it's the reverse: we are subtracting, not adding. Call it the negative imagination, if you like. We pair down an image to a bare outline—in this case, the shadow or silhouette of the centurion with his helmet and raised arm. But that's still specific enough to capture exactly what we want. That's the identity extracted from similarity you asked about, and it applies to all centurions.

LUCIAN: If we continue the process, if we make the outline even more abstract, making the centurion's shape into a square, or circle, say, its power to capture him and other specific things diminishes and ultimately evaporates.

HARMONIA: Well ... so what?

LUCIAN: The identity you claim to be extracting from similarity, like wheat from chaff, turns out to be emptiness. Don't you think that's odd? How can emptiness explain the essential features of a thing?

HARMONIA: It works just the way the diagram example works. You subtract accidental features to reveal the essential ones, the ones which remain. The point isn't emptiness; it's an outline, a concept, distilled from the flow of experience, which comes before emptiness to represent something specific, in this case a centurion.

LUCIAN: Who does this distilling?

HARMONIA: Everybody. Isn't it obvious?

LUCIAN: But not everybody sees or agrees that this is what they do. I don't.

HARMONIA: Then maybe you're just ignorant of what you're really doing!

LUCIAN: Ignorant!

AURELIA: Hold on a moment! You're both raising your voices. Maybe it's time to calm down a bit.

GAIUS: Your mother's right.

[Pause …]

AURELIA: Both of you, and everyone, listen to me for a moment. We all know the saying that someone can be so distracted by the trees that they fail to see the forest. I'm beginning to get the feeling here that the reverse can also be true: that someone can be so distracted by the forest that they fail to see the trees. Harmonia seems to me distracted by the forest, and Lucian by the trees.

HARMONIA: If by the forest you mean our power of abstraction, I may have to plead guilty.

LUCIAN: I may have to plead guilty as well. For me it's all about the trees. I don't think the forest exists, or rather it doesn't appear to us unless we can make it into something like a tree, that is, into something specific that actually appears and can be distinguished from something else. I mean by that something discreet, something we find in some context, something with parts and wholes we can perceive by sights or sounds, or other senses, including our thoughts, and as something we can remember or imagine. After all, I can see a forest from a distance as a single thing, say viewing it from a mountain top, and I can imagine it that way as well.

AURELIA: What about Harmonia's power of abstraction?

LUCIAN: I don't see that it exists, or that it's even necessary. We don't have some kind of machine in our hearts—where Stoics and Epicureans place our thinking—or in our heads, where others put it, which turns what we experience in sensation into abstract categories, or concepts. Nor do we find such a process going on in our heads, or in any other place where we locate thought. We might imagine that we have such a machine—and we can call it the *hegemonikon*—but that's something we imagine and which we presuppose to exist, but don't actually observe existing. Harmonia's giving us credit we don't deserve by creating a mysterious power that can't be found.

HARMONIA: What about the picture of the abstraction, the outline, the centurion with his helmet? Didn't we—or some human hand—make that picture? Doesn't it exist? Isn't it useful?

LUCIAN: Yes, no doubt someone painted it, probably in the Legion's workshop at the commander's orders. And it certainly exists, sitting there by the side of the road. And it is certainly useful.

HARMONIA: Exactly so. Just as I can imagine mermaids and centaurs in my mind, and even realize them in sculpture, just so I can imagine centurions in my mind, and abstract from them to create the pictographic outline we're talking about. That's exactly what the soldier in the workshop did. Such abstract symbols don't exist naturally, it's true, but they do exist through human reflection which is then expressed in natural materials. I, or someone, first have to imagine them, I agree, and then reproduce physically what I imagine in order to share it publicly.

LUCIAN: Let me try again to explain what's bothering me here. You say that we are able to extract an identity from similarity by abstraction, and reproduce it in sensation, and you offer the example of the pictograph. Is that right?

HARMONIA: Yes.

LUCIAN: And you say, if I understand you correctly, that abstraction is a process of subtraction by the imagination.

HARMONIA: Yes.

LUCIAN: And that subtracting accidental features from similar things is the opposite of adding accidental features to similar things, such as adding a man to a horse to get a centaur.

HARMONIA: Yes.

LUCIAN: What I want to say is that there is no need to invoke any such process to distil identity out of similarity. When we recognize two of Caesar's denarii as the same, as interchangeable for any possible use, as identical, we don't need to go through any kind of mental acrobatics. We see the identity immediately and involuntarily. The identity of the denarii is self-evident.

HARMONIA: I suppose so.

LUCIAN: And similarly for identical twins.

HARMONIA: Okay.

LUCIAN: Well, the same holds for similarity as well as for identity. I can *immediately* see that the items in a series of similar objects share some features, and not others, that they are similar, that is, neither strictly identical nor wholly different. I can *immediately* see, for instance, that something which appears to me now is similar to something which appeared to me earlier because it reminds me of a memory I have of the earlier appearance. I can't help but do that. It's automatic.

HARMONIA: How does that differ from what I've been saying?

LUCIAN: You're saying that this recognition is something we construct, that we somehow organize our raw experiences by abstracting or intuiting their essential features from their accidental ones. I'm saying, by contrast, that this is how things already are, that we involuntarily experience some things as similar, just as we involuntarily experience other things as identical, and still others as different. If two or more things are similar, that's something we recognize immediately; we don't need any abstruse mental process to do that, as you maintain.

HARMONIA: Really? You say that we involuntarily intuit similarity. But how can we do so unless there's some underlying identity or essence which informs what otherwise only appears to be a series of similar things?

LUCIAN: It's only what appears that counts, not what we think about what appears. There is no reason why appearances should be over-simplified, that is, reduced to some underlying identity, when they are not identical. Appearances can be blurred and vague as well as clear and distinct, just as we can have a foggy day as well as a sunny day. Both are equally and immediately apparent as what they are. Your insistence that there's an underlying identity which explains why things are similar is a fiction. It has no realization we can find outside of the imagination which concocts it, that is, unless we make a physical copy of what we imagine, just as the great statue of Jupiter in the temple on the Capitoline Hill is a copy of what we imagine Jupiter to be. But that's the exception which proves the rule. Jupiter rarely if ever appears spontaneously in real life, as I think we all would admit, apart from the representations of him which we humans have made, which are common enough. And I don't see that your abstract centurion ever appears at all, apart from the sign someone has made on the way to Gaul, and other such situations.

HARMONIA: Don't you want to understand the puzzle of similarity, of how any series of things can be somehow both identical and different at the same time?

LUCIAN: Why is it a puzzle? Interpretation is essentially a denial of what's actually happening in favour of what one believes to be happening. It is to discount something evident—in this case, the similarity in things—in favour of something non-evident: some kind of mysterious conceptualization or abstraction which is asserted but not made evident.

HARMONIA: I thought we did pretty well with the idea of sub-tracting accidental features from similar things, leaving an abstract concept which nonetheless can be pictured, as in our example of the pictogram. I thought you agreed with that. Why isn't that pictogram an evident representation of what we mean when we say 'centurion'? Why isn't it the evident representation of an abstraction?

LUCIAN: It *is* the representation of an abstraction—insofar as I under-stand that what you mean by an abstraction is a process of imaginative subtraction rather than addition—but it remains a representation of something which exists only in the human imagination, and not in nature, that is, not in the natural world of sensation—not unless we put it there, as the Legionnaires did up at the Rubicon.

The picture they made is only a particular example of a centurion, alongside all the others. It differs, it's true, in being a projection of what we imagine of a centurion, as opposed to the real centurions who appear to us naturally, but once what is imagined is realized as a sensation, as a sign at the side of the road, it's no different from any of the others, insofar as they are all more or less similar. And insofar as we recognize it as similar to other appearances of centurions, we do so immediately in exactly the same way.

HARMONIA: But the process of conceptualization is what made possible the rendering of the centurion.

LUCIAN: I'd say the rendering by a soldier in the workshop was as spontaneous as any recognition of similarity. The soldier, no doubt prompted by his commander, remembered some particular image of a centurion similar to others which he had already experienced in sensation, and then proceeded to draw it. It just 'came to mind', and he copied it, as it were. The ability to imagine a process by which accidental attributes are eliminated from a series of similar presentations, leaving only so-called essential attributes, doesn't mean that that's what's happening when one encounters one similar thing after another in everyday life.

HARMONIA: So you don't think there's such a thing as a negative imagination which produces abstractions?

LUCIAN: Yes I do. One can set out to simplify an image one already has, but the image is spontaneously generated in the first place.

HARMONIA: I can't get past the idea that you're throwing out the baby with the bathwater. Aren't we the ones who grasp our own experience, and isn't it God or the Sage who grasps all experience.

LUCIAN: I wouldn't say you're grasping anything at all, even in your imagination. Nor is the Sage. Subtracting from your thoughts to simplify them is just a way to alter the thoughts you already have, and to have new ones; it's not grasping anything, whatever that means. In our imaginations we can add and subtract thoughts more or less freely. In our sensations, we're mostly stuck with what we experience as we experience it. We can alter our sensations, of course, though only by physical effort—by putting our bodies in motion, and so on—but that quickly becomes hard work compared to the effortless freedom we enjoy in manipulating our thoughts and dreams.

HARMONIA: What about the mystery of all this spontaneous creation? Aren't you denying it?

LUCIAN: Not at all. But I am saying that the complex mechanisms of conceptualization postulated by Stoics, and Epicureans, and Aristotelians, and most other philosophers to explain what we think we know, are so many unverified fictions. They are no substitute for a valid explanation, which would involve demonstrating the mechanisms in question not only in the imagination, but in sensation as well. Sensation, after all, is the only place available to us where the things we imagine can exist independently of our imagining them.

HARMONIA: I'm saying that the forms we conceptualize out of the similarities we encounter among appearances have a real existence somewhere, even if not in the world of sensation. What we perceive in thought, in the imagination, exists somewhere. We Stoics think our concepts reveal the hand of Providence, or God, the invisible *logos* immanent in the workings of nature. The Epicureans think their concepts of the gods are subtle impressions on the mind we receive from the Void where the gods exist but remain unseen by us.

LUCIAN: The Pyrrhonists would not say the Stoics or Epicureans are wrong about this. They only point out that so far this is only something imagined to which anyone can give their assent, or not, but which cannot be established as having the independent existence that is claimed for them. Assent doesn't legitimize a belief. Imagining something doesn't make it so.

[Pause ...]

AURELIA: Lucian and Harmonia, you've given us quite a bit to think about. Maybe this is a good place to stop for tonight. The waiters have cleared the dining table, and finished cleaning up, the dogs are lying down, and the house is quiet. Time for bed, I'm afraid.

GAIUS: One last thought: we began with the Galilean idea that the truth shall make you free. If Lucian is right, there's not much of a role left for any truth which is only imagined.

AURELIA: A subject for tomorrow.

Can Anything Be Known?

RUFUS: I'm sorry I wasn't here to be the host last night, and we should all be grateful to Aurelia for skilfully managing the discussion, as I heard from Gaius. I regret that I missed an interesting conversation. Unfortunately, as you now know, there was a compelling if disturbing discussion in the Senate about the Galileans, as many call the Christians.

GAIUS: Tell us more.

RUFUS: Well, it's hard to summarize. A lot was said. The question was how to respond to their refusal to acknowledge the gods in honouring the Emperor. The debate, as usual, was between the hardliners and the moderates. The hardliners proposed a resolution for arrest and punishment, hoping to do whatever it takes to stop the sacrilege, and the moderates, like me, were for a milder penalty, one that would mark them as offenders, to be sure, but which would not inflame them further. Some of them are citizens, and suspending the rights of citizenship for any Galilean is what I'd like to see. If we did that, the folly of their gesture, I believe, would become apparent, even to themselves. There's no need to provoke them needlessly with more drastic measures like arrest and torture, or even death, as the authors of the resolution intended.

GAIUS: Did the Senate decide on the resolution?

RUFUS: No, because there were some abstentions we managed to prevent it from getting enough votes to pass, at least for now. But we were hard pressed, I can tell you. Our only hope really is the Emperor, who doesn't want to disturb the current peace and prosperity, and is inclined to be conciliatory. All gods should be respected, and none denied. It's clear, though, that we haven't heard the last of this.

AURELIA: Really! I don't understand these Galileans. Whatever they may think about the gods, they surely owe some respect to those of us who invoke them, and to the Empire and the Emperor. He's their Emperor as well, isn't he? It's impious of them to be so stubborn, is it not? We are happy enough to acknowledge any of the gods, including theirs; why can't they do the same for us?

RUFUS: Yes, of course they should, but keep in mind that the hard-liners in the Senate are just as bad, in their own way, as the Galileans in the streets. Both, after all, are sure that what they believe is true, and that the beliefs of the other side are false. There doesn't seem to be any common ground.

GAIUS: So the question of truth is not just for philosophical discussions at dinner parties, but for the Senate and People of Rome as well.

AURELIA: Indeed it is. But I'm still mystified about these Galileans. What is it about them? Or about the hardliners, the old school Senators, for that matter? Both sides are certain about what they're saying and doing, but both can't be right. Either there's one god, or there are many gods, or perhaps no gods at all.

I wonder, does last night's discussion help us understand any of this? Lucian, you argued, if I understood you correctly, that abstractions don't really exist independently of us, or maybe not at all, or at least we can't prove any of that, so that the only knowledge we can say we have is what we actually experience in sensation and thought, not in what we can further imagine to exist outside of them. That may seem a point pretty far removed from the Senators and the Galileans, but I see some similarity: in both cases we have beliefs which we imagine to be the case, but that are not necessarily the case. When you presented Pyrrhonist notions to us last month in Campania, you also focused on the difference between what we experience and what we imagine, something you continue to emphasize. Are abstractions things we can imagine, but don't otherwise experience? And what about these Galileans and the Senators opposing them; what are they all imagining? Lucian, do you have anything more to say about all this? I'm sure you do.

LUCIAN: I think so. Let me start with what we actually experience before going on to what we can imagine about what we experience. I've been following the Pyrrhonists here in pointing out that our appearances—the things we actually experience—are those of our immediate thoughts and sensations, that is, those which are currently present to us in the moment, and nothing else. They appear to us just as they are, for the moment or so they are present, and there's nothing we can do about it. Our thoughts and sensations are involuntary; we can't help but have them as long as we have healthy bodies and sense organs and minds working as they normally do. I should remember that, although our thoughts and sensations are the individual phenomena we directly experience, they seem always to appear grouped together in various fluctuating complexes or ensembles which make up the familiar facts, or *pragmata*, of life—the ordinary things we experience, the contents of our consciousness.

In Campania last summer I spoke of not being able not to see the blue sky on a sunny day if we go outdoors, and look up, with eyes wide open and working normally. I suppose it's my stock example. The same thing happens with each of our other senses: we can't help hearing the sounds we hear, smelling the smells we smell, feeling the feelings we feel; nor can we not help thinking the thoughts we think. Which is to say: we can't help experiencing the *pragmata* which our phenomena combine to present to us in our experience, these *pragmata* being the ordinary, more or less complex objects and actions which make up ordinary life. The key thing I'm trying to express is that we can't help having this or that experience when and as we are having it. Our thoughts and sensations, the Pyrrhonists insist, are involuntary.

HARMONIA: That seems a stark view, no matter how you present it. I have some questions before you go further, if you don't mind, continuing our exchange from last night. Is there anything at all we can know save for your involuntary appearances?

Since we can avoid many thoughts and sensations—by denial, distraction, substitution, drugs, motion, and so on—how is it that they are involuntary? I'm still not clear about how involuntary is involuntary. Involuntary implies that we can't avoid something, doesn't it? Can't I avoid certain thoughts and sensations?

LUCIAN: Yes, we can avoid some things, but only defer others. The rich man can avoid slavery, but he can only defer his debts, or perhaps his death, and not avoid them. But what no one can avoid, or even postpone, is the experience of a thought or sensation when it actually occurs, when it is impressed upon us, or present to us, whether we like it or not. The only way I know to avoid thoughts and sensations altogether would be to be comatose or dead. Our thoughts and sensations come into our consciousness, waking or dreaming, as long as we're alive, in a steady stream of *pragmata*, which come and go, sometimes abruptly and disruptively, like a thunderstorm, and sometimes slowly and seamlessly, like the vegetables growing in the garden. Heraclitus described the stream of experience long ago. That's what's involuntary.

HARMONIA: Let's say we accept that. But it doesn't seem to get us very far. Actually, it sounds rather trivial. It's like saying that things change, that life is one damned thing after another. Some of us want to know something more, we want to know why things are the way they are, not just that they are the way they are.

LUCIAN: You are too eager, if I may be so bold, to rush beyond your actual experience, to get to some place outside of it from which you think you can understand it. The big mistake of dogmatic philosophy —or so the Pyrrhonists say—is to overlook the experience we indisputably have in favour of what we don't have, as if we will be able to get from here to there someday.

HARMONIA: But, again, what we actually have according to you looks like little more than 'one damn thing after another'.

LUCIAN: You're still interpreting rather than accepting your experience. Let me direct at you a bit of what the Epicureans call 'frank speech', an address with regard to beliefs you hold personally. You've made a judgment—calling it just 'one damn thing after another'—that trivializes phenomena. No wonder you want to move on. You don't want to be where you actually are, yet you can't escape it. No matter where you go, after all, there you will be. The world may move, but you don't.

HARMONIA: Well, how do we know when we're interpreting things and when we're not? You still haven't answered the question.

LUCIAN: Perhaps not. Let me say that an interpretation is always two-fold. It says that this is that, in other words, that some X is really Y, that something we experience is not just what it is, that is, just what it appears to be, but that it is actually something else, something quite different. We do it all the time with metaphors and analogies.

HARMONIA: What's wrong with that? Isn't that what our often ambiguous experience suggests to us?

LUCIAN: Interpretation is a deliberate discounting of things as in fact they are. It makes the assumption, if universally applied, that nothing is simply and wholly what it appears to be, so that everything must be interpreted in terms of something else for it to make sense. It totally distorts reality.

HARMONIA: But isn't this what science does? Doesn't it reveal the underlying connections between things? Doesn't that look like a distortion of reality? But isn't it the opposite? Doesn't it show us that things as they are—say the stars as we see them in the night sky—are governed by things we can't see, by the pattern of their movements?

LUCIAN: Why do you, and so many of the philosophers, say that the pattern of the movement of the stars, or other objects, is something we can't see? We can see the paths of the stars and planets as they wheel across the heavens, can't we?

HARMONIA: I don't think so. An appearance, or direct perception, according to you, is immediate; it is present, not absent. It is something we are conscious of. We don't actually see the pattern of the movement of objects; we see only a series of objects, one after another. It's curious. You can stare at the stars and after a time you realize that they've moved, but you don't actually see them move.

LUCIAN: I can see a ball rolling across the grass of the stadium, can't I? If it rolls fast enough, I can actually see the ball begin to turn into a streak or blur, and become a continuous visual presence in my consciousness. Or if an athlete throws a javelin at the games, we can literally see it moving in an arc through the air.

HARMONIA: But there's no seeing a blur of motion in the slow-moving stars, or the sun or moon, is there?

LUCIAN: No, but I can imagine the moon, say, moving along its path, and I can even make a picture or diagram of it doing so. This is what the astronomers do in their charts of the heavens.

HARMONIA: So you've just explained one thing by another. You've given an interpretation of one thing, the moon, by another, a diagram of its path. Sounds like you're contradicting yourself.

LUCIAN: I don't think so. I'm reminded of the pictogram of the centurion from last night's discussion. That pictogram is a visual projection of something someone had imagined, and which more or less corresponds as well to the physical images we all have of real live centurions, at least in outline, at least from a certain perspective. We automatically recall, as a result, a variety of memories of individual, non-identical centurions we have actually seen. It just happens. Same thing with the diagram of the path of the moon. In each case there is enough correspondence between images—whether physical or mental—to prompt a spontaneous recognition of mutual similarity. Any one of them can become a sign for the rest.

HARMONIA: So isn't this still to interpret one thing by another?

LUCIAN: No, it's not an interpretation but a description. We're not saying that any forms displayed by images, physical or mental, of identities or similarities, represent anything other than other such images, physical or mental. They represent nothing which is independently existing, which exists outside of thought and sensation. Our descriptions simply connect some *pragmata* we involuntarily experience to other *pragmata* we involuntarily experience. Perhaps they seem to represent something independently existing simply because we can write them down, and hold on to them, and look at them later. No doubt the illusion of permanence behind phenomena was encouraged by drawing and writing. But even if our permanent written or drawn descriptions are more convenient to observe than what they describe, they remain sensations we involuntarily experience, as do the memories they prompt.

HARMONIA: Okay, call it a description. But then we still need to know how descriptions differ from interpretations.

LUCIAN: A description is a picture which to some degree or in some part accurately reproduces features of some other thing which itself may not be immediately evident, but which the description makes evident to us, provided we already have a memory of it. An interpretation does the opposite: it blurs or distorts or exaggerates or perhaps even eliminates the features of the original thing in favour of something else which exists only in the mind, and not in sensation.

HARMONIA: So a description, insofar as it is indeed a description, is some kind of accurate copy of the thing being described, or at least parts of that thing? But only things identical to one another can be fully accurate copies of one another, like Caesar's denarii as we mentioned earlier. A diagram of the path of the moon is no exact copy of the moon's path, however, not only because of differences in scale, and so on, but because it's filling in something that is not itself apparent—it suggests that the moon is moving in a way which is not apparent—but you seem not to want to go beyond anything apparent.

LUCIAN: But we know from repeated observations that the moon in fact occupies all the positions along its path, even if we can't see it in all of those positions at once. But we can imagine them all at once, as the path of the moon, and we can imagine that path being filled by the moon, and we can express our imagination in a diagram for all to see. It's a description which summarizes in one image what we otherwise can see only in separate images. It is exactly faithful to what it summarizes; it neither distorts nor denies it in any way. There is no fiction in it.

HARMONIA: And interpretations are distortions or denials? Fictions?

LUCIAN: Yes. If we say that Luna, the Queen of the Night, is the goddess of the moon and the divine force driving the moon's motion across the heavens, the moon we see becomes her symbol, if only because we have decreed it such; the moon seen through Luna then becomes connected with all that Luna represents, including feminine qualities and powers, the stories of the gods through her part in them, and so on. It's a performative act on our part, the creation of a drama we pretend to be real.

HARMONIA: What's wrong with that?

LUCIAN: It's harmless enough unless you believe that it's true that Luna really exists out there and not just in your imagination, if you believe that the moon is Luna. And it's the same with any belief. You were maintaining earlier that the things we perceive are governed by things we don't perceive, and that the former can be explained only by the latter. You were using the pictogram of the centurion not just as a reminder of centurions, as the Pyrrhonists do, but as an example of a mental process which establishes the essence of what a centurion is. I'm trying to show that there is no need to invoke things unseen, that in fact they don't explain anything. Even more to the point, such so-called explanations are unnecessary.

HARMONIA: Why are they unnecessary?

LUCIAN: Because there's nothing to explain, nothing for us to know apart from the phenomena we directly experience. My understanding of natural phenomena is deepened and extended by my ability to represent the relations among natural phenomena—as I've been trying to show with the example of picturing the path of the moon—but I don't need to invoke anything beyond my memory and imagination to make those connections. That's common sense, and science is just the refinement of common sense.

HARMONIA: I can't get past this idea that there's nothing to explain.

LUCIAN: Well, I'm not sure what would count for you as an explanation. If it's a matter of a fuller understanding of the relations among phenomena, then our ability to use our imaginations to fill in the gaps in our experience is the best we can do, it seems to me. And I don't mean to diminish that; it can reveal a great deal. It can even be a matter of life and death. An interpretation, by contrast, distorts rather than clarifies. If I say 'man is a wolf', for instance, I am offering an interpretation of men as wolves. That might be interesting or provocative, and it may well highlight certain features of men—that they can be vicious, say, or run in packs like a mob—but it really distracts us from what men are without wolves, or for that matter what wolves are without men. Your claim that forms have an independent existence as abstract entities or concepts governing what we experience looks like another kind of distortion.

HARMONIA: But an abstraction isn't a metaphor like 'man is a wolf'. It's something else: it gets at the very essence of the thing without distorting it the way a metaphor does.

LUCIAN: Well, what is an abstraction, really? You suggested last night that abstraction is a kind of negative imagination, a process of removing rather than adding features to a thing. If it has any content left at all, as I've been trying to argue, it can still count as some kind of description—like the pictogram of a centurion, which is just sufficient enough to prompt memories of other centurions. But if it doesn't have any content at all, if it's some kind of pure abstraction detached from experience, then it doesn't say anything useful or relevant to the subject in question. It prompts nothing. I'm reminded of Aristotle's notion of the one god, the prime mover, if there is one, as a kind of total abstraction which seems to dissolve into nothingness. Too bad Petronius isn't here to defend the Peripatetics!

HARMONIA: It seems to me there's a difference between the pictograph of the centurion and the diagram of the path of the moon. In the former we eliminate the different features we find in this or that or any other particular centurion in favour of something simple they all share: namely, the outline of a man wearing his helmet and holding up his hand in salute. In the case of the path of the moon we're not subtracting features but adding them, filling in the position of the moon at each point in its course. Isn't this the difference between the subtractive and additive imaginations we discussed yesterday?

LUCIAN: Not quite. I agree that the silhouette of the centurion was produced by subtracting features, and the filled-out path of the moon by adding features. Sometimes it's sufficient, as with things only similar, to ignore the non-similar parts and attend only to the similar ones; and sometimes, as with things identical, all the parts are equally deserving of attention. There's a place for simplification and a place for complication. Even the path of the moon isn't fully elaborated, after all. We don't draw an overlapping series of circles to capture the moon's shape at each point in its progress, but content ourselves with just the line indicating its path. That's a simplification. Still, we're adding something — the line of the path — so we can see the path all at once. So, yes, we can use the imagination in both these cases, once negatively and once positively. In the second case, the features introduced are not extraneous to the path of the moon, but integral to it. I have no problem with the pictograph of the centurion, as long as the simplified abstraction is not taken to represent some kind of defining reality hidden behind the appearances. And I have no problem with the path of the moon, as long as we do not introduce imagined features which do not otherwise appear, and thereby confuse our understanding.

HARMONIA: I'm not sure I follow all that, but I can accept the distinction between a description which rounds out appearances, which are in fact there, as opposed to one which falsely adds some which are not, if that's what you mean. But your claim that abstraction is only emptiness, and reveals nothing about the phenomena in question, is a harder sell. What you call a description, it seems to me, is what we Stoics keep insisting upon: the essence of things. Isn't the pictogram of the centurion we've talked about a description of the essence of a centurion? Isn't the process of simplification or abstraction exactly what captures just that?

LUCIAN: Well, then, let me try this: the pictogram of a centurion captures no more than a meagre aspect of his visual appearance. A Libyan or Scythian or Indian who otherwise knew nothing about centurions would not recognize the pictogram as representing a centurion at all. Or if he or she did, it might only be a fleeting recognition of an image they may only have briefly encountered. They might not know what a centurion really is, that he commands a hundred men, for instance, and so on. They would need to know, for a fuller understanding, not only what centurions look like, but what they can do, and not do, the contexts in which they are to be found living and acting, and so on. The pictogram only reproduces a bare visual image of a centurion in terms of some of the parts through which he is displayed, especially his helmet; a fuller understanding would be to picture as well the contexts in which the centurion acts, as he might be presented, for instance, as a character in a play or a poem or in an historical tale. The former presents us with the parts, or even just a few of them, which are enough to prompt the whole we call the centurion; the latter presents us with the whole in which the centurion plays a part—perhaps an account of what a centurion does, for instance displaying valour in battle. Both are needed to fully under-stand what a centurion is. But there's no need to insist upon any essence in any of this.

HARMONIA: I'm still confused. You're telling us that the image of a centurion is displayed by the parts that make him up, and that he himself is also a part in various larger wholes—a part of a legion, or perhaps a battle, and so on. But isn't all that a complex and open-ended process which is perhaps never definitive and which includes contradictory qualities. One centurion may display valour, as you say, but another may turn out to be a coward. And so on. Don't we need to isolate the defining qualities common to all centurions, which only abstraction can isolate? Don't we need to get the right apprehensive grasp or concept to see what a centurion really is?

LUCIAN: Well, the only centurions I can find are those who are displayed, first of all, by the parts that make them up as individuals, including their armour and insignia and weapons, and secondly, by the parts that those individual centurions play in various larger wholes. Here, as anywhere else, the parts of any whole, or the discrete thing we experience, are displayed by our sensations or thoughts — those involuntary phenomena grouped into *pragmata* which the Pyrrhonists keep talking about. Think of our sights, sounds, touches, smells, tastes, and thoughts as so many recurring phenomenal atoms, as it were, combined to constitute various things, like the neighing of horses along with their other features. It is their varying and recurring combinations which display the forms we experience, including forms within forms, or parts within wholes, but none of these forms are separate from the phenomena which display them. We cannot extract them from the phenomena which display them and independently contemplate them, though we might think we can.

HARMONIA: I hate to repeat myself, but if we can't extract forms from the phenomena which display them, then we can have no hope of achieving a deeper understanding of things. How else will we ever know what is a man, or a dog, or a god, or justice, or beauty? There will just be chaos.

LUCIAN: The fact that we can't extract forms from the phenomena which display them doesn't mean that there must be chaos.

HARMONIA: Why not? You need to explain that.

LUCIAN: Think of the letters of our alphabet, an example I brought up in Campania. In the Latin language there are twenty-three of them. Notice that they can be written or spoken. We have the written letters A, B, C, D, and so on, and the corresponding spoken letters *eh, bee, see, dee,* and so on. There is nothing about the written letter A which is to be found in the spoken letter *eh*, or vice-versa. They are entirely heterogeneous phenomena. A man blind from birth will have no notion of visual letters, nor can a man deaf from birth have any notion of audible letters. What is interesting and remarkable is that these very different kinds of letters are nonetheless both used to display the very same forms. The same forms—that is, the same words—are displayed by very different elements, visual and audible. But at the same time there is no display of forms without elements of some kind to display them. The forms displayed by phenomena, by thoughts and sensations, do not exist independently of thoughts and sensations any more than do the forms displayed by our alphabetic script exist independently of our audible and visual letters.

HARMONIA: You really mean that sensations and thoughts are like the spoken and written letters of the alphabet?

LUCIAN: Yes, as the phenomena we directly and involuntarily experience—again, our immediate thoughts and sensations—act very much like the letters of the alphabet. Just as we have different kinds of recurring letters, visual and audible, so, more broadly, we also have different kinds of recurring phenomena—in this case, the five senses plus our mental images, or six senses, if you will. And, like the different recurring letters of the alphabet, these immediate recurring phenomenal objects are different elements which are variously combined to display a variety of different forms.

HARMONIA: All right. Go on.

LUCIAN: The letters of the alphabet are arbitrary or meaningless in themselves. Only in various combinations do they display the different forms we call words, and words in turn are similarly combined into larger forms as sentences, paragraphs, and entire books. Like letters, our individual thoughts and sensations are meaningless in themselves, but in combination they are able to display the forms of the *pragmata* we experience. A dab of colour, or a simple sound, a random thought, and so on, have no intrinsic meaning, any more than do the letters A or B or C; only when combined together do phenomena display forms which have meaning, just as letters only when combined together are able to form meaningful words. The meaning is simply the reciprocal correlation of heterogeneous things displaying similar or identical forms.

In Greek, we speak of the elements which display forms as phenomena, and of the forms displayed by phenomena as *pragmata*. There are no *pragmata* which are not displayed by phenomena, and no phenomena which do not contribute to the display of some *pragma*. Or so it appears in our experience. Our phenomena are recurring universals—sounds and sights, touches, tastes, and smells, as well as elements of thought—which are variously combined and recombined to constitute the complex particular things, or *pragmata*, in which our experience is presented to us.

HARMONIA: But letters do not have to show meaning when combined. AZKTQ, for instance, is just nonsense. Doesn't your analogy break down here?

LUCIAN: No, it only becomes more compelling. In fact, combinations of phenomena, like those of letters, can be nonsensical. The thing about AZKTQ is that the forms these letters combine to display remind us of nothing beyond themselves. They can appear but they signify nothing except themselves, and so have no meaning. If AZKTQ signified something, if it was a word with meaning, there would be some object outside language, correlated with AZKTQ, which we would spontaneously recognize it to signify, which of course does not happen in this case. Similarly, in the natural alphabet of appearances, so to speak, there will be forms displayed by some combinations of phenomena, a *pragmata*, which correlate with no other *pragmata* we can find. They do not signify, except to signify themselves. We can imagine centaurs and mermaids, for instance, but insofar as we can find no independent corresponding objects outside the imagination which they can be said to signify, they too remain nonsensical, strictly speaking.

HARMONIA: Well, that's a clever analogy, I will admit, but it's only an analogy.

LUCIAN: It's a description, not an analogy. Just as the alphabet has different modes, as it were, namely the visual alphabet we read and see and the audible alphabet we speak and hear, so too we have different phenomenal modes, our sights, sounds, touches, tastes, smells, and thoughts. A Latin or Greek or any other alphabet of a language is but a miniature version of the larger alphabet of nature we all share where different sets or modes of elements—visual, audible, tactile, gustatory, atomic, and mental—can each be combined (or not) to represent the others.

HARMONIA: For instance? Exactly how does this work in nature?

LUCIAN: Well, we were talking earlier about the neighing of horses, and just now, though no one commented on it, we all heard the neighing and stomping of some horses outside in the street as the carriage drivers were taking them down to the stables for feed and for the night. We can't see the horses from here in the atrium, but if we could we'd likely see them arch their necks up and down and curl their lips in point-to-point correspondence with the sound of their neighing, and similarly we'd see the up and down motion of their feet in correspondence with the sound of their stomping. That's the alphabet of nature.

HARMONIA: But don't our thoughts differ from our sensations more than our sensations differ from one another? Our sensations are bound by the laws of nature, but our thoughts are not; they can range freely and widely in our minds, if we let them, while we are bound more rigidly by our sensations. Your example seems to break down here. And just what are the letters or elements of thought? What is a thought?

LUCIAN: Thoughts are mental copies of sensations; they are re-creations of sensations, at one remove. That's how they appear in the mind, as reflections of sensations. It's hard to put it any better. Visual thoughts somehow reflect visual sensations, auditory thoughts somehow reflect auditory sensations, and so on. Thoughts differ from sights and sounds and other sensations as much as sights and sounds and other sensations differ from one another. None of our sensations gives us any more of a clue about what it is to have thoughts than any of our thoughts give us any clue about what it is to have sensations. Just as a person blind from birth would be clueless about what it is to see, so, presumably, someone born without a mind—that is, without memory and imagination, like an animal—would have little or no clue about what it is to think.

You're right, of course, that our thoughts are far more fluid and less rigidly structured than our sensations. Nonetheless, we can reliably display in thought the same forms we find in sensation, and vice-versa. Indeed, the fluidity and ease of thought makes this easier. To achieve this, we need to combine the two aspects of mind: memory and imagination. I can imagine or recall the neighing and stomping of the horses in my mind just as I can also hear or see it. The phenomenal objects of my consciousness—physical and mental—display an immense variety of forms, which variously represent and contrast with one another. Sometimes the same forms are displayed by different phenomena, but sometimes they display similar forms, and sometimes even contrasting forms. The elements of thought are more subtle, it's true. A thought of something red, say, appears to be a kind of copy of some sensible red thing, and a thought of something heard appears to be a copy of some sensible sound, and so on. It's hard to say more about them, but such seem to be the elements of thought.

HARMONIA: By the way, you just turned philosophy on its head a moment ago, when you maintained that phenomena are universals and *pragmata* are particulars, didn't you?

LUCIAN: I'm glad you noticed that. It's no less than a philosophical revolution. The inversion of universals and particulars distinguishes the Pyrrhonists from not only dogmatists like you Stoics, and those from the other major schools, but also from the nihilistic Academics. What all of you share in common is the presumption, or belief, that our immediate experience is not only fleeting but illusory, that it's composed of unreliable, non-recurring particulars, not universals. The positive dogmatists, your Stoics included, search for universals among your abstractions, not among your sensations, and you remain hopeful of finding them, while the Academics have given up in despair, and remain imprisoned by their negative belief that universals, in which they still believe, and which cannot be found, do not exist at all. The Pyrrhonists offer a way out of this tangle by refocusing on phenomena as universals, which results in a phenomenalistic atomism.

HARMONIA: That refocusing on phenomena still needs more discussion, in my opinion, and Philia will probably want to say something about atomism from the Epicurean point of view. In the meantime, for you, and I suppose the Pyrrhonists, that seems like the end of the story. Whatever knowledge is to be had is what can be displayed by one set of phenomena to represent another set. I suppose it's not chaos, but it's hard to get very excited about it.

LUCIAN: I wouldn't say it's the end of the story, but it does seem to be the end or limit of whatever knowledge we can have, which is knowledge of phenomena by acquaintance. Truth is the ability to recognize successful representations among phenomena. Earlier I offered the example of the path of the moon, and of a corresponding representation, or diagram, in which that path is displayed, such as we might find in a chart in one of the libraries in the city, perhaps hung up on the wall. That diagram, I'd like to say, captures and sustains for us in a convenient and immediate form the actual path of the moon in the heavens. It's a successful representation. Not only that, it allows us to predict what the moon's motion will be. That is what science does — it provides us with successful representations (diagrams, notations, etc.) of *pragmata* displayed in nature which are important to us but which otherwise we can't observe together all at once. It brings together observations otherwise dispersed and allows us to contemplate them all at once, and make accurate predictions of future movements. We can thus better understand the *pragmata* or facts of nature which comprise our involuntary experience.

HARMONIA: But those sensible *pragmata* which I can represent in my imagination by thought *pragmata*, or thought images, and which I can go on to reproduce in language, or in drawing, or in some other natural inscription, as you're saying, why don't these representations signify just the essences I've been trying to talk about? Why can't I conclude that? Since the same forms can be displayed by different kinds of phenomena, it would seem that the forms are somehow independent of the phenomena which display them. It seems to me that strengthens the case for their independent existence.

LUCIAN: But they're not independent, at least not yet in our experience. What you can't do is conclude that forms have an independent existence apart from the *pragmata* which display them, tempting as that may be, because for that there is no evidence that anyone seems able to produce. Drawing such a conclusion is not a matter of knowledge, but of belief. It's a leap of faith. Accurate representation of some facts by other facts sets the extent and limit of knowledge. We can say that such-and-such a form is accurately represented only by comparing the representation with what it represents, insofar as we can make such a comparison, and often we can. Any comparison happens spontaneously; there is no hidden process behind our phenomenal display that we can determine, nor is determining any such process even necessary. Even though the same forms can be displayed by different phenomena, they remain entirely dependent on some set or mode of phenomena to be displayed at all. We have no access to forms independently of the phenomena which display them. We have no picture of the relationship which holds between a picture of something and the thing pictured. There is no picturing of picturing.

HARMONIA: I still think, Lucian, that you're evading the issue. What you're calling a belief seems to me a very reasonable, rational inference. It does justice to the experience of repeated forms we find in a variety of sensations and thoughts, the cumulative effect of which you gloss over. Isn't it precisely because different sets of phenomena can over and over display the same forms that we can separate those forms from the phenomena which display them? The forms are obviously distinct, even on your account, from the phenomena which display them. We can agree on that, but isn't that why we are justified in concluding their independent existence?

LUCIAN: On this we're going to have to agree to differ, I think. You want to step outside the circle of *pragmata* to establish beyond that circle something that can, as far as we can tell, appear only within that circle. You want a criterion of representation, which the Pyrrhonists see as unnecessary. Our dispute here seems to be a matter of distinguishing between what can be said, and what can only be shown, and not said. You are intent, it seems, on reifying abstractions. The independent existence of what is displayed in *pragmata* is a matter of belief, not knowledge, no matter how beguiling it may seem. I'm not saying that you're wrong or right about the real existence of what you believe in, only that we have no way to tell whether or not that's the case, and so, in the meantime, jumping to a non-evident belief about what's happening isn't justified, or, as I've tried to show, even necessary.

[Pause ...]

RUFUS: Well then, the original question—what can be known?—seems to remain in some question. I'm brought back again to the challenge of the Galileans and the debate in the Senate. Both sides—the Galileans in the streets and the senators in our chamber—seem to me to claim to know things that you, Lucian, deny they can know. They both infer from what is displayed by phenomena in *pragmata* that certain extra-phenomenal forms are independently existing things. They believe in them. The Galileans believe their prophet, Jesus, as I think he's called, to be the son of the one and only god, and the vehicle of their personal salvation. The senators make out the *sacramentum* to be a way for everyone to acknowledge the existence of all the gods, not just their own. Both sides hold these claims to reflect true beliefs.

The Galileans make their leap of faith on the basis of their stories of the life of their prophet. His divinity, they say, is manifest in the miracles he is said to have performed, not least his resurrection from the dead, and also in his compassion, and in the wisdom of his words, not to mention the prophecies of the Jews he appears to have fulfilled. Our senators, in much the same way, take the myths of the gods to display their divinity. Because we can imagine the stories of Zeus and

Hera, Apollo and Dionysus, Artemis and Aphrodite, and all the rest, we take them to exist independently of the stories themselves, just what you claim that Harmonia is doing when she abstracts forms out of *pragmata* and turns them into independently existing concepts.

LUCIAN: Yes, and I would add that the Galileans and the senators you describe practise not Harmonia's method of abstraction, or what we've called negative imagination, but rather positive imagination, in which they compound things which appear in sensation with those that so far can only be imagined. But the result is the same, namely projection of an independently existing belief to which one clings. It turns into a self-fulfilling criterion of reality. Assenting to such beliefs as independently existing is the road to falsehood, not truth, and it masks our ignorance of how things really are.

RUFUS: Your Pyrrhonists, Lucian, want to suspend all beliefs, if I understand you correctly. I'm not sure how that would work out, or even if it's possible. An exceptional holy man, like their founder Pyrrho, might well have succeeded in such an endeavour, but virtually everyone else is caught up in one or another set of beliefs, it seems to me. Even more, society seems to be based on beliefs. It's hard to imagine life without them. Is it even possible? On the other hand, I can also see that beliefs tend to rigidify under opposition and contradiction, and we know that contradictions between beliefs breed anxiety and conflict, as we now see between ourselves and the Galileans.

PHILIA: Let me add something here, before the night is over. This is exactly the problem the founder of our sect, Epicurus, addressed, and I think it's time to more closely consider his views on all this.

Harmonia's Stoicism is fine as far as it goes, but it seems to me that Epicurus took things a step further. The challenge is not simply to embrace one or another belief, but to find the right belief, the one that trumps all the others, the one which is true—something I take Epicurus to have achieved.

LUCIAN: And just how did he do that?

RUFUS: It'll have to wait another day. The hour is indeed late. It's off to bed, but we'll begin tomorrow evening with Philia, and see what progress we can make. It'll be our last evening together, and our last chance to resolve things. Just as the runners sprint towards the end of a race in order to get to the goal, so tomorrow we shall make our best efforts.

The Third Evening

What is Ataraxia?

RUFUS: Well, this is our final evening together. Tomorrow we will go our separate ways. This is our last chance—at least for now—to see if we can resolve the issues we've raised. Let me try to sum up where we left off last evening, if I can. Lucian made many pressing arguments, but Harmonia seemed to deflect them, or at least not be convinced. The question was what we can know, whether or not the truth of things—the significance we think they have—is self-evident and dependent upon us, or whether it depends upon something else, something we imagine to exist independently of the sensations and thoughts we immediately and involuntarily experience, something outside of us. Lucian argued persuasively, it seemed to me, that there is no warrant for anything existing independently of our immediate experience, but Harmonia maintained that the display of the same forms in different things nonetheless gives good grounds for distinguishing forms from the phenomena which display them—a distinction which supports the idea that forms somehow do have an existence independently of the elements displaying them, even if it's not exactly evident that they do, or what sort of existence that might be. They do not appear in the manner of Pyrrhonian phenomena, we can admit, yet they seem to many to be somehow embedded among the forms *pragmata* display, in ways that are hard to ignore. Is that where we left off?

AURELIA: I think so. But Philia said she had something to add at the end last night, and we promised to hear her out when we reconvened tonight. So let's start with her.

[Pause ...]

PHILIA: All right, let's see, how to begin. Perhaps this: I think last night's long discussion between Lucian and Harmonia missed a key point. It's all well and good to argue about knowledge, but achieving knowledge doesn't necessarily make us any happier. Ignorance, people say, is bliss, and that should tell us something. The more knowledge we seem to acquire, the more innocence we lose, the harder life turns out to be. Harmonia's gloomy Stoics are a good example. They make a virtue out of the inexorable laws of the universe, even as those very laws wear us down. The Pyrrhonists, by contrast, evade the issue, in my opinion. It seems there's no getting around the tragedy of life, of pain and suffering. Senator Rufus made that point on our very first evening last summer in Campania. Our greatest dramatists, the tragedians, all came to a similar conclusion. Oedipus, Antigone, Orestes, Achilles, and any number of other tragic characters can only hope, at best, for some kind of nobility in the course of their suffering.

There must be a better way, I've long thought, and it was a relief and a joy to find it in the works of Epicurus. He doesn't aim at knowledge for its own sake, nor does he deny knowledge. Indeed, he claims to possess it, and to live by it. He seeks to use it as a tool to attain what he calls tranquillity, or serenity, or imperturbability — what he calls *ataraxia*. Pyrrho may have been the first to invoke *ataraxia*, but it was Epicurus who put it in a systematic framework and showed how it can be realized by anyone. It's a kind of peace of mind which he identifies as the highest pleasure, which is the absence of pain. Rather than trying to make a virtue out of tragedy or suffering, he offers a way to minimize suffering and maximize pleasure.

LUCIAN: I'm glad you pointed out that *ataraxia* is what the Pyrrhonists discovered, even before Epicurus, when they succeeded in suspending beliefs, or as I've been saying, judgments or interpretations about the nature of things. The story is that Pyrrho encountered the possibility of realizing *ataraxia* among the holy men he met in India during Alexander's campaign, and apparently achieved it himself, and brought the discovery with him back to Greece. But, all right, back to Epicurus.

PHILIA: Yes, Epicurus was an admirer of Pyrrho's, and we know he learned of *ataraxia* from Pyrrho's disciple Nausiphanes. Epicurus and Nausiphanes had some kind of quarrel, it seems, and both of them had their differences with Pyrrho. Yet somehow *ataraxia* survived as a common philosophical goal, at least among these philosophers. Even Harmonia's Stoics cast their weary wisdom of the world as offering some kind of peace of mind.

LUCIAN: Pyrrho wrote nothing we know of, except for a poem praising Alexander, by which he was afterwards embarrassed. There are some accounts of his life, by Antigonus and others, and quite a bit from his disciple, Timon, who came and lived for a time with him in Elis. Timon compares Pyrrho to Apollo, and everyone seems to agree that Pyrrho displayed remarkable composure and fortitude in almost all circumstances, marking him out as some kind of holy man. He was honoured by the city of Elis and made a priest and was even exempted from taxes. The Athenians even awarded him citizenship. He seems to have achieved a sustained state of *ataraxia*, sometimes wandering about in a detached state of mind, but it's not clear how he did it. Epicurus and Nausiphanes quarrelled, I believe, over just how to achieve such a state. Among the Greek philosophers, Pyrrho was apparently foremost in his ability to realize and demonstrate *ataraxia*, at least by reputation.

The word *ataraxia* literally means tranquillity, a state of imperturbability or equanimity in the face of fear and anxiety. It emerged as a trait distinguishing the best soldiers in the face of battle, those who kept calm and collected in the midst of the chaos and death whirling about them. Pyrrho was a soldier too, and perhaps he adapted the term for what he discovered when he was with the gymnosophists. So goes the story.

PHILIA: Yes, no one disputes that Pyrrho opened the door to tranquillity for the Greeks, but we can debate who has the last word on the matter. *Ataraxia* has emerged among many philosophers then and since as an ultimate end, something to which other values are but a means. And an end not just in battle, of course, but in everyday life. And not only Epicureans, but Stoics and Cynics and others set it up as a goal. So it seems we can say that we're all trying to achieve the same thing.

LUCIAN: It's tempting to believe that, but disputes among the schools have clouded the question and left *ataraxia* stubbornly elusive. I'd put it this way: the Stoics, as I think we've seen, seek tranquillity in what they call the *logos*, which they isolate through abstraction; they thereby take refuge in the conceptual understanding of the world which reason seems to offer. Harmonia and I disagree about the virtue of that approach, but I think she and I can agree that that's what they try to do, and, as we saw last evening, that abstraction is a kind of negative imagination. Is that right?

HARMONIA: Fair enough.

LUCIAN: The same goes for Aristotle as well, whereby something like tranquillity can be recognized under the guise of satisfaction. It can be construed, I think, as the reward, or final end, for productive activity. Petronius isn't here, but I suspect he would agree. As for Plato, his Academy became the natural home of self-confessed nihilists like Saturninus. They embrace the impossibility of any knowledge at all as a liberation from the anxiety generated by trying to establish that knowledge in the first place—something even Plato couldn't do.

GAIUS: True. It was Plato who, in many ways, unleashed the process of debate and exchange, of question and answer, in whose wake we still find ourselves. The later Academics adopted a nihilism he resisted.

LUCIAN: Yes, they did. And how adroit Plato was, above all others, in exhibiting the panorama of dogmatic views without being caught up in any of them, though I think his theory of forms sorely tempted him, though it was Aristotle who took the bait. We have arrived at the point, it seems, where a new final goal—in this case *ataraxia*—is said to appear, marked by a sense of detachment. The problem is that in each of the current schools we find distinct and even incompatible versions of tranquillity, which nonetheless seem to advertise a common goal of liberation. It seems they can't all be right.

PHILIA: You left out the more moderate parts of the Academy, beginning with Antiochus, who backed away from Arcesilaus and Carneades' total rejection of belief, as still held by our Saturninus here. Antiochus replaced certain knowledge with plausible knowledge. We can assent to what we believe to be the most likely case in the absence of actual confirmation.

LUCIAN: Belief in plausibility is as much a belief as any other. And one is just as let down when it turns out to be false, perhaps more so, since one was expecting it to be true. Plausibility doesn't exempt anything from being overturned and ending up completely wrong. Arcesilaus mastered Pyrrho's dialectic but found a precedent for it more congenial to the Academy, namely, in the person of Socrates, who famously never expressed an opinion of his own on anything. Perhaps he achieved the tranquillity the Pyrrhonists say follows suspension of judgment, but there is no testimony from him or anyone else to that effect. Arcesilaus held that Socrates' successors gradually reintroduced beliefs into the Academy, culminating with plausibility, which corrupted its original scepticism. The Pyrrhonians by contrast are explicit, unlike Socrates, that they don't even know that they don't know. Nihilism is knowing that you know nothing, that you can't know anything. It's still all about the self, about what *you* can know. The Pyrrhonists, in admitting that they don't even know whether they know or not, erase the last privilege of the self.

[Pause …]

What do you say, Saturninus?

SATURNINUS: That's a bit unfair to the nihilist. Having nothing to believe in is a way to avoid the miseries which belief in something brings in its wake. It's important to see how belief in nothing differs from belief in something. For one thing, it can't disappoint you.

LUCIAN: But nothing still remains something you are asserting as an ultimate or final conclusion about how things really are.

SATURNINUS: But I see it as a virtue, not a liability. Who can prove otherwise?

LUCIAN: It isn't necessary to prove otherwise; it's only necessary to provide a counter-proof which neutralizes the argument. I'd say that a claim for nothingness as the vehicle of liberation carries exactly the same burden as other claims for what might liberate us, such as those of the positive dogmatists. You ask for someone to disprove your claim, but the point is that it can neither be proven nor disproven. As a result, you should suspend judgment on the question, which is a very different thing. But instead, you're continuing to play the game of assertion and negation about speculative things; but suspension of judgment is what ends the game.

SATURNINUS: I doubt it.

[Laughter …]

So let's agree to disagree.

PHILIA: Saturninus may be willing to accept a stalemate like that, but I'm not. *Ataraxia* remains a goal for Epicureans as well as for many other schools, but I believe they have the best prospect of getting there. It's about time in this discussion to turn to the Epicureans. They are distinguished from the other dogmatists by their focus on evidence and science, on the basis of the physical sensations we experience — something you're always promoting, Lucian.

LUCIAN: Well, the Aristotelians also point to their reliance on evidence and science, as do the Stoics as well, and also the Pyrrhonists. We're all scientists here, aren't we? How do the Epicureans differ?

PHILIA: It isn't enough to invoke reason, or *logos*, as the Aristotelians and Stoics do, as a kind of independent organizing principle of reality. If we are to understand the world as we experience it, we need to be clear about how it is that the things we actually experience — our sensations and thoughts — are structured. Aristotelians and Stoics presume that our immediate experience is somehow inchoate and chaotic until it is sorted out by some kind of reason understood to be more or less distinct from immediate experience. We've already gone over this, and the Pyrrhonian critique of it which Lucian advanced. Epicureans by contrast maintain, like Pyrrhonists, that knowledge comes entirely from the senses. It is contained within them, as it were, and is not imposed upon them.

They think of it like this: reason is not distinct from the irrational stuff it supposedly organizes; it is not some kind of separate principle or force. It is rather a function of the human mind—itself a subtle material thing—manifest by its ability to organize the phenomena we perceive which are not themselves rational, but simply various combinations of elements moving in the void. There is no rational living world soul which providentially governs the universe, as the Stoics claim, but only atoms of matter in random mechanical motion.

Our sensations give us recurring patterns displayed by the objects we distinguish in experience. I see one dog, then another, and another, and still more, and finally I am left with a preconception, a *prolepsis* in Greek, lodged in my mind as a distinct memory. My *prolepsis* of 'dog' arises out of the subtle ability of my mind to somehow consolidate how it is that dogs appear in nature. This allows me to recognize something as a dog, and obviously the same goes for most any object, or event, or anything else I can recognize. Such images come from sensations but are only universalized in the mind, whose rational activity allows us to sort them out so as to grasp or recognize the objects we experience.

LUCIAN: How does the Epicurean *prolepsis* differ from the Stoic *katalepsis*? You seem to be repeating the kind of argument made earlier by Harmonia. She talked about the mind 'grasping', and you talk about it 'consolidating', and I don't see the difference.

PHILIA: Although they seem similar in meaning, we might say that a *prolepsis* is a grasping derived from experience, while a *katalepsis* is a grasping imposed onto experience. Epicureans invoke no independent or final mental process to explain what they grasp in sensation, as Stoics do. Stoics propose an active mental grasping of what things really are, and how they are determined; Epicureans propose a passive reception of things arising out of our natural experience, as it comes to us contingently. They recognize a variety of sensations which overlap enough over time to display some common features, for instance, of all the various dogs one is likely to encounter. We cannot help but recognize all these dogs as similar by virtue of the forms they display in common; these overlapping forms are what we retain in the mind in memory, as distinguished from those they don't overlap. That recognition is the *prolepsis*.

Finally, our sensations and thoughts can best be understood as composed of small, indivisible, interchangeable parts which variously combine and separate and recombine, over and over. Epicurius called these parts atoms, after Democritus. The thoughts which compose the rational mind are made of finer, more subtle atoms, while sensations are made of grosser, heavier atoms, but all atoms are so small as to be unobservable to us. The greater subtlety of thought atoms, their extremely light density, is what allows them to range further than the heavier sensation atoms, and to freely represent and focus those sensations in the theatre of memory and imagination. Our sensations come to us as waves of atoms, and there is no reason to doubt that they accurately represent the external world which emits them, at least once the mind is able to review and refine them to the point of *prolepsis*, like the final moment when we complete sifting the wheat from the chaff.

LUCIAN: If a *prolepsis* is just a way of saying that we can directly remember similarities, without trying to show in what similarity actually consists, then the Epicurean view would seem to coincide with what the Pyrrhonists say about this. So perhaps we can agree. But as long as there remains a tendency to understand *prolepsis* as something by which similarity is recognized by the mind as an independent thing, somehow displayed in a singular memory, or mental image, then we have another fictional belief, it would seem, even if it's somehow passively produced. For instance, it is not possible to produce an image of the similarity of 'dog', or any other similarity.

PHILIA: So far, yes, we agree.

LUCIAN: All right, then, let's pick up on your other point, that all things are composed of atoms, of varying degrees of refinement.

PHILIA: Yes.

LUCIAN: And Epicureans are well known for holding, as you just noted, that the most basic elements, the irreducible atoms, are so refined as to be unobservable, aren't they?

PHILIA: Yes.

LUCIAN: If so, that seems like another theory about what it is that we experience, much like what the other dogmatists offer. If atoms are unobservable, how can we establish them other than by some imaginative speculation?

PHILIA: Well, Epicureans aren't theorizing or interpreting what they experience. They do not doubt the veracity of their senses, as you earlier implied, in contrast to many dogmatists, including the Stoics. Like the Pyrrhonists, they maintain that the senses are consistently reliable, and in no way illusory.

LUCIAN: Perhaps I was wrong. But if sensations are so reliable, why do we need to invoke unobservable atoms?

PHILIA: Because unobservable atoms, it turns out, follow naturally from what we know about observable sensations. It is evident that our sensations are composed of a variety of objects which are more or less in motion relative to one another. Objects and the void are the most fundamental things we can observe. The space or void between objects is what allows them to move. Further, we notice in our sensory experience that objects arise only from other objects, not from nothing, or the void. Plants grow from seeds produced by prior plants, animals are conceived from prior animals by sperm and eggs, and indeed anything at all is necessarily composed of parts from other things — utensils from pottery, armour from metal, furniture from wood, houses from stone, and so on. No thing, Epicurus insisted, can be created from the non-existent.

LUCIAN: How can we be so sure that something cannot be produced out of nothing?

PHILIA: It simply follows from what we can observe of phenomena. Any new thing, as I just said, without any exception that we can observe, comes out of some older, or pre-existing thing. Don't you agree?

LUCIAN: Yes, if only for the sake of argument. But I still don't see how Epicureans get from observable phenomena to unobservable atoms.

PHILIA: Our sensations are complex, compounded, and varied. We analyse how they are made by breaking them down into the parts out of which they are composed. But the parts of things turn out themselves to be things which are complex, and that in turn invites further analysis, and so on. Our sensations are particulars, and so stand in need of explanation. The virtue of the Epicurean explanation is that it is an inference from our sensations, not a speculation about them.

So, if everything must come from something else, and not from the void, then complex objects must in the end come from simpler objects —and not from nothing. The question then becomes what those simplest objects might be which could function as the smallest parts adequate to inform the composition of any and all of the complex objects we normally experience.

LUCIAN: That sounds like the kind of abstraction we discussed earlier with the example of the centurion's pictograph.

PHILIA: Perhaps it's an abstraction, but it's more important that it's an inference, and a sound and truthful one at that. What Epicurus proposes is that atoms must retain (if they are to be something and not nothing) the simplest aspects anything could have, and these he proposes to be shape, mass, and size. There is nothing, he maintains, that isn't composed of atoms of shape, mass, and size. And that includes, by the way, the human soul which, insofar as it exists, is the most subtle thing composed of the most subtle atoms. Our pleasures and pains are simply the effects on our subtle souls of the motions of grosser objects in the world. Even the gods are made of atoms, albeit much finer even than ours. Indeed they are so fine that they can be easily and continually replenished, so the gods can maintain their bodies forever. Such is their immortality!

LUCIAN: The pictogram of the centurion was something observable in which shape, mass, and size were evident. But these Epicurean atoms are unobservable.

PHILIA: Here's how Epicureans understand this. The variety of sensible objects is so great, and the threshold of what we can analyse so high, that we can't get down to the atomic level with direct observation. Our sensations are not granular enough for that. If we break down the parts of a stone, or a tree, or an animal, or anything else, we can only get to the smallest observable components of that particular thing, not to the smallest components that all things share in common. Those we have to infer, and they have to be the simplest aspects of something, rather than nothing.

LUCIAN: But how do you make that inference?

PHILIA: The relevant question here is what minimally distinguishes something from nothing. The Epicureans' answer is that the smallest things — atoms — are distinguished from nothing by shape, mass, and size. We're talking here about the essential features of atoms, and all the grosser things they make up. An example might help. A blank surface, say a fresh roll of papyrus, is nothing, we might say, until someone makes a mark on it, perhaps no more than a dot. Then suddenly we have something in contrast to nothing. Shape, mass, and size are all evident in the dot. It has a kind of shape — think of it as a vanishingly small circle. It has a kind of mass as well, even if no more than a speck of ink. And it has a size, albeit the very smallest we can perceive.

LUCIAN: Are you saying that these Epicurean atoms have three parts?

PHILIA: No, these are not parts of atoms, but qualities they must have if they are to combine into the larger things we see, hear, feel, and so on; they are the aspects of any atom and they do not exist independently of atoms. If you think about it, we cannot have shape without mass and size, nor mass without shape and size, nor size without shape and mass. None of these makes sense without the other two.

LUCIAN: That's very ingenious. Let's accept that for now, but I continue to be puzzled at the notion that Epicurean atoms, and their qualities, remain unobservable. Anyone can see that there is a lower limit to the smallest items we can observe. The Pyrrhonists call these phenomenal atoms, as I suggested, which are distinct from your unobservable atoms. I tried to describe them last night by invoking the example of the alphabet. We can break up a stone, say, into its smallest bits, down to grains of sand, or pour out a glass of water until we isolate its smallest bits, say the last small drops of water, or burn up logs in a fire until only minute particles of ash remain, and so on. These remainders are phenomenal atoms in the sense that they are the smallest parts of these things which we can observe. But if we keep trying to divide grains of sand, drops of water, specs of ash, or virtually any other phenomenal atom, the atom simply disappears from observation. It also seems clear as well that our phenomenal atoms are quite different from and apparently irreducible to one another: a grain of sand bears little resemblance to a drop of water, and so on.

PHILIA: This is precisely the problem the Epicureans are trying to solve. Your alphabet model enshrines the diversity of our sensations without resolving it. Your phenomenal atoms don't explain the evident variety and particularity of our sensible experience. Even though the objects we perceive remain stubbornly diverse in observation, right down to the phenomenal level, as you point out, they nonetheless constitute a single world we all experience, one which can be explained only by postulating even more fundamental atoms, even if they cannot be directly observed.

LUCIAN: So Epicureans too are trying to explain the nature or essence behind the phenomena we experience. I'm not so sure any such explanation is valid, or even necessary. I know that sounds provocative, but let me try to explain by asking some questions in turn.

PHILIA: All right.

LUCIAN: You say these common unobservable atoms are necessary to explain the actual diverse world we experience.

PHILIA: Yes.

LUCIAN: The things we actually experience, you say, are varied and heterogeneous. In other words, they are particulars.

PHILIA: Yes again.

LUCIAN: So the issue seems to be how to account for the universality which is also apparent in our experience. If everything were a particular then everything would be different from everything else, wouldn't it? Everything would be contingent with regard to anything else. The world would be a bewildering chaos.

PHILIA: I suppose so.

LUCIAN: But it's not. Is that right?

PHILIA: Well, there is order as well as chaos among our *pragmata*.

LUCIAN: So Epicurus postulated imperceptible atoms with the qualities of shape, mass, and size to explain the real or hidden nature or order of these sensible particulars?

PHILIA: Exactly. It solves the problem.

LUCIAN: And, as with his master, Democritus, these atoms are indivisible.

PHILIA: Yes, indivisibility is the limiting case of all things. If an atom were divisible, it wouldn't be an atom. It would have parts, which might be atoms, unless they too turned out to be divisible.

LUCIAN: But you can't say what these indivisible, unobservable atoms are, except that they have the qualities of shape, mass, and size.

PHILIA: We can say that anything indivisible is necessarily resistant to division. We might understand that to mean that atoms are impenetrable; we might say they are hard—that they are the ultimate bits of irreducible reality. Otherwise they wouldn't be atoms.

LUCIAN: We can agree, at least, that your atoms are necessarily indivisible, or at least that anything divisible isn't an atom. Right?

PHILIA: Right.

LUCIAN: But we don't know what an unobservable atom may be in itself, only that, whatever it may be, it must be indivisible; but we are told, according to Democritus and Epicurus, that it has certain qualities.

PHILIA: Yes.

LUCIAN: I'm curious about these qualities, and how they appear in your account of unobservable atoms. Where do they come from? You said earlier that we can't have shape without size and mass, and size without shape and mass, and mass without size and shape. Right?

PHILIA: Right.

LUCIAN: And you gave a nice illustration of that with the example of a dot on a clean roll of papyrus. That's a good picture of what a minimal item of experience can look like, isn't it? In fact it illustrates very well what I call phenomenalistic atomism—that is, the atoms we actually experience. What I don't see is how you, or the Epicureans, can invoke that example to support unobservable atoms.

PHILIA: Why not? Remember, it's no more than an illustration intended to help picture in the imagination what it is that we're talking about, but can't actually see.

LUCIAN: So the idea is to imagine in the mind what unobservable atoms might look like. The picture of an atom which emerges, if I have it right, is that of an empty abstraction, like a point in geometry, which to us must be nothing in itself, since it is unobservable, but which nonetheless has the distinguishing qualities of shape, mass, and size. Is that right?

PHILIA: Exactly.

LUCIAN: And shape, mass, and size, if we look closely at them, are visual qualities, and not audible, or gustatory ones.

PHILIA: I would argue that the basic qualities of atoms — shape, mass, and size — are in fact common to all the gross particular sensible objects we experience. Isn't it obvious, or evident, that any common object — this table with its dishes of food, the goblet before me, the pool and fountain in front of us, the starry night bending over us — all these surely display, all of them, some kind of shape, mass, and size?

LUCIAN: Really? Let's consider more fully the objects of our senses. We might find shapes and sizes in our various visual objects, but their very lightness suggests that visual objects have no weight or substance. For that we need not sight, but touch. The goblet I raise has a mass or weight I can feel, as well as a shape and size I can see, but the aroma of the wine which accompanies it, as opposed to the weight and size of the goblet, has neither shape, nor mass, nor size. The sound of clinking my goblet with yours similarly has neither shape, nor mass, nor size, though it is unmistakably a sensation like any other. I feel the mass of the wine as I put my lips to it, but the taste itself defies any notion of substance. I could go on, but my point is that a close look at the objects presented by the differing senses just as they are undermines this notion that certain qualities — such as shape, mass, or size — are common to all the objects of our senses.

PHILIA: But we don't experience sensations apart from one another, only in conjunction with one another. Different mixtures of atoms combine together to produce gross objects, and these objects will differ given the particular nature of the mixture. The shape of a horse, say, is manifest visually, its substance or weight manifest by touch, and so on.

LUCIAN: But why should a horse have one shape rather than another, or one colour rather than another, or be heavy rather than light, or make certain sounds rather than others, and so on?

PHILIA: These specific qualities which make up an object come from some proportional mixture of ingredients, much like a good cake will come from following the right recipe. I'll admit we don't have the recipes yet for how natural objects are made, but we hope to rely on what science may yet discover.

LUCIAN: So you can't explain how unobservable, invisible, colour-less, and featureless atoms can produce the rich and varied world we experience. Instead you offer an analogy from the kitchen and hope it's the truth.

PHILIA: I'd say it's an attractive hypothesis, promising as far as it goes. Time will tell. But let's go back to something we touched on just a moment ago, the recognition that observable objects are particulars, not universals. The whole point of postulating unobservable atoms, which we can imagine all objects sharing, is to make sense of the universality and common essence of all experience. Really, it's the only way to explain it. Otherwise, we have no idea of how things really stand, no way to grasp the commonality underlying what otherwise appears as a sea of chaotic particulars. Your phenomenal elements beg the question of what things have in common.

LUCIAN: But you still have not explained, as far as I can see, how these unobservable atoms can in fact inform the various particular things we experience other than as an imaginative speculation about how they might do so. And even that speculation doesn't seem to work very well across the range of sensations. Just because you can imagine that something is the case doesn't mean that it is the case. What remains lacking here is any confirmation in the sensible world of what you imagine to be the case.

PHILIA: But without postulating universals of some kind, even if we can only imagine them, we are left with the chaos of particulars—a world of heterogeneous experiences which we cannot add up.

LUCIAN: Now you are admitting that the Epicureans, like the other dogmatists, see phenomena as a chaos of particulars. I would say it's a question of finding the right universals, the ones that can do the job of making up the gross objects of our world. The cooks in the kitchen don't use unobservable ingredients for the dishes they prepare. They must have knowledge of all the ingredients they employ. They may not be able to explain how it is that certain combinations produce the flavours they do, but they come up with the right ingredients to combine to obtain the desired effect. It seems to me that Epicureans are claiming to have a recipe for how the world is made, but so far it's a secret recipe since the ingredients are a mystery. The qualities of shape, mass, and size are the only ingredients at which you hint, and they are obviously inadequate to the task.

PHILIA: Can you improve on the Epicurean account? Aren't your phenomenal atoms too diverse to play the role of atoms?

LUCIAN: I don't think so. It's a beguiling notion to insist that all atoms must be identical. It's a comforting belief, pleasing and restful, which allows us to reduce the diversity of experience to a unity, to reduce the many to a one. You're describing what you see as a chaotic world on the one hand, and an imagined way of accounting for it on the other. But that's not yet a solution to the problem; at most it's compensation for it, a comfort in our ignorance. Of course it might be the case, for all we know, that uniform unobservable atoms actually exist which make sense of our otherwise chaotic sensations, but it just as well might not be the case. This kind of solace is uncertain at best, which is the problem with all belief. To sustain that solace, it is necessary to insist that such atoms exist. Beliefs like this are expressed and sustained by making an assertion—a declaration or pledge that they are true, that something which we are only in fact imagining nonetheless really exists. This is the mark of dogmatism, and I'm afraid it applies to the Epicureans and their imperceptible atoms as well as to the Stoics, Aristotelians, Platonists, and others.

PHILIA: But the problem remains, doesn't it? Some kind of explanation for the coherence of otherwise heterogeneous sensory objects is called for, isn't it?

LUCIAN: Let me see if I can explain. Pyrrhonism is rooted in the observation of our experience. Observation is rooted in the separation of our interpretations of our experience from that experience itself. A powerful interpretation of our experience is one we've been discussing tonight, namely, the belief that our experience—what is actually apparent to us—is composed of particulars, of things so diverse as to our despairing of being able to find what is universal about them. And if experience is composed of particulars, then universals must be somehow outside of our experience. No wonder they are so hard to find.

A little background might be useful. Pyrrho, you recall, went to India with his mentor, Anaxarchus, and other philosophers and companions who took part in Alexander's expedition. Anaxarchus was a Democritean, so young Pyrrho was at least aware of atomism if not a declared Democritean. The story they tell is that Pyrrho, encountering the holy men or gymnosophists of India, was struck by the fortitude and tranquillity, or displays of *ataraxia*, some of them displayed. Here's the thing: their philosophical method, novel to the Greeks, required close attention to the direct experience of sensations and thoughts while avoiding speculation about unobservable or non-evident matters. They did not presume, as our dogmatists do, that the immediate objects of experience were unreliable or chaotic. Their concern was rather to separate out direct experience from the interpretations or speculations usually superimposed upon it and see what was left.

PHILIA: So what did they discover and what does it have to do with *ataraxia*? We don't want to forget about *ataraxia*.

LUCIAN: They discovered that our immediate experiences—our sensations and thoughts—are neither particulars, nor universals, but rather both at once. That's a kind of reunification of experience, enough to induce some peace of mind.

PHILIA: That seems incoherent, like trying to have your cake and eat it too. How does it make any sense?

LUCIAN: Let me put it this way. Among the Pyrrhonians there's a story that Pyrrho adapted Democritean atomism to make sense of what these gymnosophists were telling him. He did so, however, by abandoning Democritus's unobservable atoms, which were later taken up by Epicurus. Instead Pyrrho replaced them with the phenomenal atoms of the Indians: a very different kind of atomism. The gymnosophists, it seems, held that sensations and thoughts were made up of recurring elements—things which are minimally visible, or audible, or gustable, etc. Pyrrho, trained as a Democritean, was able to recognize sensations, as well as thoughts, as phenomenal atoms, as recurring and indivisible, like letters of the alphabet, as I have been suggesting. Who knows, perhaps Pyrrho suddenly saw the world as written in the alphabet of natural phenomena. These phenomenal atoms, in varying combinations as *pragmata*, adequately explain the various ordinary objects we experience. No need for unobservable atoms.

PHILIA: That's quite ingenious. You may yet convert me to Pyrrhonism.

LUCIAN: I hope it won't be a conversion. Conversions are for believers.

PHILIA: We'll see. In any case, let's talk a bit more about these phenomenal atoms. It looks like there are different kinds of phenomenal atoms, you say, such as visual atoms, audible atoms, gustable atoms, aromatic atoms, tactile atoms, and even thought atoms—you know, the five senses and whatever it is that goes on in our thoughts. Isn't that right?

LUCIAN: Yes.

PHILIA: And each of these atoms is indivisible, you said. That's something they have in common.

LUCIAN: Yes. Imagine, once more, atoms as the last particles remaining, so to speak, after all the other, coarser, still complex items have been broken down and sifted out, like the finest ground powder of flour left over when separated from the grosser husks and chaff of wheat. They are too small for us to divide any further and still be observable. So, as far as we're concerned, they have no more parts. Phenomenal atoms can't be divided, at least not by us, but they can disappear. That's what happens when you try to divide them. Again, imagine that dot on a clear papyrus roll. Imagine the very smallest such dot, just a speck, really, and a very faint one, the very least of what can be distinguished from its background. That's a visual atom for us, on the very threshold of nothingness.

PHILIA: And I suppose, as you've been saying, we also have audible atoms, and tactile atoms, and those of the rest of the senses, also at the threshold of nothingness?

LUCIAN: Yes, I think so. Sextus Empiricus, in his discourses, often lists these different kinds of atoms. An audible phenomenal atom, for instance, would be the very last fading tone you hear after a bell has been struck. The last, faintest aroma of a flower that's just passed before your nose would be an aromatic atom, and so on. Consider the lightest touch of a hair on the skin, or the subtlest flavour of a good wine, or a fine sauce, on the tongue, and so on.

PHILIA: What about mental atoms? You were a little vague about them before.

LUCIAN: A mental atom would have to be the smallest part of any thought or memory. Petronius isn't with us tonight, but I can very well imagine him, dressed in his elegant toga, with the very corner of his lip curled up in a confident smile.

PHILIA: That's not an atom, but a whole complex.

LUCIAN: Yes, it is. It's a *pragma*. But the smallest detail of the curl of his curled lip is no more than a phenomenal atom, a part of that *pragma*. It's just a barely perceptible point on his lip as I imagine it, something a painter might have a hard time capturing, but which could be essential to a successful portrait, and which I can present to myself in my own imagination, as all of you can. Remember that Pyrrho was a painter too.

PHILIA: But you're describing a visual atom, not a mental one.

LUCIAN: I'm trying to describe a mental atom reflecting a visual atom. Memories are *pragmata* made up of reflecting mental atoms. A visual memory is a mental representation of something visual, but made of memory atoms. The imagination is a kind of theatre of memory, where we can review the flow of what were once immediately present sensations, gone but somehow recaptured, although at a strange remove, in a ghostlike way. We don't know how this happens, but there is no doubt that it does. Anyway, our memory atoms are the smallest mental representations we can imagine. We seem to have visual memory atoms, audible memory atoms, tactile memory atoms, and the rest. That may not be very satisfying, or seem puzzling, but it seems to be the best the Pyrrhonists can offer.

PHILIA: Well, let's accept your account for purposes of argument. Now, you say, as you've been saying all along, that these phenomenal atoms never appear in isolation, but always in various combinations with one another. These combinations, or *pragmata*, are the ordinary objects we experience.

LUCIAN: Yes.

PHILIA: And you maintain that this scheme somehow explains how it is that we should understand sensations and thoughts?

LUCIAN: Yes, and it's important to see why. This is what allows us to distinguish universals from particulars without separating the latter from the former. Phenomenal atoms play the role of universals. This isn't to say that they persist unchanged forever. We don't know that. We only know that they are universals at least in our experience in the sense that they reliably recur over and over again, throughout our lives, albeit in the different formations of particular things, or *pragmata*, the flow of which makes up the whole of our natural lives. Since phenomenal atoms always appear in some combination or another, always constituting some particular object like a cup or a stone or a cloud, they have no intrinsic meaning in themselves. Their individual significance depends entirely on the other atoms with which they are combined, that is, on the particulars which they make up. The point is that phenomenal atoms, at least in our experience, are not independently existing things. They are instead dependently originated. This is apparently what Pyrrho discovered in India, some say.

PHILIA: What is this dependent origination?

LUCIAN: Dependent origination tells us, among other things, that we cannot separate universals from the contexts in which they appear, as all dogmatists try to do. This takes us back to our discussions in Campania, when we pondered whether good or evil exist. In the Pyrrhonian view of dependent origination, neither good nor evil can exist independently of the objects and events in which we seem to find them, and so neither of them can be isolated and described for what they are in themselves. And, as we saw, what's good in one context can be bad in another, and vice-versa. Like it or not, it seems we cannot step outside the circle of our experience to look back upon it as a totality separate from ourselves.

PHILIA: I still have to push back. So we have these phenomenal universals, which may or may not reappear tomorrow, and which seem of little help in determining good and evil, or any other values. It all seems like a giant step backwards in our understanding of things. There is no hope of certainty in anything, it seems.

LUCIAN: The Pyrrhonists would advise us that a longing for certainty —which means to freeze a world previously in motion—is a misplaced longing. The facts, it seems, are that we live in an uncertain if not entirely unreliable world. Our experience of phenomenally constructed *pragmata* is a mixed bag, offering joys and pains, but we can rely on the consistent connections between things to avoid the worst, and promote the best. That sounds almost Epicurean, doesn't it?

PHILIA: Perhaps, but it seems a poor consolation. And solipsistic too! You've reduced everything, including the external world, to your subjective feelings.

LUCIAN: That would be a misunderstanding of Pyrrhonism. You may be forgetting that our phenomena—our thoughts and sensations and the *pragmata* they constitute, at least according to the Pyrrhonists—are no more subjective than objective. Subjective and objective are only interpretations made or presumed about phenomena, as we've already suggested. They are not observations.

PHILIA: Well, the philosophical schools all presume our sensations are subjective, don't they? So does common sense. Hence the need to find non-sensible or abstract universals—like imperceptible Epicurean atoms!—to explain how the world hangs together.

LUCIAN: Here's how the Pyrrhonists might respond to that. They might first point out, as I already have, that there is no need to make the supposition that sensations are subjective, even if that seems to be common sense. They might note that our involuntary sensations are often if not always shared, suggesting that they are not subjective. Take this goblet which sits before us. On the Epicurean, Stoic, or any dogmatic view, the immediate evidence of a shared fact like this is somehow denied in favour of complex and abstruse theorizing— whether Epicurean or Stoic or any other dogmatic school—which alone is thought to explain how that might be possible.

Yet we can confirm without much trouble that we share at least the visual experience of this goblet. We can play a game whereby I ask you to describe the motions I might make with the goblet, like raising it to my lips, or pouring out its contents in a bowl, or laying it on its side, while I remain silent. You will have no trouble with that, as long as you're awake and attentive. We are seeing the same goblet, made up of universals we actually share as common sensations, which makes it objective and subjective at the same time.

PHILIA: I'll concede the point, at least provisionally. I have no response that can explain it away. If the Epicureans and other dogma- tists are asking the wrong questions, you say it's because they are making the wrong presuppositions. But then how is it that they made wrong presuppositions in the first place? And further, our subject, which we seem to keep forgetting, was tranquillity or *ataraxia*. What does any of this have to do with that?

LUCIAN: The simple answer is that having any presupposition at all —which is to say any interpretation or belief about anything—is a potential disturbance to our tranquillity. Our beliefs, our interpretations of the sensations we experience, are things we imagine to be real, but it seems they are not. As far as we can tell, beliefs are not realized in sensation. That's how we know they are beliefs. If we can understand how people might be ensnared by their beliefs, then we can see, perhaps, how abandoning them removes an obstacle to tranquillity, or *ataraxia*. That's how the Pyrrhonists see it, at any rate.

PHILIA: Exactly what is this error of belief? What's really wrong with it?

LUCIAN: It is the presumption, without evidence, that there are independently existing things. Or, as with the Academics, at least the nihilists among them, like Saturninus, that there are no such things at all, which merely plays off the same presumption.

PHILIA: Well, can you say more?

LUCIAN: Okay, if we examine our sensations and thoughts, that is, the immediate objects of our experience, we find that they are recurring and reliable phenomenal atoms, but they are in constant flux, ever subject to change. They come and go, and combine and recombine in a variety of *pragmata*, or particulars, which also come and go. Our experience is quite bewildering, really, and even if we do discern many regularities in everyday life which we use to guide and improve our lives, there seems to be no escaping the changes which ultimately engulf us, the most profound of which is our own death, a central concern of Epicureans, perhaps above all, but also of Stoics and most philosophers. The fear of death, no doubt, is a strong motivator to find something permanent, something existing outside the flux of experience, something on which we can rely. Needless to say, that permanent something most of us seek is some enduring version of ourselves, the souls we imagine ourselves to be, to which we cling with a desperate hope that they, that is, we, will somehow survive the changes which otherwise seem to come to all things.

PHILIA: But that's not the Epicurean conclusion. The soul is no independently existing thing, let alone one which survives death. It is no more than a subtle organization of our imperceptible atoms. And it too dissolves at death, along with the body.

LUCIAN: Fair enough. The point remains, though, that these unobservable Epicurean atoms are presumed to be independently existing, permanent entities, as are the *prolepses* which supposedly capture our experience. Dogs live and die, but 'dog' remains. As for death, what makes the Epicureans so sure of its finality? How do they know what death is, or what it is not? They do not, it is true, take refuge in an immortal soul, but they do take refuge in an immortal world of changing bodies made up of permanent unobservable atoms moving in a void. They say that death is nothing, which may remove its sting, but it helps us to accept, perhaps as a kind of consolation prize, that the world at least is immortal, along with the gods. So, in the meantime, hovering between birth and death, they navigate life following the signals of pleasure and pain, where the joy of knowledge compensates for any pains and fears. And in an infinite world, who's to say that we may not someday be resurrected by the right recombination of atoms!

PHILIA: Well, that's our version of *ataraxia*. How does that differ from the Pyrrhonians?

LUCIAN: The Epicurean atoms might provide a basis for *ataraxia*, but only if they could be established without a doubt. But it seems to me that our argument this evening has thrown that into question. Atoms are unobservable entities which we can imagine to exist independently of our imagining them, but which cannot be confirmed. They can be maintained, not on the basis of evidence, but on the basis of faith. It requires belief, from beginning to end, to maintain the existence of unobservable atoms. And since there are other competing beliefs which challenge those of the Epicureans—including the Stoics and Aristotelians, to which I'd add the Academics and the Cynics, and even the Galileans and Jews and Zoroastrians, among others, not to mention the old gods and the oracles and mystery religions—there is no end to disputation and uncertainty. The result is as far from *ataraxia* as one could get.

PHILIA: And the Pyrrhonists are exempt from this?

LUCIAN: I think so, because they refuse to credit their imaginative projections with the force of truth. They stick consistently, or try to, to what the evidence of sensations and thoughts presents. They manage to integrate them together without recourse to belief, something the Epicureans claim but do not, as far as I can see, succeed in doing. An imaginative projection, which we can observe, may or may not indicate a reality that exists somewhere, but if it does it's one we cannot observe. So the gods may or may not exist. Death may or may not be final, and unobservable atoms may or may not exist. The Pyrrhonists are content to suspend judgment on such imaginative projections.

Ataraxia, beyond the bliss of the reunification of experience, remains a profound relief from inconclusive disputation. If you don't have to maintain a belief you hold in the face of contrary beliefs, a great worry and burden is relieved. That's what they mean by tranquillity, and it's the only kind, it seems, we can expect. Even so, it is no panacea. Pyrrhonists still suffer pain and evil and face death like everyone else, just as they also suffer the joys of life. They accept the world we cannot evade—the world of flux and change. But they are relieved of the huge anxiety demanded by what it takes to prop up their beliefs, and it would be a mistake to underestimate the force of that relief.

PHILIA: It still seems like a closed and unsatisfying world, confined entirely to the flow of sensations and thoughts.

LUCIAN: Not at all. Our sensations and thoughts come and go, it is true, but their very impermanence confronts us with their absence as well as their presence. This absence is the repository, as it were, of all that uncertainty, of whether or not anything exists behind our thoughts and sensations. The point is that there are no more grounds for denial of things merely imagined or uncertain, than there is for their affirmation. Pyrrhonism is the acceptance of our ignorance, not its denial; it is the act of humility taken to its logical conclusion, with the arrogance of our beliefs put aside.

PHILIA: So do you feel liberated?

LUCIAN: Well, I'm only a student, which, by the way, is what the Pyrrhonists say of themselves as well—that they too remain students, or seekers. But I'm told that being liberated, according to the Pyrrhonists, is not what most people think it is. Ordinary life is exactly the same for them, they say, as for the rest of us. They too shuffle between pleasures and pains, between things desirable and undesirable, like everyone else—at least insofar as appearances are concerned. Liberation perhaps is easier said than done. The Pyrrhonian kind of liberation for most is less than a super-experience, where all things are resolved into some kind of ecstatic revelation, though that too cannot be ruled out. Pyrrhonnian practices of stilling the overacting believing mind help relieve us, on a case-by-case basis, at any rate, of the anxieties created by our beliefs about things, and that is no small thing.

Beliefs, Pyrrhonists insist, cannot deliver the kind of liberation they promise, it seems, and so they are bound to disappoint us. Insofar as they remain ungrounded in the evidence of appearances, they are subject to contradiction. They are vulnerable to attack, and anyone clinging to a belief thereby becomes vulnerable as well. It's a recipe for anxiety and unhappiness. You can try to go from one belief to another, of course, hoping to find the right or final belief, but that seems to be a wild goose chase.

PHILIA: But if beliefs are somehow beyond appearances, how do you explain how we can even think of them as independently existing, or as existing at all?

LUCIAN: We can't. That's the point. A belief is not the experience it purports to be; it is not the actual experience of some appearance it is said to represent. It is rather the anticipation of an experience we have not had, a judgment or projection about appearances, a fantasy, really. A belief is a judgment that something we're experiencing is really something else, something which is, say, really good, or evil. It's something we imagine to be the case when in fact, at least so far, it is not. We imagine, as we have seen, that something exists which is the good, say, and then we decide that some experience — say exercising in the gymnasium, or being rich — is a property of that imagined thing. Except that that imagined good, or evil, keeps changing and slipping through our fingers.

PHILIA: But what makes such a projection possible? There must be something incomplete about our appearances which suggest something beyond what we have. What could that be?

LUCIAN: I can know only what I experience, as Sextus keeps telling us, but that also includes experiencing the absence of what I experience. I know the blue sky of a cloudless sunny day only because I can see it for myself with my own eyes. But things come and go and change. Clouds turn the sky grey; nightfall brings an end to the light; then it might clear up and the moon might come out, and so on. The knowledge of things, their presence to me, is variable — sometimes reliable and recurring, sometimes not. Things are defined not only by their presence in some *pragmata*, in some complex of parts and wholes, but also by their absence.

PHILIA: This seems an interesting twist.

LUCIAN: Yes, it is. Absence is evidence of the incompleteness of our experience; it seems to be a condition of experience, at least as we know it. Or, we might say, we come to understand experience in part by its absence. Anything that can be absent as well as present — including our own mortal selves — is unstable, and in some sense empty or illusory. Our own absence eventually becomes evident to us, bringing fear to most of us. We try to plug our sense of absence with one or another belief. But, as I've been trying to suggest, following the Pyrrhonists, that only compounds our problems.

[Pause …]

RUFUS: Well done, Lucian and Philia. But I'm afraid we must stop here. The night is late and you've left us much to ponder. My thanks to all for an excellent discussion over the last three days. I hope we may meet again in Campania next summer, and continue our exchanges. In the meantime, farewell, with much love, and good night. The slaves will bring around a couple of litters to the front door to take Gaius and Saturninus back home.

Part III

Dialogues on Life and Death

Characters:

Rufus, a Roman Senator

Aurelia, wife of Rufus

Harmonia, a Stoic, their daughter

Lucian, a student of Pyrrhonism, their son

Philia, an Epicurean, a friend of Harmonia's

Petronius, a Peripatetic Philosopher

Saturninus, an Academic, friend of Rufus and Aurelia

Time:

The reign of Antoninus Pius, second century CE

Place:

The Villa of Rufus in Campania,

Overlooking the Sea

Are Beliefs Necessary?

AURELIA: I am grateful we can all be together again here in Campania, on a warm summer evening, with a moonlit sea swelling before us. I regret I missed the discussion here a year ago. Back then, as I understand it, you racked our brains about good and evil, trying to clarify how they are understood, and misunderstood. Later, last winter most of us were able to continue the discussion in Rome, where we explored understanding itself, or truth. Lucian surprised me then, and I think the rest of you on both occasions, with his consistent application of sceptical Pyrrhonian arguments against Harmonia's Stoicism and Philia's Epicureanism, as well as Saturninus's nihilism. But, I have to say, though hard pressed by Lucian, both Harmonia and Phylia held their ground, while Saturninus has remained implacable, as usual.

Those discussions now may seem rather high-minded and theoretical, more in the way of clearing up our understanding of what good and evil and truth might be, rather than addressing the realities of actual life which can be as uncertain as the claims of the philosophers. We are faced with life's choices, where we try to sort out the good from the bad, and the true from the false. If I understand you, Lucian, you say your four opponents here—Harmonia, Philia, Petronius, and Saturninus—share dogmatic beliefs about what is valuable or not, which guide their behaviour, for better or worse. Pyrrhonism by contrast seeks to reject all belief. Is that right?

LUCIAN: Yes. A life without beliefs.

AURELIA: What does that mean? I keep wondering what to make of the Pyrrhonian way of actually doing things, of what kind of life they would recommend we practise from day to day, and how it would be an improvement over how we live now. On the face of it, trying to live without beliefs seems outlandish and absurd. How is that even possible?

Let me suggest, therefore, that we continue to put Lucian to the test, with the aim of getting him to demonstrate just what a Pyrrhonian way of life looks like. I think we're all curious to hear more.

RUFUS: It's hard to disagree with Aurelia. Philosophical discussions, it's true, can be no better than an exalted passtime unless we bring them to bear on how best to live. The philosophies of our day all claim to do that in one way or another, or so they say, but each offers its own path to the realization of virtue. Pyrrhonism is perhaps more elusive on this point. It may be the difference between telling us how we ought to live, and showing us how to do so. Let's proceed, then, by our usual question and answer method, with Lucian as our respondent, if he agrees.

LUCIAN: Of course.

RUFUS: Excellent. Who would like to begin the questioning?

PETRONIUS: I would. Pyrrhonism is elusive indeed! More like absurd. By now most of us have heard the crazy stories about Pyrrho, about how his friends had to follow him around to keep him from being run over by carts and wagons, or falling into a ditch, or off a cliff. He suspended judgment so much, it seems, that he hardly knew how to put one foot in front of the other. Perhaps you can explain away these stories, Lucian, but at the very least they suggest someone impractical to the point of helplessness, as far removed from Aurelia's call for practical sense as one could possibly be.

LUCIAN: I don't believe them. They seem to be caricatures born of hostility or envy, and hardly plausible. But consider the prophets and magicians of our times, like Apollonius, or Cynics like Diogenes and Peregrinus, or earlier figures as diverse as Pythagoras or Thales or Empedocles, perhaps even Socrates and the Christian Jesus. Like all of these, Pyrrho was reported to display extraordinary qualities of self-control and concentration, reinforced by periods of withdrawal and isolation. He was widely recognized, as they were, to be a holy man possessed of an unusual wisdom. Yet others, like you, judge him to be a madman.

PETRONIUS: So he seems a wise man to one person and a madman to another. We often see this. The power of an unusual person, the disruption posed by his or her character and behaviour, all of that can be seen either as a benefit or a threat. But to me, the very wisdom, as you call it, which Pyrrho is reputed to possess, only reinforces a disturbing picture. His disciple Timon glorified him almost as a god. And this because he claimed we can say nothing true or false about anything, just as you were arguing about good and evil a year ago in this very place. Similarly, for Pyrrho nothing is beautiful or ugly, just or unjust, rich or poor, a virtue or a vice, or any other judgment anyone would normally make. Such judgments, he supposedly said, are all just so many empty opinions, or beliefs.

And, if that's the case, there is no reason to prefer one thing over another, or to avoid one thing over another. That's what a life without beliefs looks like to me. There's nothing left over, which seems dangerously close to nihilism. But those of us who disagree with that negative line of thought, who judge some things to be better or worse than others, and act accordingly, then we must be in error according to the Pyrrhonists. Isn't that right?

LUCIAN: You have just agreed that someone can seem wise to one person and mad to another. A lesson we can draw from that is not that one can be one or the other, but rather that one cannot be either one or the other precisely because one can be said to be both one and the other. So Pyrrho is neither a god nor a madman because he can be said to be both a god and a madman, and because we know (or think we know) that gods can't be madmen and madmen can't be gods. I think Timon understood this.

PETRONIUS: Well, if that's the case then there's very little if anything left for us to say about anything. We might as well go to bed early. The only things we can make judgments about are those things already evident, or that can be made so. That's the life of an animal, a life lived wholly on the surface of things. Now no one, except the Cynics, would deny that we have a deeper understanding than animals. We are rational creatures, after all, the rest of us agree, and that allows us to deliberate over how to respond to sensations far better than animals can, yet what you are proposing would push us back to the level of animals.

I think it's safe to say that Peripatetics, Stoics, Epicureans, and the Platonists of the Academy — all the major schools — not only agree that humans are distinguished from animals by their use of reason, but that reason reveals a dimension to experience beyond the immediate phenomena to which you Pyrrhonists would reduce us. It not only opens us up to another world denied to animals, but, even more significantly, it allows us to recognize ourselves as who we are. Animals don't know who they are because they are unable to significantly detach themselves from the sensations which command and monopolize their attention. We, by contrast, can deliberate our options at length and choose among them. Reason, in its ability to review the past and contemplate the future, to compare things and infer other things which follow, all that allows us to detach ourselves from our sensations, and to make our own decisions; it frees us to know who we really are. It allows us to become conscious of ourselves in a way that animals cannot.

LUCIAN: Pyrrhonists, as you expect, would say your claim to be a rational being is a belief you have about who you are, a belief like any other. It asserts a separate, independent but undemonstrable identity for your soul, or a part of it, the rational mind, apart from the actual sensations and thoughts you experience through your body. The Pyrrhonists don't deny that something like the power of reason is what distinguishes humans from animals, as you describe it; but neither do they affirm it. In any event, they think they can describe the same functions in simpler terms, as combinations of memory and imagination. The idea that we are rational beings looks like another interpretation of who or what we are.

PETRONIUS: Your idea of suspending judgment may not entirely rule out what we call an independent rational soul, but it is no less effective in rendering it moot. As long as a judgment about something is suspended, it will remain unavailable to us, and that thing then might just as well exist or not. So, for all practical purposes, it amounts to a denial of the thing in question. We are left, again, by the Pyrrhonists, with our immediate phenomena, and nothing else; we are reduced to the sentient soul of an animal.

LUCIAN: Certainly the human animal remains an extraordinary animal—one whose memory and imagination far outstrip those of other animals, and which allow him or her to reliably imagine, for instance, that footprints observed on a beach were made by another human, or that the smoke that's seen from afar is caused by a fire. These are connections ordinary animals sometimes make as well. They too can 'read' the 'alphabet' of nature, for their own purposes, but they don't seem to be able to 'write' it nearly as much as we can. Birds can build nests, bees hives, spiders webs, and so on, but these are limited and fixed talents. People, by contrast, are able to build new and different things in endless variety, seemingly without end. What seems evident is that we take memories of past experiences and review and freely compare them in our imaginations. And that makes all the difference. It gives us foresight. Animals, from what we can tell, command no such power.

PETRONIUS: What is evident, at least to me, is that it is I who am doing this reviewing and comparing. I am my rational mind at work. You're saying something very different: that it just somehow all happens by itself, that I'm not the one doing it.

LUCIAN: You're right. What is evident here, as the Pyrrhonists would say, is that there is reviewing and comparing, and nothing more, even if it's unique to human beings. Your conclusion that it is you that is doing the reviewing and comparing takes a step beyond what is evident. That leaves us distinguished from animals, who do far less reviewing and comparing. We might call it a process of reflection. You want to say that it's you who's doing the reflecting, and that you're somehow in control of it, but the Pyrrhonists want to say only that it's happening and that we don't know who, if anyone, is doing it.

PETRONIUS: That is perhaps the nub of our difference. What makes me evident to myself is precisely my command over all this reviewing and comparing of things. That certainly seems evident to me. I can decide to review something in my memory and to compare it in my imagination with other things. Or I can choose not to do so. And I can act or not act as a result. It's all up to me. To deny that seems absurd.

LUCIAN: Wouldn't it be more accurate to say that these things simply happen, or do not happen, that something is reviewed and compared, or it isn't? The agency you claim for yourself remains invisible. Consider an example: to stop my chariot, the horses' reins have to be pulled. The immediate agency here—the pulling in of the reins— seems evident enough. If I pull them, it reliably follows and we expect that the horses will stop. But the decision to pull in the reins is not itself evident—even if our language suggests otherwise. Indeed, it is not uncommon when driving at full speed, say on the open road, that the sudden sight of an obstacle I might hit is immediately followed by a pulling in of the reins, all without my having a chance to think about it at all.

PETRONIUS: Well, sometimes we act instinctively, no doubt, but that doesn't preclude our acting rationally. If you're right, if everything somehow happens automatically, then there's really no role left for me or for anyone else in the conduct of life, from the most trivial matters to the most serious. It all becomes a matter of action and reaction, with me and you simply going along for the ride. Without the ability to control events, there is no skill, no virtue, no character, no morality. It's insane, really.

LUCIAN: The Pyrrhonists often hear this objection, and they usually offer the same answer. They readily admit to living by appearances, and not by any belief in their own independent agency. They simply follow their sensations and thoughts (including memories and imaginings), foremost among them being the needs and drives of both body and mind. Being hungry, they seek food, being aroused they seek a mate, being attacked they seek defence, being humoured they laugh, being cheated they get angry, being praised they feel love, and so on. Similarly, seeing what conduct is necessary to secure peace and cooperation, they are prompted to acknowledge custom and piety, and seeing the benefits of the arts, they are prompted to perfect the skills needed to sustain productive activity.

PETRONIUS: You make it sound easy. Yet what you say suggests a radical detachment from oneself.

LUCIAN: Indeed it does. They sacrifice the self entirely. When the Pyrrhonists repeatedly state 'I determine nothing', they aren't asserting that some belief or other is necessarily indeterminate, but only that they themselves are not able to determine it for themselves. Having given up the pretence of believing they control things, while accepting the sensible and mental *pragmata* which we have no choice but to experience involuntarily, they abandon entirely the commanding sense of agency you value so much, and the identity which goes with it. They recognize that they are not in charge of what is happening in experience, but entirely dependent upon it. They abandon the very self most philosophers, like you, take to be an independently existing free agent. That self disappears entirely. It's gone.

PETRONIUS: Astonishing. What's left, I wonder, if you detach yourself from yourself? Is there no self left at all?

LUCIAN: What remains, it seems, is something like a witness which experiences phenomena, as I suggested a year ago here, though you may have forgotten. Appearances, after all, are not free floating and independently existing. Instead we each have specific appearances which come to us as *pragmata*. Appearances appear to you and me and it seems to every sentient creature. They are the world. But the active, reasoning self, the witness, is not among these appearances, at least so far as we are able to tell; and insofar as we do not appear to ourselves, who we really might be remains indeterminate.

PETRONIUS: So there's no free will. Everyone is like a puppet.

LUCIAN: We can't conclude that either. The Pyrrhonist answer is that we don't know and can only suspend judgment about it. Free will, like the self, does not appear among our sensations, but I can imagine that it exists. I can also imagine that I exist and that I deliberate among alternatives and choose some and reject others, like the captain of a ship who is determined to set one course and not another. Just as I can imagine the captain putting a hand to the tiller to pick out for the helmsman the desired setting produced by his deliberation, so I can imagine a miniature person—call it my real self—located somewhere inside of me (let's say in my head) similarly commanding my body to act or not act in response to what my body experiences, much like the rational mind of the Epicurean or the Stoic *hegemonikon.*

Now to confirm a belief like that, to realize it as a fact, I would have to demonstrate that such a miniature person actually exists inside the human body. That wouldn't be an easy thing to do. Something like a dissection of the body would seem to be required to pursue the question. Perhaps we should consult that bold physician in Rome, Galen, who's made a name for himself examining dead gladiators and animals by dissecting them. Of course, even though we might be able to locate this miniature real self within the bodily self, we still wouldn't be able to see how such a miniature person could actually deliberate and command without taking a step further to look inside of him or her, and so on, in what becomes an infinite regress. Any discovery is endlessly postponed. We can't seem to locate the real active, deliberative self at any point. That doesn't prove that it doesn't exist and operate somehow, somewhere; it only shows that, at least so far, we can't find it.

PETRONIUS: How do you even know you're a witness? That seems a mysterious and rather unsettling idea.

LUCIAN: Only because what appears to me seems to appear only in relation to what does not appear, to an absence which seems to accompany all that is made present to me. Call this the awareness, or consciousness, of appearances, of their presence to us. Thoughts and sensations come and go in consciousness without any further clue to explain how or why they do so. All we have, it seems, is their appearance before an absence which seems to be a witness. And we seem to be that witness. It is simply evident, I would submit, that there is consciousness, or the witnessing of appearances, by us. And this consciousness, although neither a sensation nor a thought, appears as well, but only as an absence confronting thoughts and sensations. Whatever the witness is, it is neither body nor mind. It is present, but only indirectly as an absence, and thereby as indeterminate, and that's all we seem to be able to say about the witness. The witness, of course, is only a witness insofar as there are phenomena to witness. That seems about as close as we can get to what you presume to be the self.

PETRONIUS: So the Pyrrhonists are sleep-walking through life! Or so it seems. What a strange conclusion.

LUCIAN: On the contrary, they are very much awake, and not asleep. If anyone's asleep, the Pyrrhonists would say, it's the dogmatists who dream about themselves, and of a freedom and agency that they can only imagine, however, and cannot realize in real life.

PETRONIUS: So there are two kinds of people: those who live by their beliefs and those who don't. Can we say that?

LUCIAN: I think so. To be truly free is to detach yourself from yourself, that is, from your belief in yourself as something existing independently, as something that has the kind of particularity we find in thoughts and sensations. To be in bondage is to be enthralled by your beliefs, above all by a belief in a false self. It is to imagine you are free when you are not. It is to imagine that you have some control over your thoughts and sensations.

PETRONIUS: How strange and depressing! You take away our reason and our free will and our very selves, and leave us entirely passive in the face of experience, and yet you claim this is freedom! For the rest of us freedom is exactly the opposite—the ability to deliberate among various courses of action and to select which of them to follow. If what you say is what the Pyrrhonists maintain, it would be a scandal if it were not so absurd.

LUCIAN: I'll grant that it can seem unsettling.

PETRONIUS: Unsettling is putting it mildly. If the rational mind is no more than a fiction, a belief, and not a fact, then all responsibility for human action would be eliminated. That way lies madness—a world in which anyone can do what they like without being held accountable. I can rob my neighbour, murder my mother, incite people to violence, cheat and lie—the list is endless. No one would be able to blame me for anything since I would only be naturally responding to what experience prompts me to do. Nor would I have anything to feel guilty about. All I would have to say in my defence is that the gods made me do it, or nature, or society, or anyone or anything else, and I'm off the hook. If I'm only reacting to involuntary sensations and thoughts I'm living like an animal. Even if I'm more capable than an animal, I remain bound by impulses over which I have no control.

LUCIAN: Hear me out a bit further. Philia brought up the Epicureans a year ago here in Campania, and we continued the discussion of their philosophy last winter in Rome, which you missed. It seems fair to say that Epicurus took over some notions developed by Pyrrho, and others, and made them his own. It's also true, as we discussed, that Epicureans rely on their belief in the power of an independent rational mind—by way of preconception or *prolepsis*—to grasp the common features presented by sensations and retained in memory. And it's also true that the Pyrrhonists point out that that is just another belief about how the mind works, not so different from the Stoic's *hegemonikon* or the conceptualizing mind of your own Peripatetics, Petronius. Even the Academics of Plato's Academy think they have rational minds, if nothing else; indeed, if anything, they worship its 'divine' powers.

So Pyrrhonists may share some things in common with Epicureans, and not with the Stoics, nor with Socrates and Plato, nor their Peripatetic and nihilists successors, namely, that we respond to our involuntary and immediate thoughts and sensations in terms of the impact upon us, of the pleasures and pains they present to us, and that these are the only basis we seem to have for what we can know and how we can respond. The phenomena we experience have qualities which fall into a wide range from pleasure to neutrality to pain. We are naturally attracted to pleasure, indifferent to neutrality, and repulsed by pain. Pyrrhonists and Epicureans both claim to remain within the circle of what presents to us. The other schools, the Stoics with their notion of a rational Providence, and the forms of Plato and Aristotle and their schools, in one way or another step outside of the natural world and invoke something beyond it to clinch their arguments.

Philia, before going further, I must ask if you think I have licence to speak this way about the Epicureans.

PHILIA: Yes, as far as you've gone.

LUCIAN: All right, then. The mind for the Epicureans and Pyrrhonists is not some separate entity as it is for the other philosophers. For them it's just as natural as the body, just as mechanical, if you like, just as much a matter of atoms in motion. They differ, however, over the nature of the atoms, as we've already noticed. Pyrrhonists are entirely naturalistic in their reliance on phenomenal atoms, while Epicureans insist on non-phenomenal atoms underlying the everyday facts or *pragmata* of life we actually experience—their famous invisible atoms. In both cases the atoms are understood as natural and not divine, meaning that whether or not we can observe them they would turn out to be phenomena just like those we do experience. The difference is that Epicureans don't think we can observe them, while Pyrrhonists think we can.

This means that the mind—the sum of thoughts we encounter in memory and imagination—is just as phenomenal as the body, though no doubt more subtle. Remember the workshop of Daedalus, where minds were manufactured along with bodies to accompany them?

PHILIA: Yes, Epicureans are in whole-hearted agreement on the physicality of minds.

LUCIAN: And this is where the notion of an independently existing soul exercising free will disappears.

PHILIA: Yes, our existence is but temporary and fleeting. And free will turns out to be no more than the indeterminate swerves of atoms. The death of the body means the death of the mind and the end of any self. The subtle mechanism of the mind depends upon the grosser mechanism of the body, and with the dissolution of the latter the former can no longer be sustained, and it disintegrates as well. The witness you suggest seems designed to avoid that.

LUCIAN: Insofar as our minds and bodies will no longer exist, there will no longer be any Lucian, or Philia, or Petronius, or my parents, or Harmonia or Saturninus, or any of us. On this we agree. However, the witness within each of us, the mysterious absence which accompanies our sensations and thoughts, which observes our bodies as well as our minds, including the drama of our personalities, that ever-present consciousness, is neither body nor mind, if the Pyrrhonists are right. And if that's the case, then the dissolution of the body and mind is not necessarily the dissolution of the witness. For the witness is already dead in a way; it is already a dissolved thing, something indeterminate. We can't say that it's nothing—as the Epicureans would—only that we don't know what, if anything, it might be. To say it's nothing is to define it negatively as a non-phenomenon, as a kind of mirror which reflects everything but itself. But that too is a speculation, a belief, something we can only try to imagine but which we have no evidence, at least not yet, to substantiate.

PHILIA: But it hardly seems to matter. Once we're gone—both as body and mind—we're quite dead enough. You even suggest that the witness is more or less dead as well, or perhaps is a kind of living death.

LUCIAN: Fair enough. I only wish to establish suspension of judgment about the nature of the witness, just as we should suspend judgment about the nature of thoughts and sensations, such as the idea that they are made of invisible atoms. As far as who we are as living personalities, that is entirely a natural, which is to say a mechanical or mental, matter, by which I mean that we are entirely reactive to our involuntary phenomena, and indeed appear to have no free will. Or to put it more carefully, free will is nowhere apparent in a natural system. This is what Petronius was objecting to.

PETRONIUS: Yes, and you have yet to address the consequences of that. If there is no free will and no rational action, then there is no responsibility, no morality, no civilization, nothing except living by animal impulses, even if the humans turn out to be exceptionally clever animals.

LUCIAN: I would put it to you that the notion of an independent self with free will explains nothing and is not necessary at all.

PETRONIUS: Well, I'm all ears.

LUCIAN: Instead of imagining that you are responding freely to what you experience, as if you could freely choose among options, consider that every action you take is prompted by the collective force of your thoughts and sensations up to the moment you act. The actions you Peripatetics and Stoics and most others think we take voluntarily, and for which they believe we deserve praise or blame, as the case may be, can be reduced to the automatic calculations balancing of pleasures and pains. The moment of action for the Pyrrhonists does not appear a free choice, but seems determined by necessity, by impulses which can no longer be deferred but demand to be resolved, by the involuntary force of appearances. You free-will dogmatists flatter yourself that you're in charge of your own destiny, even in some small part, when you are to all appearances only actors in a script which writes itself for us every day.

PETRONIUS: Doesn't that lead to total passivity?

LUCIAN: Not at all. The actor on stage is hardly passive. It's hard work being an actor, after all. Have you ever tried it? He or she has lines to recite and acting tasks to carry out. From beginning to end the show must go on and actors must do their part. As this might suggest, there is no difference in everyday life between the Pyrrhonist and anyone else. The parts we play may be as dramatic or boring as anyone else's.

PETRONIUS: So if I murder my mother, it's all the same. I just have a bad part in the script.

LUCIAN: Basically, and tragically, yes.

PETRONIUS: Where is the tragedy?

LUCIAN: Suffering is still suffering.

PETRONIUS: But society doesn't tolerate that kind of thinking. I would be dragged before the magistrates, charged, put to trial, and perhaps made to drink hemlock, like Socrates. We don't punish actors for the roles they play, but we do punish real people for theirs, when and if needed.

LUCIAN: Actually, we do punish actors. It's all part of the script, of the evolving story of the lives we are compelled to live. It's a script that's being written for us every moment as we live. The script normally includes behaviours born out of our imagined beliefs, as well as our natural reaction to sensible things. Families and tribes, assemblies and monarchs, and societies at large all practise the beliefs they hold—including beliefs in guilt and punishment—and act accordingly. They impose what they imagine in belief on what they do in the sensible world, and behave accordingly. They will presume the idea of free will and personal responsibility if prompted by what they believe. And they will accept punishments as deterrents. It's all as if they said, 'Let's pretend to believe in this!'

PETRONIUS: But most people don't just think you're following a script when you murder someone. They think you've chosen to do so, by which they mean you could have just as well have chosen not to do so. They presume that you're not an automaton acting out a script like some Daedalean machine, but a free person responsible for his or her actions. That's why you're punished for murder.

LUCIAN: What I'm suggesting is that a society acting in response to the dictates of involuntarily experienced phenomena, and suspending beliefs, will choose to deter murderers, not because they are morally guilty but because murder—when not justified by some belief—is too unpleasant to tolerate, too upsetting, too painful for too many people. The preponderance of natural involuntary phenomenal experience is all that's needed to dictate that response.

PETRONIUS: But don't free will and responsibility help deter crime?

LUCIAN: They only make things worse, Pyrrhonists would say, because they punish people for who we think they are in addition to what they actually do. It superimposes a layer of guilt and self-righteousness on top of the natural unfolding of events, compounding our problems.

PETRONIUS: But our whole culture is based on personal responsibility. We raise our children to develop self-control and an ability to command their actions. The reward of the good life isn't just material success but the satisfaction that comes from doing the right thing, and avoiding the bad thing. We take a justifiable pride in achieving and maintaining self-control. It lies at the heart of living the good life for the Peripatetics and other philosophers; it lies at the very heart of the virtue cultivated by the Stoics.

LUCIAN: The Pyrrhonists would say that any so-called virtue based on responsible self-discipline and the presumption of an independent self controlling one's destiny only creates a prison of pain and suffering. The final product, taken to logical extremes, is all too familiar—a fictitious ego inflated beyond measure by overweening pride on the one hand, or crushed by shame and guilt on the other. This kind of 'virtue' turns into self-satisfaction, and then pride, and ends in the arrogance of narcissism, before its fall. For the prideful person lives in fear of contradiction and reversal of fortune. The height of such egotistical belief is matched only by the depths to which such a person may fall. Along the way, all those who follow this path, and struggle with elusive success, are left frustrated and depressed, for they have only themselves to blame for not succeeding.

PETRONIUS: How harsh and uncompromising the Pyrrhonists seem to be. They would starve the seeds of ambition which lie in most persons' souls without which the good things of life would never come to pass. Neither Homer, nor our great playwrights, nor the architects of our temples and cities, nor ingenious craftsmen, nor great generals and statesmen like Caesar and Augustus, Titus and Trajan, and others, would have achieved anything at all if they followed your philosophy. There would be no poems and plays, no great buildings, no comforts of life, no peaceful Empire.

LUCIAN: Not at all. As the Pyrrhonists repeatedly point out, we cannot help but respond to the phenomena we experience, to our actual sensible and mental *pragmata*. They are what command our attention and demand a response. They elicit within us various talents and skills. We see the beauty and sadness of life, and we are prompted to tell a story or write a play, or find a spouse, or build a house, or defend a city. We see how nature works and how to arrange its functions to benefit us, as best we can. We see how plants grow and animals are raised and roads are built, and so on. I can see how blowing my breath through a reed makes a pleasant sound, and I can see how to fashion a flute and play a song. But in all of this, it's not I who is making it all happen; rather it all happens through me. The gods, we might say, play the notes and we only discover how to move our fingers on the instrument. We are only the vessels through which all this happens. Involuntary appearances, by the way, can't be said to be either determined or contingent. We see that *we* aren't the ones determining any of them, but whether anyone else is, or whether they are purposeful or random are questions over which we must once again suspend judgment.

PETRONIUS: That's an intriguing defence of a shocking vision, I'll admit, but I still can't get past what seems to me to be the profound passivity of it all. There is no room for human intention, for its role in desire and purpose. You say the life of the Pyrrhonist is as active as any other, but it's a very strange activity. Earlier I called it sleep-walking and I still can't shake that image. The sleep-walker can be said, applying your argument, to be as active as a wide-awake person. He or she, after all, walks about and might even talk or be engaged in some complicated activity. Maybe a sleep-walker can even give a speech! But it's sleep-walking all the same, not real waking life.

LUCIAN: Let me expand on a point touched upon earlier. You and other dogmatists who imagine the independent rational self intentionally deliberating and acting in the world identify it with freedom itself. To be free, it seems, is to be able to act under one's own power without constraint. It's the difference, after all, between a citizen and a slave. Is that a fair observation?

PETRONIUS: Yes.

LUCIAN: Now I have been following the Pyrrhonists in maintaining that this so-called free self is in fact a prisoner of his or her beliefs. There's nothing free about being harnessed to the demands of one's ambition, is there?

PETRONIUS: My freedom lies in my ability to choose between one thing and another.

LUCIAN: But your bondage, the Pyrrhonists would say, lies in your having to live with the consequences of your choices, which you might regret. Your ambition to achieve something can be seen as a compulsion to choose, a force which entrains you in the outcome for better or worse. It can be a hard lesson.

PETRONIUS: Perhaps, but it allows me to act and to change the world.

LUCIAN: Like a god? But only a god, or perhaps a Sage, could possibly know enough to make the right choice, that is, one he or she would never regret. But we are like children playing with fire. We enjoy the illusion of our freedom and power, but we may burn down the house because we really don't know what we are doing.

PETRONIUS: So it's better just to do nothing, except, of course, as prompted by sensations and thoughts?

LUCIAN: That's right. You know that Sextus Empiricus, the Pyrrhonist philosopher, is also a physician. The first rule of medicine, from Hypocrates, is to do no harm. The quickest way to do harm is to blunder ahead out of the arrogance that we know what we're doing.

PETRONIUS: But nature, whose dictates you'd have us follow slavishly, which is to say involuntarily, cannot be counted upon to reliably prompt us to do the right thing. There's no guarantee that we won't end up suffering no matter what. Pain, it seems, will come into my life, even if I am a Pyrrhonist. Even a wise man, like Diogenes the Cynic, for instance, who also professed to be merely following nature, ended up sold into slavery.

LUCIAN: It's true that the dictates of nature can be as painful as they can be pleasant. But even the most painful experience need not be devastating. When put up for sale in the slave market, Diogenes asked for, and got, a master he could command, and so turned his slavery upside down. We spoke in earlier discussions of gymnosophists and others minimizing if not eliminating even physical pain. No one would deny the world is fraught with dangers which cannot be eliminated, but it seems, not being gods or Sages, we are not in a position to explain that away. Arguably, our pains can be mitigated only by abandoning our pretensions.

PETRONIUS: So you would have us give up the freedom we find in the active soul, and its potential for some kind of achievement, and for the satisfaction that brings, in return for accepting a problematic world over which we have no control at all. And, by the way, don't those gymnosophists exercise some kind of free action in controlling their responses to unpleasant conditions? Aren't you contradicting yourself?

LUCIAN: I don't think so, and this gets us to the heart of the matter. The gymnosophists, like the Pyrrhonists, who seem to have adapted their understanding and practice to experience, find freedom in necessity, not in attempts to evade necessity by embracing a belief in the fiction of free will. We don't know whether the phenomena which compel us are themselves determined or free, only that we must respond to them. There could be free will intervening in nature, yes, but whose? What the Pyrrhonists discovered, paradoxically, was that the abandonment of belief in free will on the part of an independent self (in which they included their own selves!) puts necessity—the phenomena we are compelled to experience in immediate sensation and thought — in an entirely new light. The suspension of judgment, or belief, over free will versus determinism is at the same time the end of the distortion of our experience, and the cessation of the pains that come with those distortions. Our sensations and thoughts are freed of our interpretations of them, and we can see them for what they are.

PETRONIUS: And what do they turn out to be?

LUCIAN: That is perhaps best answered by some Pyrrhonian more practised than I am. What I have heard said, though, is something like this, as a kind of preliminary indication: insofar as we succeed in separating out our interpretations of things from things as they are, we also dissolve our appropriation of things which occurs by virtue of our interpreting them. And when and if that happens, when the desires and fears about things created by our interpretations of them are dissolved, then we're left with the things themselves.

PETRONIUS: You report the Pyrrhonists to say that our beliefs, or interpretations of things, distort those things. How does that distortion happen?

LUCIAN: Suppose someone asserted — a sophist, perhaps, or a demagogue — that 'man is a wolf', to bring up the metaphor again, and the idea catches on. What happens is that the imagination is thereby prompted to combine memories of men and wolves into a singular image, an imagined wolf-man. This isn't hard to do. Think of centaurs, or mermaids, or unicorns. If you combine the two such images, common features are retained while uncommon and contradictory ones are discarded. Wolves, at least in most peoples' minds, are vicious and beady-eyed; they run in howling packs which hunt and kill their prey. Men, that is to say human beings, are intelligent, rational calculating creatures, it is popularly thought. If you combine the two images you get a composite mental figure — a cunning, howling predator. Does that make sense?

PETRONIUS: Yes.

LUCIAN: Notice that we are anthropomorphizing wolves and canining men, if we can talk that way. So when I see a man, and if I believe that men are wolves, I will project onto the man my imagined wolf-man; and similarly, when I see a wolf, I will project onto the wolf my imagined man-wolf. That is how I will see, that is, interpret, each of them in terms of the other. This profoundly distorts what men and wolves are really like, and how they actually appear. The features unique to each are edited out, and suppressed. Insofar as we continue to believe in wolf-men, we remain bound by an image we repeatedly impose on men and wolves which prevents us from fully understanding either. Even worse, it leads to incomplete and erroneous conclusions about men and wolves, and results in harmful outcomes for both.

PETRONIUS: I suppose the solution is to suspend judgment about wolf-men and man-wolves. A belief in wolf-men is anyway a trivial example which proves little if anything. A truly rational mind will see pretty quickly that wolf-men is a flimsy, superficial idea, nothing anyone would take too seriously. It will insist on a deeper, more pervasive comparison of the features of our experiences to uncover compelling principles not otherwise understood.

LUCIAN: Exactly, the point is to suspend judgment about wolf-men, and other beliefs as well—even the belief that there is no free will. Free will—the idea of an agent outside of experience somehow intervening to change experience—is something we can imagine, but not demonstrate. It may or may not be the case. What is interesting is that the believer becomes a prisoner of his or her belief. Believers think they are made free by their beliefs; they think they will be liberated from the compulsions of necessity by finding in some belief or other an explanation of the real or true nature of their compulsive experience. This includes both positive and negative dogmatists. But they are only exchanging one bondage for another. The beliefs they embrace determine their behaviour; they can even override the natural necessity of experience. Belief adds another layer of bondage. And they do so only for the worse, insofar as beliefs require a distortion if not a suppression of experience.

PETRONIUS: But the rational mind remains free, does it not? It has the ability to resist our reactions to natural necessity so as to allow us to assess what free choice can really offer us. This is what suspension of judgment is really about, I would say. Free will, to be more precise, is negative free will. It does not bring anything into being, I'll grant you that, but by being able to put our impulses on hold, as it were, and to resist immediately embracing and acting upon any of them, it allows for a consideration of alternatives, and eventually for a rational choice regarding which of several options in a situation to accept.

LUCIAN: You dogmatists consistently flatter yourself that you can penetrate behind appearances to their true nature. But the only reason why we would pause in our reaction to something which natural necessity prompts us from doing is that some countervailing natural necessity neutralizes our impulse to go ahead. It suggests an alternative response, a different course of action, and so leaves us, at least momentarily, stymied. It is not the rational mind, but natural necessity, which gives us pause.

PETRONIUS: Even if that were so, it still remains up to the rational mind to weigh the alternatives and come to a resolution.

LUCIAN: But the same difficulty reappears. Any resolution of the impasse will come only when one or another of the options presented by natural necessity is stronger than the others. As long as the options remain balanced, or equally desirable or undesirable, then the impasse will continue. In such a situation even the most trivial impulse one way or the other—perhaps the tossing of a coin, or the weight of a feather in the scale—will be enough to prompt one outcome over another.

PETRONIUS: Isn't the tossing of the coin a free decision to resolve the question?

LUCIAN: No, because the very thought to toss a coin is itself determined by a prior association, by an antecedent thought or sensation. I am stymied, and the thought comes to me: why not toss a coin? And that of course is to abandon any notion of free will and leave the decision up to chance.

PETRONIUS: If that's the case, if even our apparent ability to pause or suspend our reactions to what we experience is itself determined by the kinds of experience which we have, why doesn't that apply as well to the Pyrrhonists' famous suspension of judgment about beliefs? Given what you're saying, any suspension of judgments about my beliefs would also seem to be determined by my experience up to that point. Depending on how I am prompted, I will either accept some belief, reject it, or suspend judgment. It would be an automatic process, if you're right, not any kind of free choice.

LUCIAN: Yes, that's right. Even our liberation from belief, if it comes, does not depend on any rational free will, but on the circumstances of our prior experience. This is perhaps the final blow to our idea of independence based on free will. The Indians call it *karma*, and like Pythagoras and Plato and Apollonius and many others, understand it to operate over many, even indefinite lifetimes. The suspension of judgment comes precisely from the equipollence of conflicting thoughts, which is involuntarily imposed on us.

PETRONIUS: Then why all this talk of therapy and liberation and so on?

LUCIAN: Because you still end up liberated. Insofar as I and the Pyrrhonists use the language of a soul with free will—such as 'I believe this' or 'I do that'—we necessarily speak with the vulgar, as it were, precisely because our common language, distorted as it is by belief, makes it more or less impossible to do otherwise. The belief that we're active independent agents in control of our destiny is, at least to some degree, deeply ingrained in how we think and talk. But it's important to keep in mind that liberation from beliefs can nonetheless occur in spite of that, only that it's not something, if the Pyrrhonists are right, that we can freely will.

PETRONIUS: Then it seems to me that we've reached an impasse. It looks like there's nothing for a Pyrrhonist to do, except to respond to sensations and thoughts as they come and go.

LUCIAN: Yet this is precisely the release which enables tranquillity. The recognition that we have no independent will, no agency in directing the course of events, lifts a great burden from us all. I've tried to show that the Pyrrhonist is as active as any dogmatist in everyday life. There is no lack of feeling. He or she responds with joy or sorrow, pleasure or pain, curiosity or boredom, and even neutral indifference, as the case may be, to the impulses of nature and society, depending on the quality of the uninterpreted experiences at hand. Far from being distracted from appearances, as is the dogmatist, the Pyrrhonist is deeply immersed in them, and fully conscious of them.

As a witness, however, he or she will gaze as well upon their own behaviour; they will watch themselves from outside themselves, as it were, as they react now one way and now another. They will see the impermanence of their own bodies and souls, and of the beliefs their souls feverishly attempt to establish.

By contrast, if I am acting out of my beliefs, that is, out of my interpretations of my experience rather than absorbing those experiences at face value as they come to me, my understanding of what's going on will be seriously distorted, as I've tried to suggest, and my reactions will be similarly exaggerated. My pleasures and pains, and desires and fears, will all be inflated. When I believe something, I necessarily affirm it and thereby identify with it. Only a fictional self, after all, can affirm a belief. To believe in something is not only to offer an interpretation of some experience, it is to seal that interpretation with the imprimatur of one's identity. The fiction of my independent self is the ultimate belief, the mother of all beliefs, the home we build to house and nourish the rest of them.

PETRONIUS: Well, you're not afraid to spell out the implications of Pyrrhonism, I will admit. It's a lot to swallow. Still, I can't get over that you've reduced us to so many Daedalian automatons who somehow watch themselves be themselves, and gain tranquillity to boot. It's a hard sell, I'm afraid. Why should anyone believe it?

[Pause ...]

AURELIA: Are there any comments, I wonder, from our silent listeners? Harmonia? Saturninus?

HARMONIA: The Stoics may have a word or two to add about free will, but it's late and we can take it up tomorrow.

SATURNINUS: Pyrrhonism still seems to be what I've thought all along—a subtle version of nihilism, of trying to have your cake and eat it too. I think Petronius's objections brought that out. To me a judgment suspended remains as good as a judgment denied. But any further comment I have can also wait until tomorrow.

AURELIA: Perhaps, then, we've reached a good place to stop. Lucian, with Petronius' help you've revealed something of the Pyrrhonian life, I must say. It's not exactly what I expected, but I have to admit you've provided us at least some measure of what it would take to lead a life without beliefs. I for one would like to hear more about the differences in attitude and emotion between the Pyrrhonists and the Dogmatists. Perhaps we can take that up tomorrow evening. Good night, then, for now. Off to bed!

Is the Soul Necessary?

RUFUS: We're fortunate to have another pleasant evening to continue our discussion, and to cool off after a hot day. So let's begin. The Pyrrhonists, Lucian tells us, seem to have discovered not only that it's not necessary to believe in free will to live a full life, but that doing so is actually a hindrance to living a full life. And similarly, that it's not necessary to deny free will to live a full life, and that doing so is also a hindrance to living a full life. That seems to take in Saturninus's nihilism as well. In any event, Petronius, if I understand him, remains unconvinced, if not unmoved, by Lucian's Pyrrhonian speeches last night.

PETRONIUS: Yes, though Lucian was very ingenious, as we've come to expect. Aurelia's question of how the Pyrrhonist can expect to live a life without beliefs led us to debate, as I recall, whether or not we are independent agents with free will, and if not, then who or what might we be, or not be? I'm not sure I can carry on much further with Lucian on that slippery issue, but the rest of you might, and I'm sure he's ready, as usual. Here's where I stand: I'm not ready, not yet, to give up my free will, and I suspect most of you aren't either, and I'm not sure anyway that I could if I wanted to, or what it would take for me to do so. Harmonia at the end last night said she had something to add. Maybe she should start.

RUFUS: Yes, let's begin with Harmonia.

HARMONIA: Thank you. As Lucian well knows, the Stoics are determinists, though in their own way. Unlike the Epicureans and Peripatetics and other dogmatists, the universe for Stoics is the realization of

God in nature. God, the supreme being, is coherent in his wholeness as manifest in nature, which means that nature, being divine, must be entirely rational. The divine *logos* necessarily plays itself out perfectly, with everything determined by a preceding impulse.

I bring it up because Lucian and I debated this point last winter in Rome. He had little patience then with the idea—he dismissed it as just another belief—that human reason, manifested in the power of abstraction, is able to grasp, at least in part, the larger rationality of God's nature. Stoics arrive at the same conclusion, it seems to me, that the Pyrrhonists do: that we are determined by the phenomenal world we experience, and that there is no apparent free will. But by conforming to God's will, manifest in phenomenal nature, and acting in accordance with God's plan as it unfolds, we Stoics realize a kind of freedom. We find that freedom through recognizing and accepting the necessity of rational nature, instead of blindly following it, resenting it, or denying it. It's the freedom from ignorance achieved through the pleasure of knowledge.

LUCIAN: Keep in mind that Pyrrhonists suspend judgment about whether actions are free or determined, and do not conclude one way or another about that. They just do not know. But you Stoics believe in the determination of our behaviour by nature, or God, which seems to preclude any kind of independent deliberation and action on our part. You also believe, as I understand it, that we retain a small part of divinity within us, manifest in our limited but real powers of reasoning. Exercising our reason to gain knowledge will somehow liberate us, you seem to think, and you call that freedom. You say we can see deeper into God as a result. Insofar as we act rationally, we don't do so out of our own autonomy, but as part of God's autonomy. If there's any freedom to be had, it looks like it's really God's freedom, not ours, just as it seems to be ultimately His reason, not ours, though we may be able to tap into it. This is a way of smuggling in freedom in the face of determinism, or trying to, it seems to me. Unfortunately, the notion that God is the active rational principle of the world looks like an unfounded speculation, another belief, to the Pyrrhonists.

You Stoics, Epicureans, and other dogmatists all cling to a belief in reason in some form as a refuge for autonomy and identity. Reason becomes your God. The Epicureans too locate human identity in the rational mind, which they imagine can directly penetrate to the invisible internal workings of things, to their version of atoms and the void. But for them there's no God, only nature. Stoics see the whole world as animated by a divine rational principle and imagine that humans have a unique ability to recognize and identify with it, even if only in an indirect way. But that is enough, it seems, for you to claim some kind of contact with the divine and thereby justify who we humans are, and our place in the world. Did I get that right?

HARMONIA: A forceful summary, but not quite. At least we dogmatists try to understand who we are. You Pyrrhonists seem intent on eliminating any vestige of the natural individual soul, leaving at best what you call the witness, a kind of receptacle of consciousness, a tabula rasa, which has no identity at all and no freedom of any sort, primary or secondary. Saturninus commented at the end last night that he didn't see a difference between his nihilism and what results from suspension of belief, and neither can I.

LUCIAN: Here is a difference: I press you again, Saturninus, as I have before, that you hold at least one belief the Pyrrhonists don't: the belief that there is a reality out there which allows us to know who we are. The problem is that you've concluded that that reality cannot be found, and yet you retain the presumption that it is what is somehow necessary.

SATURNINUS: The only difference between us, as I see it, is that you hold out that the reality of what we imagine could still be realized. I suppose that's why the Pyrrhonists say they are still inquiring into the nature of things. But I see no *practical* difference between us. It seems to me that your attempt to keep the question open is also a belief!

LUCIAN: Not at all. A belief is an affirmation, positive or negative, about the existence of something non-evident, like a centaur or a mermaid or a God. Suspending judgment about things non-evident is a recognition that they would have to be made evident to settle any question of whether they exist or not. It's not a belief, but an appeal to facts, or *pragmata*. That's the opposite of belief.

SATURNINUS: My point was that there is no practical difference.

LUCIAN: The difference is between a world with beliefs, and a world with no beliefs at all. The practical difference is enormous. As long as the former persists there is the possibility of a refuge in some kind of fictional self. Without such beliefs, no such refuge exists, and all fictional selves are dissolved. If there is going to be a self, it would have to be a real one, not just one we imagine to be real. This is why the Pyrrhonian life without beliefs is so important.

AURELIA: Let me interrupt, now that we're back to last night's question. In a world without beliefs, if I understand what Lucian has been trying to spell out for us, there is no independently existing self acting as a deliberative rational agent, which is the common view of the philosophical schools, of Stoicism, Epicureanism, the Aristotelians, and the various Platonists, including the Academics, in spite of their differences. For the Pyrrhonists, however, there is only a passive witness to what we experience, including our experience of what we otherwise believe to be ourselves. Is that right?

LUCIAN: Yes, at least there's no such self anyone has yet found.

AURELIA: All right, but holding beliefs, you maintain, is the source of our troubles. And being released from them is to escape from those troubles. Surely this is to gain some kind of freedom?

LUCIAN: Yes, but it is a freedom from something, not a freedom for something.

AURELIA: All right, but none of this liberation from desire happens deliberately, or by free will, ours or God's, as you've been insisting. How then do we come to have beliefs in the first place, and how do we get over them?

LUCIAN: The phenomena we experience in sensation and thought, variously grouped into *pragmata*, affect us directly and involuntarily in different ways. These affects we call feelings. Here the Pyrrhonists agree with the dogmatists in describing the feelings we suffer from *pragmata* as falling along a continuum from pleasure to indifference to pain. As the Epicureans point out, we are naturally attracted to pleasure and repulsed by pain, and this is what puts us on the path to belief.

AURELIA: How is that?

LUCIAN: Pleasure gives rise to desire, and pain to fear. These are emotions, or interpretations or judgments about feelings. We naturally seek more pleasure and less pain. Or, to be more accurate, we can't help following our pleasures and avoiding our pains. We don't need to calculate at all. We naturally hold on to our pleasures and pains, in their absence, by reflecting upon them in imagination and memory. Desire is the emotional force unleashed by the pleasures upon which we reflect, and fear is the emotional force unleashed by the pains upon which we reflect.

AURELIA: We still haven't arrived at belief.

LUCIAN: The key role is that of the imagination. When we reflect imaginatively on our memories they aren't just replayed; they are also compounded, extended, embellished, and otherwise reshaped. Our memories are thus transformed into new imaginative creations with new and compounded powers of pleasure and pain. Desire and fear in this way are inflated well beyond what we normally experience in sensation. The best account I can offer about the origin of belief is that our inflated desires and fears arising out of what we imagine to be the case are what drive us to posit the real existence of the things we only imagine.

AURELIA: Are we doomed to give in to our desires and fears? That's hardly surprising.

LUCIAN: One likely reason for it is the sheer emotional force desires and fears accumulate and concentrate over time. They distract and overwhelm us. It's hard for us not to believe that our imaginings, at least some of them, represent something beyond themselves, something strong enough to elicit desire and fear, to command our behaviour. They must come from somewhere, we think, so the immediate explanation is that what we imagine exists somehow independently of us.

If I believe in the gods, it is because I am prodded by the emotional power of what it is that I imagine about them. I take them to exist and act accordingly. There is the old myth about Zeus, that he went about in disguise as a wandering stranger. If you believe that a stranger begging at your door might in fact be Zeus, you would invite him in, make him warm, provide a meal and a bed. He might leave you next morning with a blessing of good fortune. If you refuse him, however, he might curse your home and family, beat and rob you, and burn down the house. There's the desire, and the fear.

AURELIA: It's a story we all grew up with. But what would change my mind to dispel such beliefs?

LUCIAN: Over time we naturally speak with our relatives, neighbours, and friends about what we believe or don't believe about the gods, about Zeus walking about the countryside, or even around the city, knocking on doors. One of us, perhaps a sceptic, asks: 'How do you know it might be Zeus instead of an ordinary itinerant or runaway slave? Wouldn't Zeus have to reveal himself, display his divinity, perhaps perform a miracle, say restore sight to the blind, or raise someone from the dead, and so on.' Yes, you'd likely think, that makes sense. You might then naturally investigate, as the Pyrrhonists say. You would seek out times and places where strangers might be expected to visit, where Zeus might become manifest as imagined. You might interview them, find out who they really are. If you couldn't do it yourself, you might seek out other witnesses and collect their testimony, and so on.

AURELIA: What would it take to establish a lack of correlation between the myth and actual real sensible experience? It's hard to prove a negative, as they say.

LUCIAN: And that's why Pyrrhonists are content to suspend judgment. It takes a nihilist like Saturninus to think he can prove a negative, when all he's done is embrace it. To prove a positive, we would need a confirming case, a real example of the realization of

Zeus in ordinary life. Even better, a number of such examples. What would be convincing would be indisputable phenomenal experiences of a range and type to be so overwhelming as to invoke divinity: for instance, repeated miracles and other extraordinary and supernatural events on the part of the reputed divinity.

AURELIA: That's just what the Galileans claim about their holy man, Jesus.

LUCIAN: Jesus, of course, like Apollonius and others, including Peregrinus, is reputed to have done a number of such things (raising a man from the dead, walking on water, changing water into wine, rising from the dead himself, etc.) and by virtue of these supposedly factual but miraculous events he seems to have convinced a lot of people in his day and ours that he possessed some kind of divinity.

One can quibble with any and even all of these examples—maybe they're just hallucinations, the madness of crowds, bad faith, or whatever—just as one could quibble, as we've already seen, with what we take to be ordinary, unproblematic experiences (say, the goblet of wine in front of me). Given the preponderance of evidence, however, we accept goblets of wine as facts, and I submit we would accept the Galilean belief that Jesus is the Son of their God if we had a similar preponderance of evidence. All we need to turn belief into reality is a good enough match between what someone imagines about something and whether or not there is a corresponding involuntary phenomenal experience to substantiate it. If Zeus turned out to walk around in ordinary life, with an occasional display of divine power, we'd have to take him seriously indeed.

Of course, no such preponderance of evidence seems to exist for our examples, even for this Jesus, and we can only conclude, involuntarily, that divinity for such individuals is a mere belief, a myth about them, at least so far. But the benefit of suspending judgment about Jesus's divinity and others' is that we are thereby released from the burdens of that myth, not least from the excess of emotions that it or any belief of importance produces. It is their emotional burden which weighs most heavily upon us, and whose lifting is our greatest blessing.

PHILIA: Perhaps I can chime in here. The emotions are a central concern of the Epicureans and I'd like to hear in more detail about how the Pyrrhonians understand emotions.

LUCIAN: We might think about it this way: our desires are stimulated by pleasant sensations, passed into memories, and revisited in our thoughts, such as the warmth of a touch, the beauty of a sight, the harmony of a sound, the smoothness of a taste, the aroma of a smell, the attraction of another person. We are involuntarily drawn to renew these pleasurable sensations. Similarly, our fears are emotions stimulated by unpleasant sensations, and these are also separately preserved and revisited in our thoughts, such as the jab of a knife, an ugly sight, a dissonant noise, a bitter taste, a stench of smell. We are involuntarily drawn to avoid these sensations. These kinds of pleasures and pains we share with the animals.

PHILIA: So far, so good.

LUCIAN: But, unlike animals, we have vast realms of thought which run parallel to our sensations. Seemingly endless memories constantly recycle through our minds in a dizzying variety of revisions and recombinations. We ruminate almost endlessly, don't we? Because of this we are liable, unlike animals, to find both our desires and our fears swollen out of control. More accurately, emotions are automatically magnified for us by the material we find in our imaginations.

PHILIA: An example of how beliefs are developed out of emotions would be useful. The story of Zeus as a wanderer was helpful, but something more in the normal course of events would be good here.

LUCIAN: Imagine a young woman, perhaps much like yourself, Philia, but raised in more difficult circumstances. Let's call her Diotima. She inherits a small estate, blessed with a fine olive grove, as her only property. With attentive good management, possible only through mental activity—including continuous detailed reviews of estate operations in her memory, and their comparison and re-evaluation in her imagination, and on paper—she manages to increase production and makes a good profit. This accumulated wealth allows her to purchase a neighbouring estate, and to expand her production of oil. She is a shrewd manager, and she continues making more profits and buying more estates, and in the end becomes a very wealthy woman.

So far, you might say, so good. But the contents of her consciousness are largely the worries of her estates, and the demands they make on her take their toll. This mental activity which has so preoccupied her has largely shaped what she has become, and she comes to identify with the personal empire she believes she has created and which she deserves. What was at first a straightforward desire to maintain a small estate is gradually transformed into a relentless and unnatural desire to build a vast enterprise of scores of villas and farms with endless groves and fields and workshops filled with numerous clerks and foremen, and slaves and animals, all toiling on a grand scale on her behalf.

At some point, without her realizing it, what was a natural desire for simple security has morphed into an obsession which cannot be relinquished. Her success, to complete the picture, has become her very identity, and her pride and her habit of command have settled into arrogance. She becomes insensitive, imperious, even cruel. She is prepared to do anything, at any cost, to maintain her properties. Now all of this was made possible only because of her ability to imagine this fictional identity for herself, as something she created, something no animal could do.

PHILIA: You call it a fictional identity, but why isn't it a real identity, as most people would say, and why do you make it turn out so badly? Why couldn't she have managed her estates with grace and charm and compassion?

LUCIAN: Her identity is fictional because it exists only in her imagination, and only by extension from there in how she behaves, and so finally in how others in reaction imagine her as well. It is the picture she has of herself as the mistress of her estates, an autonomous, demanding woman with a never-ending series of desires — another estate, another villa, more slaves. It is what she has become in her mind; it is her identity, it is who she is. And she imposes it on others and the world. She really can't help it. It's true, she might have turned out differently, more modest and generous, perhaps, but even a less aggressive identity would retain many of the inflated desires of a person in her position.

PHILIA: Surely the Pyrrhonist therapy has something to offer here?

LUCIAN: The challenge is to deconstruct our imagined personalities. From early on, for most of us, they are hardened into a set of dispositions which channels how we react to any situation.

PHILIA: Exactly how does that work? How do we deconstruct a personality?

LUCIAN: Suppose Diotima, our imperious landowner, is notified by the local magistrate that a neighbour disputes her title to some recently acquired land. On one level, any such dispute is an objective matter, to be settled by fact-finding and testimony and records on file. On another level, it is a subjective matter. Her right to the land, arrived at by her own efforts, with proper payments and fees, and time and labour spent, she now presumes to be part of her identity. And now that identity is also called into question. The land isn't just something she owns; it's part of who she is. She will be disposed, as a result, to take the dispute personally. Rather than seeing the issue solely as a question of fact, she will also see it as an attack on her integrity. She will be angry and resentful; she will, not surprisingly, come to see her neighbour as an enemy, and she will be open to thwarting him in any way she can. This is something we see all too often and it can happen even to someone with a reputation for grace, charm, and compassion, if they are threatened enough.

PHILIA: But if our Domitia had not developed such an imperious personality she would not have been upset as she was over the lawsuit. She might have dealt with her neighbours' claim as a factual matter and relied on the magistrate's impartiality to weigh the evidence pro and con. More to the point, if the finding was in her neighbour's favour she would recognize and welcome the justice of it, just as much as if it were in her favour. That would be unusual behaviour, you might say, almost too good to be true. But then that's the goal, isn't it? It's what the Sage would have done.

LUCIAN: No doubt. It's true that people are not always corrupted by their personalities. We all know of examples, a few anyway, of people who would have acted in such a situation without being governed by their emotional dispositions. And yes, the best of such people we can think of as sages, full of virtue.

But those are the exceptions, rare enough to prove the rule. The sage, I think we all agree, is an ideal, I'd say a belief, one which fulfils a desire for perfect pleasure, for the Epicureans, or for perfect knowledge, for the Stoics. There is no Pyrrhonian sage, by the way, since there is no complete and perfect mind available to always calculate the right thing to do. The best Pyrrhonists can offer is someone more or less shorn of belief and at the mercy of appearances. Most people more or less identify with beliefs, but beliefs are inherently unstable, and often interchangeable; they inflate our emotions and upset our tranquillity. Since the independent existence of what is believed, that is, its status beyond mere opinion or fantasy, cannot be secured, any belief remains vulnerable to challenge. Any belief can be contradicted. If you say you believe such-and-such is the case, absent evidence to that effect, anybody can deny it. And if you identify with that belief, you will be distressed by such a challenge.

PHILIA: The later Epicureans, I should point out, Philodemus especially, explored issues involving the power of our dispositions to dictate our behaviour. He pursued in detail the distinction made by Epicurus between natural beliefs and empty beliefs. The former are matters of fact which can be settled by the objective evidence of phenomenal sensation. The latter offer no such resolution. Natural beliefs lead to natural feelings, the kinds of pleasures and pains which arise out of ordinary sensory experience. Empty beliefs lead to unnatural feelings, or emotions, such as those of our Diotima. You Pyrrhonists seem to be talking about the latter.

LUCIAN: A point of clarification. Of course, we often say in ordinary speech that we *believe* the sun will rise tomorrow, and since we have considerable phenomenal experience to anticipate confidently that it will do so again, it's reasonable to call that a natural belief. It is subject to the test of confirmation or disconfirmation. It's pretty clear that the Pyrrhonists, in their idiom, use the term 'belief' for what the Epicureans call unnatural or empty beliefs, that is, imaginings which do not admit of any such test, but which are asserted or presumed to be true, to have an independent existence.

Such an assertion or presumption turns something we imagine — take again our stock examples of mermaids and centaurs, or even the gods — into a belief. It also holds for things we cannot imagine at all, or only negatively imagine — such as the geometers' points without parts or lines without breadth. For in these cases we can still imagine that someday we might imagine something we can't imagine now.

PHILIA: But finding evidence to confirm or disconfirm what we imagine to be the case often isn't so easy.

LUCIAN: No it's not. We might scoff at mermaids and centaurs and even the gods, but consider that we already have exotic animals, such as elephants and giraffes and monkeys from Libya and Asia which we would have never expected to see. Who's to say that anything that can be imagined might not be out there somewhere, perhaps in another world? Closer to home, maybe in the mountains of Asia there are centaurs, we hear, and maybe in the far Ocean there are mermaids, as reported. And perhaps the gods may appear again, as many in the past have claimed they once did. Perhaps Zeus will come to the door after all.

But until any of that actually happens, until such things actually appear, we cannot presume that they exist. If we do, we are imposing fictions upon reality, with all the problems and anxieties that it raises. Like Diotima, we get into trouble over our beliefs because our emotional well-being has become entrained by our identification with them. The difficulty with beliefs is that they lead not only to unnatural or inflated emotions, but that there is no easy way to correct such emotions once they are unleashed.

Diotima is outraged by what she takes as a challenge to her dignity. There is nothing to check her anger; she can give it free vent, and can hardly resist doing so. The only restraint on her emotional reaction can come from outside of her. Unfortunately, that's likely to come in the form of an opposing inflated emotion, in this case from the neighbour who is challenging her claim. He too has a personality formed by his own history and interests, and his claim to the land in question could well be just as personal in nature as hers. If so, we have a recipe for conflict with no mechanism of resolution.

PHILIA: Some beliefs, such as in mermaids, are trivial, but others, like the soul, are quite significant. For the Pyrrhonists, therapy, it seems, means the deconstruction of the entire personality, or the soul as we think we know it; the Epicureans don't go that far.

LUCIAN: No they don't. The Epicureans, like all philosophical dog-matists, retain the personality, though they have shrunk it down to the rational calculating soul, but the Pyrrhonists would dispense even with that. To them, the soul, even the rational soul, remains a firmly held belief, a fiction.

PHILIA: Assuming, for the sake of argument, that it's desirable to deconstruct the belief in the soul, how can it be done? Or maybe I should ask 'how does it happen' since, lacking free will, there isn't anything we can do about it anyway?

LUCIAN: There is no easy answer to that. The soul, a combination or melding of body and mind, evolves over a lifetime, perhaps many lifetimes. We learn early on to distinguish the sensible *pragmata* evident to us which make up our bodies, from those which do not. This bodily identity, or body soul, we share with other sentient creatures. But, unlike the other animals, we have, as we've seen, the capacity to retain memories, that is, to form mental *pragmata* which reflect the sensible *pragmata* imposed upon us, and to reorder them in what we call the imagination. We automatically recognize among both sensations and thoughts comparisons which we see as identities, similarities, and differences. We are able, particularly in thought, to regroup our memories of sensible *pragmata* not only in the order in which we experience them, but in various other orders as well. We can, for instance, combine things disparate in sensation (horses and wolves and men) into things unified in thought (centaurs and wolf-men).

PHILIA: I suppose you're going to say that these mental creations have something to do with how we construct our souls.

LUCIAN: Yes. Animals, lacking mind as we know it, are aware of themselves, it seems, but only as bodies in nature. We have that awareness as well, of course, but it is supplemented for us by a further awareness of ourselves as thinking beings unique to ourselves, thinking being the picturing we find ourselves doing in our imaginations. Much of what others before us have thought, the various reorderings of mental *pragmata* they have encountered, have not only been captured in memory, but also been accumulated and written down and taught to us by our parents, family, teachers, priests, rulers, and by the general life of the city. This flow of phenomena through cultural memory gives us a strong personal identity on top of our natural or animal identity.

PHILIA: How much of this mental education is belief and how much is not?

LUCIAN: We already know the answer. The mental *pragmata* we can imagine—those which are not beliefs—are those which can be shown to accurately represent sensible *pragmata*. Because we remember our sensible *pragmata* through our mental *pragmata*, and can more or less freely compare and otherwise reorder them, we can anticipate the course of our experience in a way that animals cannot.

This proper work of the mind we call reflection, for it is no more or less than our ability to literally capture and represent to ourselves the sensible experience which otherwise would simply flow through us and be gone, as seems to be the case with animals. We can, then, in turn, also turn around and represent the mental *pragmata* of our imaginative creations as sensible *pragmata* (this is what we do in art, literature, politics, tradition, religion, and culture). In this way we bring our thoughts back into the sensible world, where they did not exist originally.

None of this reflective activity has to involve belief. A belief, by contrast, is an imaginative construction which cannot be shown to represent sensible *pragmata*, but which is nonetheless presumed to represent something non-evident somehow independently existing. Insofar as we make that presumption our own, it becomes part of our identity. And of course we can project that mental *pragmata* back into sensible *pragmata* as well.

PHILIA: Are you suggesting that the soul, that is, who we are, is constructed out of mental *pragmata*, that is, beliefs ungrounded in sensation?

LUCIAN: Well, it seems evident that we have sensations and thoughts, a body and a mind. The body is evident among our sensations, but the mind, curiously, is not evident among our thoughts, where we might expect to find it. The body is unambiguously demarcated among our sensations. I am in little or no doubt about distinguishing my body (my eyes and ears, head and trunk, arms and legs, and so on) from the rest of nature in which I find myself. The mind, however, is not unambiguously demarcated in thought, as one thought among others. There is no thought of my mind the way there is a sensation of my body. Our experience differentiating the body from other sensible *pragmata* is perhaps what tempts us to imagine differentiating a parallel mental body we call the soul. We might think, for example, of the soul as the container of our thoughts, much as we can think of the body as the container of our sensations. Or we can imagine, as you Epicureans do, that a subtle part of our body, made up of very fine and unobservable atoms, is what actually constitutes our mind. But these are all beliefs. There is no evident manifestation of mind as such, as something we can think of. It seems we can't think the mind.

PHILIA: And you propose that we deconstruct this belief in a soul?

LUCIAN: It looks like we have to if we wish to avoid anxiety. Our identity with the soul is what makes the other beliefs we posit into *our* beliefs; the soul exercises ownership over whatever it believes, and is subject to mortal threat by whatever challenges its beliefs. Or rather, the soul gives us an identity we can use to appropriate beliefs as needed, for better or worse.

PHILIA: You have argued that, since our sensations and thoughts are involuntary, we have no free will, that all our actions are determined. You've said our liberation from belief is also involuntary. So why worry about liberation of the self, which is what I take deconstruction of the soul to mean?

LUCIAN: Liberation is possible only if the impulse to believe in the reality of something we imagine is checked by a counter-impulse to deny it. This comes out best in therapeutic dialectics, the kind of dialogue I think we are having here, and in which the Pyrrhonists excel. Only then, it seems, are we put into a position to see that a belief we hold can be contradicted, and that it does not necessarily represent something other than what it is — a product of our imagination. At that point, our innocence is lost, even if we resist the conclusion. The Pyrrhonists have developed long lists of what they call 'modes' setting out common assertions and counter-assertions, or dialectical strategies, about various beliefs to induce suspension of judgment.

PHILIA: But, as you suggest, the believer may still resist this demonstration. In fact, isn't that what usually happens? The very fact that people identify with their beliefs is what makes it hard for them to give them up. It's a very strong bond.

LUCIAN: No doubt. We have to remember that whether or not one gives up a deeply held belief isn't a matter of free choice, or at least it can't be presumed to be that. One will continue to maintain a belief as long as the impulses promoting it remain greater than those opposing it, and conversely abandon it when the impulses demoting it are greater than those supporting it.

PHILIA: But doesn't an equally plausible contradictory argument sufficient to balance the argument supporting the belief lead to the equipollence of which the Pyrrhonists speak? Doesn't that dictate suspension of judgment? How can our impulses remain in favour of the belief or against it if the arguments are in balance?

LUCIAN: Because simply recognizing that something we believe in may be false or non-existent is only a first step in exhausting the impulses which determine whether or not we accept the belief in question. Challenging the truth of something believed isn't the only relevant factor in whether or not it is believed.

PHILIA: I'm not so sure. What are some of these other factors?

LUCIAN: Let's consider Diotima again. Her identity, her consciousness of herself as a sentient thinking being, was not left up to her alone. Had she been raised by a she-wolf, like Romulus and Remus supposedly were, her sense of self would have been based largely on her own body, like any animal. But she was raised in a good family, and well educated. She was given a name, learned to speak, and was loved and educated and praised for who she was. She began to think about herself in her mind, as we all do, in addition to reacting to things through her body. Her identity was reinforced in memory and imagination by a preponderance of pleasant impulses, not only from her family, but from her city and its culture. She was not only told in countless ways that she was Diotima, but she was also told to take responsibility for herself and her actions. In her mind, she came to believe that she, Diotima, existed as a soul associated with a body and engaged in the autonomous exercise of her free will.

What could be more natural? Given all that, when confronted by a Pyrrhonist who pointed out that no such Diotima could be found among her thoughts to correspond to what she imagined herself to be, and that Diotima therefore really did not exist, this apparent equipollence of arguments for and against her real existence would likely have little effect.

PHILIA: You seem to be discounting the Pyrrhonian exercise of suspending judgments over beliefs.

LUCIAN: Yes and no. Resisting a notion contradicting your belief in something is a common initial response. People tend to dig in their heels when first challenged. But the recognition by Diotima that her very self might not exist — that she may be no more than an illusion of an independently existing self — is not something, once recognized, that will go away. There is instead, at some point, a loss of innocence in the face of contradiction; a more subtle involuntary impulse is introduced which can gradually force a re-evaluation of everything that she has thought and imagined about herself. Equipollence of beliefs, if it persists, is the continuation, not the end, of dialectics.

PHILIA: So all those positive impulses which went into creating and sustaining the illusion of her independent self continue to support Diotima's self-illusion even when challenged?

LUCIAN: Yes, they do, and they will persist. But if she is honest with herself, she will slowly realize that she has no choice but to separate the positive impulses she has enjoyed all her life from from the illusion of an independent self she has mistakenly taken them to reinforce.

PHILIA: What kind of a mistake was that? You said earlier that our desires and fears condition us from the start to have beliefs. You made it sound like a natural process, apparently not under our control at all.

LUCIAN: Falling into belief isn't an intentional mistake. It's a consequence of ignorance; it's an honest and seemingly inevitable mistake, unintentional like any other. In the world of sensation, the involuntary self-evident truth is that some of our sensations, those which comprise our bodies, are the conditions for others, the thoughts we entertain in our minds. So yes, what could be more natural, then, than to look for an analogue of the body in the mind? The natural mistake is to think about ourselves in our thoughts after the way in which we see and otherwise sense ourselves through our bodies, particularly because of the involuntary force of our sensations coloured as they are by desire and fear. We may notice that we do not immediately find a self among our thoughts, but what could be easier than to presume that it's hidden there somewhere, that we have a soul as the container of our mind just as we have a body which is the container of our physical world. This is especially so in the absence of any suggestion otherwise.

PHILIA: If we accept all that, what does it mean not to have a soul, or self?

LUCIAN: It means we're thrown back onto the direct and immediate experience of our involuntary and self-evident thoughts and sensations. But there is a sort of consolation prize for the loss of the soul, that is what I have been calling the witness. For to live without beliefs, that is, without the soul, is to continue to live with the consciousness which nonetheless accompanies our thoughts and sensations in their direct immediacy. We are aware, as witnesses, of the determining, involuntary physical and mental *pragmata* we can't help but experience, just as they come and go in the presence of consciousness.

PHILIA: You said earlier that this doesn't mean total passivity, that in fact we are just as active in response to the pleasures and pains *pragmata* impose upon us as when we believe ourselves to be autonomous souls, or agents deliberating and acting freely. I can see that, perhaps, but the surrender of autonomy and responsibility seems to imply a deeper disruption of some kind. Certainly, our learning and philosophy are based entirely upon the illusion that we are independently existing, freely functioning souls. What happens to our culture? I think Saturninus was getting at this last night. For instance, what about guilt and punishment enshrined in the law for deliberate offences? If I'm not responsible for a crime that I have clearly committed, how can I be punished?

LUCIAN: Just exactly the same way as when you believe you are responsible. If you physically committed a crime, you can be punished insofar as you have violated norms of behaviour which sustain a pleasant society as opposed to a painful one. It doesn't matter how you feel about it.

PHILIA: So I need not feel any guilt or shame? As long as I'm willing to take my punishment, I can be dismissive or even contemptuous of the law.

LUCIAN: Yes, as long as you take your punishment. Even if you resist it, getting punished is all that matters. But this hardly seems a worry. Punishment is painful enough to dissuade most people from being contemptuous of it. Following the law is the practical thing to do; it is piety itself, whatever you think about it. What you think about it is not important.

PHILIA: I'm not so sure. You make me feel a bit like an insect that's been pierced with a needle and stuck onto a display board. I'm left totally helpless.

LUCIAN: But that's your liberation. There's nothing to worry about because there isn't anything you can really do about anything.

PHILIA: Why does that sound so shocking?

LUCIAN: Because you're not used to it. You still think you have some control over things, and you feel anxious if you think you don't. But the real anxiety comes from thinking you have control when in fact you have only the illusion of control, which is part of the greater illusion of the self. This control you believe in, after all, is too unstable and subject to failure to rely upon. To maintain the illusion you have control you have to overcompensate. You have to insist at all costs that you are in charge, at least of your own destiny, if not of the world. And when things break down, as they seem to do sooner or later, then you go to pieces, wailing and gnashing and blaming yourself, or at least quietly grinding your teeth. That's the price of illusory responsibility.

PHILIA: You've already suggested that desire and fear are inflated by our beliefs. Are you saying they reflect this instability?

LUCIAN: Yes, it's always the same dynamic. The fictitious soul and its pretentious freedom have to be pumped up if they are to be maintained at all. This is manifest in the inflated emotions which accompany all this, pride above all, along with pride's accompanying vices of condescension, arrogance, certitude, self-righteousness, superiority, vanity, authority, greed, presumption, imprudence, ambition, and others I'm sure we could add.

PHILIA: And the price of pride, I suppose, is the special suffering it entails, the deflation which follows the inflation.

LUCIAN: Yes, the inflation of pride is the inflation of desire. And the price of pride is fear. You have more to gain, you think, because you're so special. You deserve more good things, more pleasures, and it's all very exciting. But you also have more to lose. The house of pride has no foundation, no real independent existence. It can be knocked over at any moment. The inflated fear which follows is manifest in anger above all, accompanied by resentment, contempt, unscrupulousness, malice, vengeance, self-loathing, mendacity, and others too I'm sure we could add.

There are some interesting secondary effects as well. The prideful person is one thing; but he or she also victimizes others. The victims respond to their prideful masters with depression, flattery, envy, evasion, insincerity, obsequiousness, resignation, passive-resistance, emulation, conspiracy, gossip, and so on.

PHILIA: Is there anyone not caught up in this dynamic? Pyrrho, I suppose.

LUCIAN: Anyone who's constructed a fictitious self which they think really exists is more or less subject to these emotional overreactions. And that's almost all of us. Those with more pride, with a more developed self, tend to dominate others. Those with less pride tend to be the victims of the more prideful. But their emotions are inflated all the same. The inflated emotions become ingrained and habitualized all round; they turn into personal dispositions recognized by repeated patterns of behaviour: the man quick to anger, the obsequious woman, the flatterer at court, the self-righteous official, the hypocritical politician, and so on. But yes, the Pyrrhonists follow Pyrrho in recognizing the possibility of liberation, of *ataraxia*.

PHILIA: So to be liberated is to be free of these conflicting dispositions?

LUCIAN: Well, yes, but it should be clearer now how difficult that is.

PHILIA: What advice do the Pyrrhonists have to offer this recalcitrant soul you describe?

LUCIAN: The first step is the recognition that any belief we hold of our soul, meaning the self, as an independently existing thing, can be denied; that calls the existence of the soul into question. The second step is the recognition that our inflated emotions stem from our commitment to this belief, and our need to defend it, a need aroused when it is denied by someone we expect to accept it. That becomes the price and burden of sustaining the belief in the face of uncertainty and challenge. The complexity and emotional history of our beliefs must be respected. The third step is to consider that abandoning our belief in an independent existence is what allows us to abandon all these inflated emotions as well. This release from inflated emotions makes possible the peace of mind or tranquillity we call *ataraxia*.

PHILIA: You make it sound so easy.

LUCIAN: In a way, it is. It finally just happens, or so the Pyrrhonists say. The main obstacle is the sheer force of the emotions involved, particularly those with which we identify. By presuming that I am an independently existing autonomous being I allow myself a range of pleasures not otherwise available. I can act like a god, or at least a minor god, or mortal god, or I can think that I can. My desires are aroused. I can impose my will and make things happen, or so it seems to me. I may have some power over slaves, clients, tenants or soldiers, as the case may be. That's all very seductive. At the same time, I am exposing myself to a new range of fears. Another autonomous self can come along and interfere in my activities, even seek to destroy me. It's a recipe for endless conflict.

PHILIA: So there's no way to dampen these emotions without abandoning the belief in the autonomous self which generates them?

LUCIAN: In the end, it seems not. But in the meantime endless conflict and anxiety bring on a weariness, a disillusionment of sorts. It may be that what emerges over time—perhaps over many lifetimes—is a gradual realization that nothing is gained by this heightened dynamic of desire and fear, repeated over and over. We find ourselves on a kind of treadmill, and eventually we realize we are going nowhere. The self we are trying to realize never materializes, and each effort ends in frustration.

PHILIA: And then we get off the treadmill?

LUCIAN: Perhaps, but only when the time is right. Or so the Pyrrhonists caution us. Remember it's not in our hands. There is no formula to follow. No real therapy. But what may become evident, once we see that what we think we are doing isn't getting us any-where, is that we find ourselves gradually accustomed to witnessing a process we do not in fact control. Abandoning our belief in the self, when and if that happens, leaves us with what is evident: with our sensations and thoughts and our consciousness of them, and the involuntary force of their commands.

PHILIA: This remaining consciousness we have of sensations and thoughts—the witness, as you call it—still seems to be some kind of a residue of the self, doesn't it?

LUCIAN: You might say that. It's what's left when the self is totally gone. But there's not anything to identify with. We can't objectify it. It's not an entity we think exists somewhere, like the old self. It has no qualities or attributes. There's nothing we can say about it. It's entirely indeterminate, it seems to me. Call it a mystery, if you like.

PHILIA: If consciousness is not the self, then maybe it would be God or the gods, at least for the Stoics, and others.

LUCIAN: That would be another interpretation, wouldn't it? We can't say that the absence of self is anything other than the evident aware-ness we experience of the coming and going of *pragmata*, physical and mental.

PHILIA: So *ataraxia* comes down to the peace of mind which supposedly comes once we've abandoned any sense of self and the emotions that go with it, reducing us to mere observers of our own destiny. Doesn't this leave us, as Petronius was objecting, no different from animals? As passive creatures who respond to the dictates of nature, and no more?

LUCIAN: Unlike animals, we enjoy the gift of imagination and the capacity for reflection it makes possible. We are given knowledge which eludes the animals, in their innocence. I may have given the imagination a bad name in my complaints about belief, but it is the imagination which allows us to reflect upon the sensible world and come to understand better how it functions. It is what makes possible science and art. Animals don't do that.

PHILIA: But I can't get past the passivity that bothered Petronius. We may better understand the world than the animals do because we can reflect upon it in ways they cannot, but we remain just as subject to its involuntary constraints as they are. You said last night that realizing this made no difference in outward behaviour, and perhaps you are right. But this total surrender of the self remains somewhat frightening nonetheless, like a living death, or sleep-walking, as Petronius put it. We end up playing our involuntary parts in the drama of life where anything can happen. Does the gain of *ataraxia* make up for the loss of our god-like freedom? There would be no point even in a philosophical discussion such as we're having.

LUCIAN: There is a sense in which Pyrrhonism is the end or limit of philosophy. It's true that the final status of our beliefs is left suspended, and that the Pyrrhonist, unlike the nihilist, keeps an open mind as to whether any beliefs can be realized or not. But Pyrrhonism takes to its logical conclusion the determinism which already looms so large in the fatalistic world of the Stoics as well as in the calculus of pleasure and pain you Epicureans take so seriously. There is no escaping our determination by our own sensations and thoughts, whether or not they are themselves determined, as Stoics maintain, or simply happen by chance, as the Epicureans hold.

Perhaps, it is true, even the soul might someday be found among our thoughts, just as the body is already found among our sensations.

But even the discovery that what we are can somehow appear to us would not necessarily establish us as autonomous agents armed with free will. For that would not explain how we got here, which can only be shown by the whole of our experience, but not, it seems, explained by our experience, whether the agent of change is imagined as God, or Nature, or the rational Soul. But that is no doubt a topic for another time.

It is late, and I'd like to offer one last thought for tonight, or image. To understand the nature of belief and of release from belief, we might think of a magic show. To believe in the real existence of something that we only imagine is no different from believing in the illusion of a magician. In the darkened theatre, we forget ourselves as we sit in our seats and the torches are dimmed; then the magician comes on stage and we are invited or distracted to enter into our imaginations along with him or her, and to take as real the sleight of hand or story or drama presented to us, whatever it may be. We fall into a spell and suspend disbelief. When the show is over, the curtain pulled shut, and the torches lit up, we wake up, as it were, out of a dream, and shuffle out of the theatre and into the noisy streets of the city. We re-enter reality like a traveller suddenly coming home from a journey, and for a time we see the ordinary world afresh. And similarly, perhaps, when we suspend judgments about our beliefs, including the belief in our very souls, so do we wake up and see afresh the reality we have missed while transfixed by our beliefs. And who knows what that would be, if anything.

RUFUS: A solemn note, no doubt, on which to end tonight. Lucian is right. It is late indeed, and tomorrow is another day, our last together. Until then, good night and pleasant dreams to all!

Is Death Necessary?

RUFUS: It's been a year since we began our discussions and I believe this is the ninth occasion on which most of us have gathered to learn what we can about philosophy. It may be our last evening ever, for all we know. We've lingered long at dinner, and there will be early departures in the morning, so our time for discussion tonight, like life itself, may be briefer than we'd like. Let's make the best of it.

Now I don't know about the rest of you, but a strange feeling has come over me since last night's discussion. Lucian's Pyrrhonian responses in our exchanges have been a strong challenge to most of us, insofar as we remain dogmatists to one degree or another. Any attempt to refute Pyrrhonism seems to rely on us promoting some belief or other, and so plays right into its hands. At the same time, we've learned, it seems, how deeply entrenched our own beliefs seem to be, especially the most cherished of them all, the belief most of us hold most dear, that of our own independent existence as wilful beings of action. If overcoming our own self is what it takes to be a Pyrrhonist, it looks like most of us have a ways to go.

The Pyrrhonists are reported as saying that no matter what we feel and think and do—whether we are enslaved by our beliefs, or free of them—what happens turns out to be determined by the involuntary nature of our direct phenomenal experience. If I understand Lucian, it's not really up to us to liberate ourselves from our beliefs. We couldn't do so even if we tried since the very thought that we can try to do so itself turns out to be a belief, a myth. That's not to say it can't happen, only that it isn't up to us. So much for therapy, as we usually understand it.

If we accept this for the sake of argument, we are left with an understanding of our experience that is as unsettling as it is simple. On one level, Lucian assures us, nothing in life is really any different after it becomes clear to us that everything about us is determined for us. In our responses to the imperatives of our involuntary experiences we will still laugh or cry, be heroic or cowardly, be moved by beauty or be blind to it, believe we can act freely, and so on, just like everyone else. Which reaction we have any any time will depend, it seems, on the accumulated history each of us has built up, the countless streams of phenomenal atoms which blend together in our *pragmata* to shape our inclinations and dispositions. Since none of us has a history identical to anyone else's, our responses will differ, and thus we behold the great diversity of life.

It's a relief, I suppose, to hear that we don't need to be responsible for anything. Even if we involuntarily continue to believe in our independent existence and freedom to act, we can begin to see at least some of the consequences of that belief. As discussed last night, we can now see where some of our strongest emotions — pride, anger, bitterness, envy, and many others — may come from. Even if we can't help having these emotions, understanding them as the ramparts of the soul seems a step in the right direction.

As an older man, I'm perhaps more disposed towards Lucian's message to us than I would have been in my youth or middle age. The excitement over life's novelties slowly diminishes over time, ambitions are tempered, and the cycle of anticipation and disappointment becomes more apparent. It is evident that the roles assigned to us in life vary enormously, but here too the diversity which often exalts or enrages us loses its promise of an ultimate resolution. We cannot change the world, it seems, but if Lucian is right, we still have to endure what we have made of it, or rather, what it has made of us. But we can, it seems, change ourselves, or at least be changed, albeit involuntarily. It is possible, it seems, to drop out of the world of belief and end up instead living on the sufferance of nature.

I've gone on talking long enough, except for one more thing. The Pyrrhonism we've been hearing about seems to capture the mystery of life in some way dogmatists do not. In one form or another, if Lucian is right, dogmatists drain life of its mystery by substituting one or another fixed interpretation of experience for the flow of experience itself. Interpretations shut things down. And these interpretations are rooted, if he's right, in the power of the imagination to reconfigure our sensations and memories, and ultimately to reconfigure them into the commanding fiction of the now somewhat battered independent self. But that attempt to nail down the mystery of life inevitably fails, it seems. In which case, instead of doubling down and insisting we have our way, as it were, it seems the truer piety is to accept the mystery, if we can. And it seems that the greatest of mysteries, and the ultimate challenge to our pretentious selves, is death, which more than anything else puts our vanities to an end.

So, if the Pyrrhonists are right, the last thing we should do is advance some interpretation of death—a conclusion, it seems, also reached by Stoics and even Epicureans. Any interpretation of death can only reify it, turn it into some kind of absolute. The Pyrrhonist way of suspending judgment over death seems unique to them, however, and may be a better way to defuse its power, than simply enduring it, as the Stoics do, or ignoring it, like the Epicureans. In any event, death remains the spectre that haunts us as the ultimate threat to our desperate belief in our own identities as independent, autonomous selves.

Something like that, at any rate, seems to be the promise of Pyrrhonism. So let's end tonight discussing the subject of death.

[Pause ...]

PHILIA: Epicurus certainly put the question of death at the centre of his philosophy. I won't say he ignores it. Peace of mind cannot be achieved as long as we are dogged by fear of death. Death is nothing to fear, he argued, because, once we are dead, we no longer exist to experience it. Since death is not an event in life, its relevance to us is moot. And it seems indisputable that once I, Philia, have gone from this earth, then Philia no longer exists and has nothing to suffer, not even death.

LUCIAN: But this too is something we do not know, it seems, but Epicurus thinks he knows. For him, human existence is entirely material, and nothing else. His version of the autonomous self is a material self, a mechanical self, and on that belief it's hardly surprising that death becomes irrelevant. Do machines die? They fall apart, I suppose, and lose the functional integrity which is their purpose. That seems to be a kind of death. Often they can be fixed, though, and brought back to life.

PHILIA: We know your qualms about Epicurus. You may not like how he reached his conclusions, but many have found his way of removing death and other confusions from the list of human anxieties to be a great relief.

LUCIAN: No doubt. His strength of mind and influence and place among the greatest of philosophers is not to be denied. But how satisfying can a belief about death be, given everything we've said about belief? Epicurus too railed against beliefs, even if he didn't eliminate them all, just the ones he didn't like, perhaps.

PHILIA: Well, I obviously find his argument very satisfying. I suppose that's the conclusion that my life experience, according to you, has determined for me.

LUCIAN: It looks that way. Pyrrho, in any event, reached a different conclusion about death than Epicurus. Pyrrho spent a lot of time observing the flux of *pragmata*, as did Epicurus, but better resisted the impulse to interpret what he was observing. His method of observation may have been a technique of the gymnosophists he encountered in India. The idea, they say, is to still the mind, and above all not to give any special status to the operations of the imagination, but to observe them just as phenomena in exactly the same way we observe sensations just as phenomena.

PHILIA: I suppose that's one way to disable belief.

LUCIAN: Yes, it is. Perhaps the only way.

PHILIA: How does it work?

LUCIAN: The Indians have elaborate techniques, from what I've heard. But it may be enough just to be still and concentrate on what is passing in consciousness. The key seems to be to suspend one's own activity, to stop jumping around both physically and mentally, which only confuses things.

PHILIA: So what did they, and presumably Pyrrho, discover?

LUCIAN: Well, I think you can anticipate the answer. It's what I've been suggesting all along. If you carefully observe your immediate experience, your experience of what is present to you, you gradually come to recognize the recurring phenomenal elements that make it up: the sights, sounds, touches, tastes, and smells we call the sensations, plus the memories and imaginings we call thoughts.

PHILIA: Yes, we've been over this. Is there more to the story?

LUCIAN: There is. I touched on this earlier but perhaps we can go a little deeper. Our sensible and mental elements come and go; they are alternatively present and absent. We notice not only the *pragmata* they compose, which we sense and think, but also their motion, their coming and going. We notice that they are alternatively present and absent, often but not always recurring. In other words, we notice absence as well as presence. What I want to suggest now is that we also notice that we notice. We notice, in other words, that we are conscious of presence *and* absence. Or, perhaps more accurately, we notice not only that there is presence and absence, but also that we are conscious of presence and absence and therefore we realize we are somehow distinct from them.

PHILIA: Are you sure you're not slipping in some idea that you'd like to be the case? Maybe something to believe in? The presence of phenomena is something we might agree to. Maybe even that they are atoms. The presence of their absence is a little tricker, but all right, let's see. Here it seems you want to add something else, a third thing, to the basic mix: the consciousness of consciousness of presence and absence. How does that work?

LUCIAN: Yes, we could call it the consciousness of consciousness. The point is to observe, as much as possible, our direct and immediate experience. Everything has to start somewhere. There is no reason to doubt our appearances, nor to doubt their absence. They come and go. Nor is there any reason to doubt our awareness of their coming and going. Awareness, or consciousness, is also something we notice, directly and involuntarily. And it too comes and goes. Every night we fall into sleep and the waking world disappears. We may dream, or not. And then we return to the waking world, and round and round we go. This is another gap in our experience, different from the gap between the presence and absence of phenomena. It is the gap between waking and sleeping. Notice of this other gap brings consciousness itself to consciousness. It is precisely because we are not always aware, not always conscious, that we notice it when we are. We become aware of awareness because it too comes and goes. It seems to be that we can only know something when we re-encounter it after it has gone away. That seems true of sensations and thoughts, and also of consciousness.

PHILIA: Does that complete your inventory of the most basic experiences?

LUCIAN: Perhaps it does. I'm not sure.

PHILIA: It's a compelling description, audacious in its simplicity. You, that is, or let's say the Pyrrhonists, are asking us to reach points of common evidence together. The coming and passing of phenomena, present to us as *pragmata*, seems evident enough to elicit agreement; but consciousness is another matter. Suddenly you're introducing this term. How is it evident? It needs a fuller description.

LUCIAN: Well, to clarify we should ask whether consciousness is a belief. Is it something which can be imagined, but is not realized, like mermaids or the gods? Could it be a fiction of some kind?

PHILIA: It would seem not. Consciousness seems like an experience of some sort. It is having experience, isn't it? Being awake?

LUCIAN: But consciousness does not exist the way a *pragma* exists, as one among a number of discrete things. Even though it comes and goes as they do, consciousness is apparently another dimension, the third dimension, if you like. We might put it this way: sensations are the first dimension, thoughts are the second, and consciousness the third. Sensations arise, thoughts in turn arise in reflection on sensations, and consciousness arises through reflection on both. It becomes aware of itself through its own alternating absence and presence. Consciousness has a kind of singular invisibility. It is indeterminate and transparent. It's like a hall of mirrors. It is the lens through which we watch the first two dimensions.

PHILIA: You mean it is not itself a *pragma* but somehow it contains all of our *pragmata*, all of our experience of sensations and thoughts.

LUCIAN: It seems so.

PHILIA: Our subject is death. Does consciousness die along with the body and the mind?

LUCIAN: Only complex things can die. Death is the breakdown of a *pragma*, the dissolution of a structure into a disorganized, disintegrated state, back into its constituent phenomena, its devolution into disconnected parts which no longer function together. In this broadest sense even a machine which falls apart can die. Consciousness, however, doesn't seem to be complex in a way that would allow it to die. It's not phenomenal or mechanical. But it can disappear.

PHILIA: So what happens when consciousness ceases entirely, as in dreamless sleep, or when someone has a stroke or wound or other trauma which leaves them unconscious, or in a coma?

LUCIAN: I don't know; who does? But it's pretty clear that loss of consciousness as we experience it is not death; it happens all the time to us without our dying. We even welcome sleep. Consciousness reliably returns; we sleep and then we reawaken and find ourselves conscious again, more or less where we left off. The dead, by contrast, stubbornly do not return to consciousness. Consciousness, like phenomena and their absence, is something we witness, something which also comes and goes.

PHILIA: But if the body and mind die, as they do, where does that leave consciousness? Does consciousness depend on sensations and thoughts? You said it arises out of them. Can it exist without them? Is this some kind of immortality?

LUCIAN: The death of body and mind dissolves the contents of consciousness. As far as we know, the death of the body necessitates the death of the mind, so there are no new sensations, or memories of sensations, or recombinations and other refashionings of those memories. Once body and mind are gone, consciousness is left blank, it would seem.

PHILIA: Couldn't consciousness retain thoughts, once it has them, even without a body? It would not be able to make new memories, but perhaps it would still be able to reflect on the old ones? Doesn't that describe the world of the dead, and of ghosts and other spirits?

LUCIAN: It also describes the world of dreams. Epicurus speculated that thoughts were the apparent features of our subtle physical minds, constructed out of very fine, unobservable atoms and reflective of their motion and force. That's a belief in a mind existing independently of its thoughts, like a machine operating out of sight under the surface of things, or behind the curtain at the theatre. The Epicurean Daedalian mind-machine supposedly receives thoughts in much the same way as the body receives sensations, by importing them from somewhere outside. The Stoic *hegemonikon* is similarly imagined as a command post.

None of this works for the Pyrrhonists. All we have are sensations and thoughts, they say, not some stage machinery behind them to explain it all. The idea that the consciousness we discover through sensations and thoughts can retain thoughts in the absence of sensations, and reflect upon them, is supported by our dreams, where this seems to be accomplished. That much we can observe. But we don't know how it's done, or whether it can happen without the body. We know that our bodies are alive while we sleep; they are standing by, so to speak, breathing, and waiting to awaken. We see this in others who sleep, and in their reports as well as in our own experience.

PHILIA: But it remains a possibility that consciousness might retain memories and continue to reflect upon them, does it not?

LUCIAN: Yes, a possibility which might or might not turn out to be the case. Do we believe in ghosts and spirits? Many do. Here we have a clear instance of where judgment should be suspended.

PHILIA: But by the same token the death of consciousness does not necessarily follow from the death of the body. Perhaps this is what happens in the reincarnations imagined by Pythagoras and Plato and others, and by the Indians. A tangle of memories might somehow be carried over by consciousness latently from one physical life to another. I say tangled because already in dreams we see a marked confusion by comparison with waking life; such confusion would likely be far greater between separate lifetimes than among the dreams within a lifetime. That could explain why so few people report memories of past lives.

LUCIAN: You make belief in reincarnation very plausible. But— except for those who actually retain memories of past lives, if we can believe them—it can only be an unconfirmed hypothesis, another matter for suspended judgment.

PHILIA: What about those people who insist they remember past lives? Don't we have to respect their testimony?

LUCIAN: Believers always deserve a hearing, but they should not expect their beliefs to be accepted. What's required is pretty straight-forward. We would have to find corroborating evidence for claims of past lives. So, if someone gave a detailed past life description with examples of time and place and artefacts which could be independently checked, and with due precaution against fraud, and if enough such cases could be substantiated, then past lives would enter into the world of fact and become a part of our lives, just like anything else.

We hear that's the case in India. I think it's fair to say that that hasn't happened here, at least not as far as we are aware.

PHILIA: Still, it seems that the possibility that consciousness might function this way, through many lifetimes, staves off the certainty and finality of death. Epicurus, by contrast, embraced that certainty and finality and found in it liberation from fear. You may not approve of the dogmatism behind his conclusion, but surely that's a useful outcome, and a help to many.

LUCIAN: Dogmatism has its upside. Organized thinking seeks certitude, and the excitement of certitude is always invigorating and satisfying, certainly in its early stages. There are leaders and followers, teachers and students, enthusiasm, new ideas, a plan to follow, some kind of satisfying closure, a permanence that is proclaimed and embraced. Epicurus makes death into something permanent, the backstop to all his talk of calculating pleasure and pains. He sweeps past the limits of evidence, past the true empiricism of phenomena, onto his vision of the unobservable. He had his vanity, his reluctance to acknowledge his predecessors, including Pyrrho, his pretension in founding a school, a way of life, some would say a cult. Is that too harsh?

PHILIA: Maybe. Unlike Pyrrho, no one said Epicurus was a god, at least not seriously. So you maintain that we Epicureans, like all dogmatists, will be disappointed by our beliefs in the end? Perhaps not. Not all dogmatisms are made the same. Belief in the gods, and their wrath, will increase one's fear, for instance. But belief in death, as Epicurus argues, will decrease it, in fact, eliminate it.

LUCIAN: Perhaps it may, but you don't have to believe in death to assuage the fear it promotes. All you need to do is suspend judgment about it. The price of the Epicurean embrace of death is too high. It requires the sacrifice of consciousness, which can find no place in his system. The Epicurean world is really a Daedalian world. There is no way that a mechanical interpretation of sensations and thoughts can admit consciousness. It makes us entirely into automatons necessarily unaware of what we are doing. There is no recognition of reflection, only of particles bumping into one another. It's as if Epicurus took the sensation of touch, based on physical contact, and forced all of nature into that narrow mould. But our *pragmata* don't just touch or not touch one another; they literally represent one another. Consciousness arises out of the recognition that they do so. It is the awareness of reflection. It is the recognition that reflection is happening.

PHILIA: But consciousness is also what allows us to anticipate our own deaths.

LUCIAN: Yes, certainly the death at least of the body and the mind. The nature of consciousness itself remains in suspense, as you've been agreeing, I think. I will add one more thing. Consciousness of phenomena, and their absence, and even consciousness of consciousness, prompted by its own waxings and wanings—all this comprises the experience (as far as we can tell) of the witness. The witness doesn't seem to be *any* of the things he or she experiences, not even consciousness itself. The recognition of the impermanence of consciousness, whatever it is, distinguishes consciousness from the witness, leaving the witness an even deeper mystery.

[Pause …]

AURELIA: Our time is running down, and on such a topic as death we must before bed hear from those who have been quiet tonight. Harmonia? Petronius? Saturninus? Your thoughts?

HARMONIA: Perhaps, I've been thinking, we dogmatists can continue to hope that our beliefs are not entirely without virtue, even though Lucian has put them in such a bad light. It is well to keep in mind that they are not disproven by his attack, but only suspended. That seems some kind of comfort to me. It may still turn out that the world, indeed the cosmos, is a rational place after all, unfolding under divine guidance. That we cannot demonstrate that such is the case, at least not yet, is a sobering check on our pretensions, to be sure, and we should be grateful to the Pyrrhonists for pointing that out. But we should not forget the beauty of what can be imagined and its power, and we would say its promise. It would be a dreary world indeed if our imaginings were discounted to the point where they counted for little more than amusements to pass the time.

The Pyrrhonists, in seeking to suspend our beliefs, raise the question of how we are to regard phenomena if we don't have a right to believe they testify to some independent existence. Their suggestion is to treat them as imagined hypotheses subject to confirmation or disconfirmation by the senses. How narrow that seems. The possibilities of the imagination seem so much grander and far more interesting. Homer and Virgil and the other poets and the playwrights create marvellous and profound worlds which don't have to exist in reality in order to be compelling to the beholder. And the same is true for the great painters and sculptors and for all art. We can be deeply moved even if we can't explain why.

LUCIAN: Yes, the Pyrrhonists can be analytic and clinical. Perhaps it's the medical influence. Regarding their alarm instead of joy at the power of human creations bred out of the imagination, they would probably say that poets and artists are but the vehicles for the thoughts which come to them, and which they share with us. How alarmed or enjoyed they or we might be depends on what those thoughts actually are. To believe that their visions have an independently existing reality, however, would be to interpret them, to give them a heightened existence of some kind apart from what they already are. That belief is what gives those visions legs to walk. Artificial legs, I might add. The only existence our creations enjoy is to appear and persist in our consciousness, in thought or sensation; they do not appear anywhere else. Their power in the imagination is already strong enough, I agree; it doesn't need to be exaggerated.

[Pause ...]

PETRONIUS: Well, if it's my turn, let me say this. My thoughts this evening keep going back to the uncompromising determinism of the Pyrrhonists. You put a nice gloss on it, Lucian, but it still looks to me that you reduce us all to little more than Daedalian automatons, with all other questions postponed, or tabled indefinitely. This consciousness you've introduced tonight doesn't seem to help either. Indeed, it only makes things worse by showing us how it is that we can see that we're automatons. It's all very well to say that the great achievements of culture and art are somehow passively transmitted through us, but if they are, what exactly is the point? That's awfully close to positing some kind of force or god of your own who does the transmitting. The dogmatic autonomous independent self which you seek to dispense with is perhaps not so easily evaded. At least it gives us the thrill of achievement and purpose. Yes, it also raises anxiety and fear of loss and failure, but for many of us that's a price worth paying for the joy of exercising our will.

Your witness—the last hope you offer for a self, after you dismiss consciousness—seems a starved, disembodied nothing, a mere place-holder for who knows what. The dramatic panorama of sensations and thoughts flowing through our consciousness is a mystifying, inexplicable story which nobody understands. Is it supposed to instruct us? It's hard to see how. You say that contemplating it with-out the distraction of belief is the road to tranquillity, to *ataraxia*. Death has been the theme tonight, but it seems to me that *ataraxia* is a kind of living death, peaceful perhaps, but dead all the same. On the other hand, to openly declare the self and free will is to choose life over death, with all the rewards and risks.

LUCIAN: Perhaps we need to die in this life in order to be reborn in another. Perhaps life is a dream from which we may one day awake. We can't say where our phenomena come from, can we? There's plenty of excitement in the drama life presents to us without having to insist that we're in control of it, or that anyone else is, or no one. As to whether one embraces the self or abandons it, the Pyrrhonist remains indifferent. After all, it's a predetermined or involuntary matter, as far as we can see. Even if you believe you have some choice in your destiny, what you call the mystifying, inexplicable story which nobody understands remains unchanged. All the Pyrrhonists try to do is point to what is self-evident and what is not, to what is a belief and what is a fact.

SATURNINUS: Looks like I'm the last to chime in tonight. Honestly, I'm happy enough to embrace a living death. I'm willing to say that nothing has any meaning. That doesn't mean I can't have a good time, or that misfortunes won't pile up on me. I don't know whether my will is free or not. Sometimes it seems to be, and other times not. Nor do I know whether I have a self or not. Nor do I particularly care. I seem to have one, but who knows? I don't think the difference between a nihilist like me and the Pyrrhonists is very great. Holding beliefs is a lot of nonsense. There we agree. What is the difference, then, I wonder?

Lucian seems to think it's that I have a residual belief that there should be a belief which explains, or interprets, what I actually experience, that I'm still presupposing belief, in other words, but that my despair at not being able to find any belief that can be realized has led me to conclude that no such belief is possible. I think that's fair enough. The consistent failure to realize any of our beliefs is itself what strongly suggests to me that we will never find one that can be realized, or confirmed; it seems to me that to draw such a conclusion is entirely reasonable. The Pyrrhonian idea that we should suspend judgment because someday, somehow, our beliefs might be realized, that is, find a sensible expression, seems a distinction without difference. I suppose it's possible, yes, but for most of the beliefs which concern us it seems so unlikely as to be practically if not theoretically impossible. So I'm not sure what the Pyrrhonists are trying to prove by holding out on this point.

LUCIAN: Well, Saturninus, I'd say there's a big difference, not a small one, between us. Once you conclude that no beliefs can be realized, you ensure that anything you actually experience will be measured by a non-existent standard and found wanting. It's a recipe for a built-in disappointment with experience as it is, whether it's pleasurable or painful, your bravado, as I see it, notwithstanding. It's a way of holding back from fully accepting what nature has to offer us; it's a way of proclaiming your own independence, of finding a way to stay aloof. I'd say that's the last resort of the independent, autonomous soul, hanging on to the shadow of an identity it cannot find. You seem to be saying 'if I can't have a belief, no one can have a belief'.

SATURNINUS: Not so fast. I'm only speaking for myself, not anyone else. To me, however, experience calls out for interpretation, something you Pyrrhonists dismiss too quickly. I agree that trying to interpret our experience is self-defeating in the end, but it also seems unavoidable. It's virtually a universal impulse, isn't it? Why are we given a rich and beautiful imagination by the gods, if not to interpret things? The appearances we have are evident enough, as you say, as are the absences we encounter when they cease to appear. Even the consciousness you point to is a nice way of tying together how our experience of sensation and thought is evident to us. But consider the ambiguous nature of our experience, its combination of pleasure and pain, good and evil, beauty and ugliness, and so on. Eventually it wears most people down. That is hardly reassuring. How can you begin to explain it, say to your children, if you ever have any? How can you tell them that what's left if we suspend our beliefs, including the belief in our own souls, is a problematic world that seems impossible, in the long run, to live in happily.

LUCIAN: You talk as if they would be bitterly disappointed to learn how problematic are our beliefs, but I'm not so sure. It's true that life is not all sweetness and light, as children learn in due course. And it's true that our beliefs are often a comfort in a difficult world. A life without beliefs would lose that comfort, it seems. But we should not prejudge the consequences of a life without beliefs. The first step is to recognize the involuntary nature of experience. The involuntary inflow of physical and mental events which goes into moulding our characters or dispositions will be of one sort for one person, and an entirely different sort for another. The variety of possibilities, we should remember, is practically unlimited. Some people are lucky, and others doomed, it seems, while most end up somewhere in between. It seems that some suffering enters every life, but it can range from the overwhelmingly tragic to the mildly inconsequential. In spite of the prosperity and comforts of your own life, the weight of sadness for you seems greater than that of fulfilment, perhaps because it's based on an unfilled longing. At least that's how I understand your nihilism.

SATURNINUS: I don't deny it. But it shows that we can't help being who we are, as you keep telling us. If I'm disposed to being a nihilist, I suppose Harmonia here is similarly disposed to being a Stoic, Petronius to being a Peripatetic, Philia to being an Epicurean, and you to being a Pyrrhonist. We seem to have been involuntarily determined to be who we have turned out to be. Even those who believe in free will turn out, if this is right, to be determined by the force of their experiences to adopt the belief that they are free. This suggests to me that there's very little we can do to escape what fate has wrought for us.

LUCIAN: We are, it seems, like a ship at sea ploughing a course. Everything that has happened up to this moment—all the way back to the very first idea of the ship in someone's imagination, to the actual building of a ship, to its launch, to the stocking of provisions and the recruitment of a captain and crew, to setting sail and beating a course downwind—all that collectively is what propels the ship forward. Its course cannot be changed immediately, or even in a short time. If the helmsman sees shoals ahead too late, the ship will run aground no matter what he does.

Our lives are very much like that. The sheer force of the involuntary impulses we call sensations and thoughts keeps us on the course they set for us. At the same time, we continue to receive new impulses which contribute to the sum of our experiences. These continue to modify our experience, usually in an incremental way, sometimes more dramatically. Sometimes, we may be led to change course. As the ship's helmsman confronts new thoughts and sensations to prompt him to adjust his setting, he will do so. He'll swing the rudder to one side, and slowly the ship will come about. The very impermanence of our *pragmata* guarantees change.

We are determined by our experience to be who we are, but that determination only brings us to the current moment. We've only reached a certain point, the now, the present. Our experience is determined in the sense that it is forced upon us; but it is open in the sense that we don't know for certain what will be forced upon us next. All that is determined by an appearance is its appearance. As long as we live, we are subject to further determinations which can change

who we are, even unravel who we are. A sudden, powerful determination — a shock, a trauma, a vision — can overturn our personalities.
And, of course, even a moderate change in our experience can modify
who we are over time, even significantly so.

SATURNINUS: Still, change can be for the better or the worse. The
ship might miss the shoal and find safety, or crash onto it and break
up and sink. We can only wait, it seems, for our fate to be revealed to
us. In the meantime, it is what it is.

LUCIAN: The acceptance of our fate includes accepting that it will
change. Again, the past does not wholly determine the future, only the
moment. How likely we are to be changed by what happens next is
unknown. The Pyrrhonists, at any rate, cultivate a respect for our
involuntary sensations and thoughts, and this is what they mean by
piety. Piety is not only the observance of custom, as we usually think
of it; it is also the recognition that our customs, that is to say, the roles
we play in our individual and collective lives, are cumulatively all we
have to go on. Experience not only makes us who we are, but also has
the potential to make us into something quite different. As you point
out, Saturninus, it's a terrible uncertainty we face, with the all-too-
obvious possibilities of good and evil all-too-evident to us, as are the
illusions of belief and the inevitability of death. Piety is born of the
soberness which that terrible unfolding potential puts into our hearts,
and the deference we must thereby give to the mighty unseen hand
which we can imagine, if not believe, moulds our fate.

SATURNINUS: So is piety *ataraxia*?

LUCIAN: It seems it must be. It may be useful here to step back and
recall something Cicero says about Pyrrho in his *De Finibus*. He writes,
if I remember correctly, that Pyrrho's 'conception of virtue leaves
nothing as an object of desire'. That conclusion seemed shocking to
Cicero, who, along with other Academics, remained sympathetic to
the dogmatic project in principle, in spite of its elusive uncertainty. For
Cicero, as for all dogmatists, virtue remains an object of desire. Yet he
reports accurately the point Pyrrho was trying to make. By abandoning all beliefs, including any belief in the rational understanding of

virtue and the world in general, Pyrrho eliminates all the objects of desire. To him virtue, we might say, is what is left over when all beliefs are abandoned; it is the absence of desire, and therefore the absence of fear as well, the price of desire. Out of this double absence arises *ataraxia*, also called tranquillity, or peace of mind. It is the end of the struggle to establish any control over the impermanent *pragmata* which endlessly come and go in the flow of consciousness. Once this effort to control our experience is gone, however, and the involuntary nature of experience is made apparent, we are relieved of the anxiety produced by that effort, and *ataraxia* naturally follows.

SATURNINUS: But this isn't something we do ourselves, you say. It is rather something which happens to us.

LUCIAN: Yes, it's what happens to us involuntarily when our experience brings us to that point. Wisdom comes to us, if it will; we cannot conjure it up out of nothing.

AURELIA: In the meantime, I hope we can harvest the fruits of the imagination and place them alongside the fruits of piety, and sidestep the confusions of belief. The beauty we find in what we imagine in our minds we possess in addition to the beauty we find in the natural world of the senses. By that count, we are doubly rich. Even if something exists only in imagination, its failure to be realized as if it were a sensation does not mean that the feelings it arouses in us are any weaker or inferior than those aroused by our sensations. If there is a divine power in humans, surely it's the imagination, especially when free and liberated from belief.

[Pause …]

RUFUS: Well put, my dear. I think that brings us to the end of tonight's discussion. Tomorrow is another day, and we have to get up early to prepare to go our various ways where, no doubt, we will find what new changes fate has in store for us. So to bed then, and pleasant dreams. The ship will be ready at the dock at sunrise for those leaving by sea, and the carriages will be ready down at the stables for those leaving by land. Aurelia and I will return to the city, after a few more days here, and we hope to see you there, the gods willing.

Glossary of Individuals Named in the Dialogues

More information is available at the *Stanford Encyclopedia of Philosophy*, the *Internet Encyclopedia of Philosophy*, *Wikipedia*, and other sources.

Alexander the Great. 356–323 BCE. King of Macedonia, head of the Hellenic League, and conqueror of the Persian Empire. Alexander's conquests transformed the ancient world.

Antiochus (of Ascalon). 125–68 BCE. A head of the Academy who rejected its previous radical scepticism, and sought to reintroduce dogmatic ideas of Peripetitics and Stoics.

Antigonus (of Carystus). 3rd century BCE. Greek historian whose works, now lost, were quoted in antiquity as a source of information about Pyrrho and others.

Antipater (of Tarsus). 2nd century BCE. Stoic philosopher who maintained the identity of God and fate; his Stoic morality emphasized the moral virtue of truth.

Appelles. 4th century BCE. Famously skilled portrait painter at the courts of Phillip and his son Alexander the Great.

Apollonius. 3 BCE–97 CE. A widely travelled Pythagorean philosopher, holy man, and magician (a seer and miracle-worker sometimes compared to Jesus).

Arcesilaus. 316–241 BCE. A nihilist about knowledge, who as head of the Academy turned it into a sceptical school strongly influenced by the Pyrrhonists.

Archimedes. 287–212 BCE. Astronomer, physicist, and engineer, he was the inventor of mathematical physics and the Archimedian screw and other technological devices.

Aristarchus. 311–231 BCE. Greek astronomer and mathematician who was the first to propose the heliocentric theory in which the earth revolves around the sun.

Aristotle. 384–322 BCE. Student of Plato and systematic synthesizer of most earlier philosophies. His extensive works largely defined the terminology and disciplinary fields of Western philosophy.

Augustus (Caesar Augustus/Octavian). 63 BCE–14 CE. First Roman Emperor. Established the *pax Romana*.

Caesar (Julius). 100 BCE–44 BCE. Roman statesman, famous general, and dictator. Instrumental in ending the Republic and establishing the Empire.

Carneades. 214–129 BCE. A head of the sceptical Academy. Infamous for arguing both sides of philosophical questions in Rome, and perplexing the public.

Catullus. 84–54 BCE. Roman writer famous for his poems of love and personal life.

Cicero. 106–43 BCE. Roman orator, politician, and philosopher. Author of numerous philosophical dialogues and other works. Adherent of the moderate scepticism of the Academy.

Chrysippus. 279–206 BCE. Influential head of the Stoic school and prolific author; he developed Stoic logic and sought to balance determinism in nature with personal freedom.

Cleanthes. 330–230 BCE. Successor to Zeno as head of the Stoic school. He emphasized self-control in ethics, and a fluid theory of active matter in tension, including a material soul.

Clitomachus. 186–110 BCE. Carthagian philosopher who became head of the Academy and continued the radical scepticism of his predecessor, Carneades.

Democritus. 460–370 BCE. The 'happy philosopher'. Principal developer of the atomic theory of physics who promoted a naturalistic view of nature, life, and ethics.

Diogenes (of Sinope). 412–323 BCE. First Cynic philosopher, who spurned the schools and society and lived as a homeless person, almost an animal, and who praised the freedom of his austere asceticism.

Dionysius (the Younger). 397 BCE–343 BCE. Ruler of Syracuse who Plato attempted, unsuccessfully, to turn into a philosopher-king.

Empedocles. 412–323 BCE. Cosmologist who imagined a fluctuating universe composed of four natural elements (earth, air, fire, and water) animated by two forces (love and strife).

Epicurus. 341–279 BCE. Influential Greek philosopher renowned for his application of an atomistic material philosophy to social life focused on pleasure and pain. Founder of Epicurean school.

Epictetus. 50–135 CE. Stoic philosopher born into slavery and later emancipated. Taught in Rome on the practical aspects of living as a Stoic.

Eratosthenes. 276–195 BCE. Greek mathematician, astronomer, and geographer. He was the first to accurately calculate the circumference of the earth and its axial tilt.

Euclid. Late 4th century–early 3rd century BCE. Greek mathematician active in Alexandria, famous for his *Elements*.

Flavius Arrianus (Arrian). 95–175 CE. Historian and geographer as well as Stoic philosopher, who transcribed and promoted the works of his teacher, Epictetus.

Galen. 129–216 CE. Greek physician who pioneered autopsies and anatomical research, and discovered the localization of biological functions in various organs.

Glaucon. 5th century BCE. Plato's older brother. An interlocutor in several Platonic dialogues, especially *The Republic*.

Heraclitus. 535–475 BCE. Secretive and misanthropic, the 'weeping philosopher', he became the pre-eminent writer on impermanence, flux, becoming, and sorrow in a world unable to stop changing.

Hippocrates. 460–370 BCE. He pioneered the systematic observation and categorization of diseases, establishing medicine as an independent science.

Homer. 8th century BCE. Canonical Greek poet. Legendary author of the *Iliad* and the *Odyssey*.

Jesus (of Nazareth). 1st century CE. Jewish prophet and holy man, preached love and compassion, and the forgiveness of sins; acclaimed founder of Galilean or Christian sect.

Kalanos. 4th century BCE. Indian holy man or gymnosophist, attached to the entourage of Alexander the Great, and noted for his self-immolation before Alexander's court in 323 BCE.

Lucretius. 99–55 BCE. Roman poet and philosopher whose only surviving work, *The Nature of Things*, is a primary source of the physics and natural philosophy of the Epicureans.

Nausiphanes. 4th century BCE. A Democritean philosopher who was a link between his teacher, Pyrrho, and his student, Epicurus.

Parmenides. 5th century BCE. In his poem, *On Nature*, he introduced the abiding contrast between a pure and timeless 'way of truth', and an impure and ever changing 'way of opinion'.

Peregrinus. 95–165 CE. Greek Cynic philosopher, famous for immolating himself at the Olympic games in 165 CE.

Phidias. 490–430 BCE. Renowned sculptor and artist. His statue of Zeus at Olympia was acknowledged as one of the wonders of the world.

Philo (of Larissa). 159–84 BCE. A head of the sceptical Academy and teacher of Cicero. He developed a form of mitigated scepticism allowing for probable knowledge.

Philodemus. 110–30 BCE. Greek Epicurean philosopher who wrote extensive works—many recovered from papyri scrolls found in Herculaneum—on ethics, including the virtues and vices, and on the emotions.

Plato. 427–347 BCE. Very influential Greek philosopher. Author of numerous dialogues featuring Socrates and others exploring many philosophical issues from a variety of perspectives. Known for his theory of forms and his myths.

Plutarch. 46–120 CE. Greek Platonic author of extensive biographies and essays. Priest at the Oracle at Delphi.

Posidonius. 135–51 BCE. Famously learned Stoic philosopher who was also a mathematician, astronomer, geographer, and historian. He sought to integrate Platonic and Aristotelian ideas into Stoicism.

Praxiteles. 4th century BCE. Renowned sculptor known for his anthropomorphizing statues of the gods.

Pyrrho. 360–270 BCE. Founder of Pyrrhonian school of scepticism. Travelled to India with Alexander the Great where he encountered Indian philosophers or holy men. Developed a Buddhist-like suspension of judgment about beliefs as a way of life.

Pythagoras. 570–495 BCE. Philosopher, astronomer, and traveller who promoted the mathematical structure of the universe, along with a mysticism centred on metempsychosis. Founder of an ascetic community, or cult, in Italy.

Seneca. 5 BCE–65 CE. Roman Stoic philosopher in Nero's circle. His *Letters* emphasize personal self-control and fortitude in reconciling rational providence with adversity.

Sextus Empiricus. 2nd century CE. Pyrrhonian Greek physician and author of numerous surviving works outlining Pyrrhonian practices, with detailed criticism of other schools, especially Stoics and Epicureans.

Socrates. 470–399 BCE. Made famous by Plato's dialogues, Socrates radically questioned the common beliefs of his day, and was tried and executed in Athens for corrupting the youth.

Strabo. 64 BCE–24 CE. Traveller, philosopher, and historian known for his *Geographica*, a comprehensive compendium of the known world of his day.

Thales. 626–548 BCE. Regarded as the first Greek philosopher and scientist for replacing mythological accounts of events with natural-istic explanations. Predicted the eclipse of 28 May 585 BCE.

Theophrastus. 371–287 BCE. Aristotle's successor as head of his school, the Lyceum. Best known for his work in natural science and plant biology, among a wide range of subjects.

Timon (of Phlius). c. 320–235 BCE. Most important disciple of Pyrrho, well known writer of satirical poems.

Titus. 39 CE–81 CE. Famous military commander and Emperor of Rome. Suppressed the Jewish revolt and sacked Jerusalem and destroyed the Temple.

Trajan. 53 CE–117 CE. Emperor of Rome at the greatest extent of the Empire. Noted for his philanthropy and public works.

Virgil. 70 BCE–19 BCE. Poet and author of the *Aeneid*, the epic national poem of the founding of ancient Rome.

Xenophon. 430–354 BCE. Author of military memoirs and philosophical dialogues featuring Socrates.

Xenophanes. 570–475 BCE. Perhaps the earliest Greek sceptic. He distinguished between knowledge and belief and denied there could be a criterion of truth.

Zeno (of Citium). 334–262 BCE. Founder of Stoicism who held the universe to be a divine, rational entity accessible to human knowledge and a source of solace. He sought to distinguish true knowledge from false by a purported ability to correctly assent to sensory phenomena.

Bibliography

Selected Readings

Ancient Sources:

Cicero. *On Academic Scepticism*, Charles Brittain, trans. Indianapolis: Hackett Publishing, 2006.

-----. *The Nature of the Gods*, Horace C.P. McGregor, trans. Middlesex: Penguin Books, 1972.

-----. *On Ends*, H. Rackham, trans. Cambridge: Harvard University Press, Loeb Classical Library, 1931.

-----. *Tusculan Disputations*, J.E. King, trans. Cambridge: Harvard University Press, Loeb Classical Library, 1945.

The Cynic Philosophers from Diogenes to Julian, Robert Dobbin, trans. London: Penguin Books, 2012.

Diogenes Laertius. *Lives of Eminent Philosophers*, R.D. Hicks, trans. 2 vols. Cambridge: Harvard University Press, Loeb Classical Library, 1925.

Epictetus. *Discourses and Selected Writings*, Robin Dobbin, trans. London: Penguin Books, 2008.

Epicurus. *The Art of Happiness*, George K. Strodach, trans. London: Penguin, 2012.

-----. *Letters, Principal Doctrines, and Vatican Sayings*, Russell M. Geer, trans. Indianapolis: Bobbs-Merrill, 1964.

The Hellenistic Philosophers: Volume. 1, Translations of the Principle Sources, with Philosophical Commentary, A.A. Long & D.N. Sedley, eds. Cambridge: Cambridge University Press, 1987.

Lucretius. *The Nature of the Universe*, R.E. Latham, trans. Middlesex: Penguin Books, 1951.

Marcus Aurelius. *Meditations*, Martin Hammond, trans. London: Penguin Classics, 2006.

Plutarch. *Essays*, Robin Waterfield, trans. London: Penguin Books, 1992.

-----. *Selected Essays and Dialogues*, Donald Russell, trans. New York: Oxford University Press, 1992.

Seneca. *Dialogues and Essays*, John Davie, trans. Oxford: Oxford University Press, 2009.

Sextus Empiricus. *Outlines of Pyrrhonism, Against Logicians, Against the Physicists & the Ethicists, and Against the Professors*, R.G. Bury, trans. 4 vols. Cambridge: Harvard University Press, Loeb Classical Library, 1933–49.

Modern Sources:

Annas, Julia. *Hellenistic Philosophy of Mind*. Berkeley: University of California Press, 1992.

Beckwith, Christopher I. *Greek Buddha: Pyrrho's Encounter with Early Buddhism in Central Asia*. Princeton: Princeton University Press, 2015.

Bevan, Edwyn. *Stoics and Sceptics: Four Lectures Delivered in Oxford During Hilary Term 1913*. Cambridge: W. Heffer and Sons, 1965.

Flintoff, Everard. "Pyrrho and India." *Phronesis*. XXV, No. 2, 1980.

Hadot, Pierre. *Philosophy as a Way of Life*. Oxford: Blackwell, 1995.

Kuzminski, Adrian. *Pyrrhonian Buddhism: A Philosophical Reconstruction*. London: Routledge, 2021.

-----. *Pyrrhonism: How the Ancient Greeks Reinvented Buddhism*. Lanham: Lexington Books, 2008.

Long, A.A. *Epictetus: A Stoic and Socratic Guide to Life*. Oxford: Clarendon Press, 2002.

-----. *Hellenistic Philosophy: Stoics, Epicureans, Sceptics*. 2nd ed. Berkeley: University of California Press, 1986.

Nussbaum, Martha C. *The Therapy of Desire: Theory and Practice in Hellenistic Ethics*. Princeton: Princeton University Press, 1994.

Sandbach, F.H. *The Stoics*. 2nd ed. Indianapolis: Hackett Publishing, 1975.

Seneca. *The Stoic Philosophy of Seneca: Essays and Letters*, Moses Hadas, trans. New York: W.W. Norton, 1958.

Sharples, R.W. *Stoics, Epicureans and Sceptics: An Introduction to Hellenistic Philosophy*. New York: Routledge, 2005.